PRAISE FOR
THE POCKET MARKETER

"Takes the marketing-naive and equips them with a comprehensive set of the fundamentals."
—David J. Reibstein, Vice-Dean and Professor of Marketing, The Wharton School

"A terrific reference . . . . Step aside Harvard and Wharton, I've got Marketing 101 right here on my desk!"
—Yosi N. Heber, Director of Marketing, The Dannon Company

"Extraordinary . . . . This unique primer speaks clearly and concisely to the needs of marketing professionals."
—Karen Angelini, Harvard Business School Class of '93

"A hands-on winner . . . clearly one of the most insightful, easy-to-use marketing tools to come along."
—Harold Bevis, Manager, Corporate Business Development, General Electric

"An MBA course in your pocket. Everything you need to know about big company marketing techniques."
—Seth Godin, author of *Business Rules of Thumb*

"A gold mine for anyone who needs a basic background in marketing to succeed."
—Jeff Slutsky, co-author of *How to Get Clients*

"An incredible module for executives . . . . A must for every marketer and required for my whole staff."
—Stephen Adler, CEO, JAMI Charity Brands Services Inc.

Brian Scott Sockin was born in Forest Hills, N.Y. Brian received his M.B.A. in marketing from the Wharton School of Business, University of Pennsylvania, in 1985, and his B.A. in psychology from the State University of New York at Binghamton in 1982.

Brian's professional experience includes marketing management positions in entertainment, telecommunications, and packaged goods industries, including brand manager at Kraft General Foods and divisional marketing manager at Northern Telecom, Inc. Brian is currently vice president and director of marketing at Alba Kids, a leading U.S. kids marketing and promotion agency, based in Bethel, Connecticut.

Brian lives with his wife, Darlene, and their two computer-literate cats, Jazz and Clio, in Stamford, CT.

Janet M. Grottalio received her M.B.A. from St. John's University in Queens, New York, in 1989, and her B.A. in English and Journalism from the State University of New York at Binghamton in 1982.

Janet's marketing experience comes from working both with an agency and as a client. She is currently a promotion manager at Kraft General Foods, Inc., in White Plains, New York. Previously, she was an account executive at FCB/Leber Katz Partners in New York.

THE POCKET MARKETER

Your Portable Professional Real-World Marketing Companion

Brian Scott Sockin, M.B.A.
Janet Grottalio, M.B.A.

WARNER BOOKS

A Time Warner Company

The case examples presented herein are fictional. Names, characters, places, and incidents are either the product of the author's imagination or are used fictitiously. Any resemblance to actual events, locales or persons, living or dead, is entirely coincidental.

Copyright © 1991, 1992 by Brian Scott Sockin and Janet Grottalio
All rights reserved.

Warner Books, Inc., 1271 Avenue of the Americas, New York, NY 10020

W A Time Warner Company

Printed in the United States of America

First Printing: December 1992

10 9 8 7 6 5 4 3 2 1

Library of Congress Cataloging in Publication Data

Sockin, Brian Scott.
   The pocket marketer/Brian Scott Sockin, with
      Janet M. Grottalio.
      p.   cm.
   ISBN 0-446-39376-2
   1. Marketing—Handbooks, manuals, etc.   I.
      Grottalio, Janet M.   II. Title
HF5415.S686   1992
658.8—dc20   92-24254
                                              CIP

Cover design by Julia Kushnirsky

We dedicate this book to everyone we ignored while we wrote it. We'd like to say that we'll make up for it, but we can't . . . we're starting our next book tomorrow.

Special thanks to Bruce at Business Computers, who helped to save us after the great crash of Feb. '92 (computer crash, that is). And to Dawna Genander for her help and enthusiasm.

Contents

Foreword

Global changes are shaping the evolution of marketing in both the services industries and product corporations themselves. Understanding these changes and their implications will help you to understand how THE POCKET MARKETER was organized and to make the best use of what it has to offer.

In the earlier decades of the twentieth century, using a message to reach a potential consumer or business was referred to as "advertising." Promotion, packaging, and publicity were all considered parts of advertising—the "catchall." As markets and product offerings became more segmented, and therefore more complicated, the catchall split into four major marketing functions: advertising, promotion, packaging, and public relations, and specialized industries surfaced to provide these services.

Each of these industries had its own territories or media. Advertising worked through television, most print (i.e., magazines, newspapers), radio, outdoor media, cinema, and some direct response. Packaging utilized the physical package itself, its importance only now being realized as a strategic element in the marketing mix. Distributing coupons, sweepstakes, or premiums was in promotion's domain. And, public relations used the media without purchasing the space. The lines were pretty clear.

Today, as the industries and media themselves have become more sophisticated, the four functions of product marketing have begun to merge, and those lines of distinction are blurring. We see advertising agencies doing promotional sweepstakes on television, promotion houses doing newspaper inserts without coupons, ads containing coupons in magazines, and electronic media in stores delivering both advertising *and* promotion messages.

And where do commercials on home videos fit? And what about future trends, such as viewer profile advertising, where "on command" a consumer gets a coupon printed off an outboard computer printer on his/her television set for the product being advertised on the screen? Advertising or promotion?

As the business environment for suppliers of the different functions grows increasingly competitive, change is ongoing. Perhaps the strongest push to change lies in the sophistication of the markets, the companies playing in them, and the products themselves. As competition mounts and budgets are squeezed more tightly, all four functions must work in harmony to produce efficiency and economy. One chorus of messages is more cost-effective than four individual scores. In essence, a merging of the functions may be re-emerging, and the supplier service industries are organizing to provide "full service" capabilities.

Especially in the largest corporations, where once all functions were accountable to "product or business managers," advertising, promotion, packaging, and public relations and nonmarketing functions have become almost autonomous. Turf battles sometimes exist where there should be team efforts. While the smartest companies have begun to apply the team approach to business planning and decision making, they still have a way to go in optimizing the functional interrelationships.

We've written this book with the hope that it *will* help to optimize the way that corporations utilize the functional areas in marketing. The functional areas should not merely execute or design—they should play a key role in developing the strategies and tactics that will help the business to achieve its marketing objectives. Each function should have a basic understanding of the others and where they best fit into the mix. The marketing manager should communicate, clarify, and direct this process, to focus all functions toward effectively reaching the final goals.

THE POCKET MARKETER will show you how the functional areas can and should cooperate with and contribute to the marketing plan, its execution, and its evaluation. It is the marketing manager's job to ensure that this happens.

INTRODUCTION

BACKGROUND AND REASON FOR BEING

Hundreds of marketing textbooks and resource guides teach theory and practice on just about every topic in the marketing domain, but few can be used on a practical, real-world basis. And few of us have the time or patience to sift through voluminous information to get to the real "heart of the matter."

Specialists exist in the areas of marketing research, marketing planning, product development, packaging, advertising, promotion, public relations, and sales. Product or marketing managers try to pull all these functions together for a common goal: to present the consumer with the best product and with the singular, best message about the product.

Once upon a time, being an expert in one area was enough. But today, as marketing has become more sophisticated, competition more fierce, and marketing methods more plentiful, it has also become necessary for functional experts to operate in a different way. Today, the concept of the business team—where everyone works together and depends on one another's support of the marketing directives—has expanded into nearly every organization where people regularly interact with their marketing counterparts. This has even gone beyond marketing—marketers find themselves working hand-in-hand with other specialists to solve their own problems, such as operations, finance, and manufacturing.

Marketers and those outside of marketing now must be able to communicate with their marketing counterparts and to understand how decisions they make affect what happens elsewhere with the product. They must not only be expert in their fields but also have a basic knowledge of all other marketing fields.

The promotion manager and staff need to know how advertising works; the marketing research manager and staff need to get a grasp of product development; the sales manager and staff need to understand how pricing is set. This doesn't mean that a packaging engineer has to be an advertising maven, but the engineer should understand, for example, how a change in packaging will affect the overall image of the brand.

With this in mind, we began developing a book that

attempts to address these issues—a practical real-world users' manual for:

1. **Marketers** who want to gain a basic understanding of the big picture and how the different functional areas contribute to it;
2. **Marketing students** who want to make educated career choices by understanding their potential roles should they specialize in a particular marketing function;
3. **Other business professionals** who relate to marketers and wish to gain insight into how best to work with them.

FORMAT

THE POCKET MARKETER (PM) is designed to be a comprehensive, user-friendly marketing sourcebook and briefcase business companion. It begins with the "Big Picture," an overview of how to develop a marketing plan for a product and how all of the marketing functions work together in doing so.

Following are eight chapters or "modules" (because they interlock), one for each marketing function: marketing research, product development, packaging development, distribution, pricing, advertising, promotions, public relations.

Each chapter is a tutorial and reference unit containing not the lengthy information you'd find in textbooks, but real day-to-day stuff that's used in companies across the United States. Each module consists of three sections, all tied together to produce a layered reference guide. In this way, you can get an overview of a particular topic, look up terms, or use standardized charts and tools.

1. **TOP-LINES:** Each topic begins with a 15 to 30 page "top-line" or summary, which provides an overview of the subject. Then, top-lines are broken down to illustrate the step by step process of each function. For example, if what you want to know about advertising is how the media planning process works, read only that self-contained section. If you simply want to become familiar with the terms used in advertising, you can turn to the topic glossary at the end of that chapter.

2. **TOPIC GLOSSARIES:** Each PM topic has its own glossary, which is cross-referenced both with the Top-Line and within itself, through the use of bold-face and

italicized words. Wherever applicable, PM offers examples and discussions to help illustrate the meanings and applications of those terms.

3. **TOOLS:** PM provides state-of-the-art charts and tools to help you research, organize and plan in each function. Each module includes a series of these management tools to use to organize and streamline your jobs. They are designed for simplicity and usability, based on actual practices in leading companies across America. You can modify them for your needs, enlarging the forms as you photocopy, and translate them into tangible action in your job.

The final chapter of PM brings all you have learned together in a sample marketing plan. We have created a hypothetical company called SolarTech, with a new product launch called *SunSplash,* for which we built an actual marketing plan from beginning to end. While the case scenario is fictional, it simulates the dynamics of the consumer suncare market and reflects the structure and issues confronting manufacturers in that industry. The marketing plan walks you through the mental processes of preparing a marketing plan from start to finish, as well as each of its functional components. The background of the case and setup of the problem are provided in Chapter 1, The "Big Picture."

ONE

THE MARKETING PLAN

OVERVIEW

Marketing exists side by side with its sister-business functions such as finance, operations, and human resources, which are governed and bridged by senior management. The Business Plan outlines how these business functions can work together to achieve a common goal.

The business plan can be the blueprint for either an entire company or a single product. Where the ideas and opportunities are found and planning begins depend upon the organization. Ideas for planning, development, and execution of products can come from within the marketing domain, from other business functions, such as manufacturing, or from outside the company itself.

Wherever ideas originate, ultimately they filter up (called "bottom-up" planning) or down (called "top-down" planning) through the corporate structure. Companies usually adopt one of these planning philosophies; but philosophy aside, ideas for products and how to develop and market them usually slide up and down the corporate ladder many times, evolving and ever changing.

The marketing plan is the "commercial" portion of the business plan—what has to be done to develop products and get consumers and businesses to buy them. Within the parameters imposed by manufacturing and finance, marketing is the core of business planning, linking the company and all its layers to the end-user of a product. As such, marketing plays a dominant role in most modern competitive businesses.

While marketing plans are structured in many different ways, there are many common elements that usually go into a plan. The following is an outline for writing a typical marketing plan. It will help you organize your own marketing plans and streamline the flow of information and ideas. If the marketing plan is being written for an existing product or line, we begin with a recap of the prior year's activities. If we are planning for a new product, we begin by stating the premise for its development. The next step in both cases is the preparation of a situational analysis.

I (a).   RECAP (for existing products only): Overview of last year's marketing plan: what worked and didn't work and why. Major

	lessons learned and implications for the future.

or

I (b). PREMISE AND BASIS FOR PREMISE (for new products only): statement of the overall new product initiative and how it came to be.

II. SITUATIONAL ANALYSIS:
Business Objectives and Strategies—the context for the creation of your plan
Market Analysis—marketing sizing, segmentation, dynamics, trends at all levels
SWOT Analysis—strengths and weaknesses, opportunities and threats
Competitive Analysis—study of competitors to understand the dynamics of the market, anticipate their moves, and prepare offensives (can include competitive SWOTs)

III. STRATEGIC DIRECTION:
Overall product direction, target audience, positioning, marketing objectives, and strategies
Functional Roles and Guidelines—impact and role of each function in the overall plan

IV–IX. FUNCTIONAL PLANS

X. BUDGETS

RECAP/PREMISE

If you are writing a marketing plan for an existing product or line, you want to take a good, hard look at how your marketing plan did over the past year (or to date if your planning is done in midstream). Evaluate all of your objectives and see if your strategies and tactics fulfilled them. What worked and what didn't? List major lessons learned and state the implications of those lessons for your present planning endeavor. Each function is also advised to do a recap in its own area.

If you are writing a marketing plan for a new product, begin your marketing plan with the idea. State the idea in one or two sentences, such as "An unfulfilled need in the market exists for _____ and we should develop a _____ for inclusion in next year's line." This is simplistic example, but your premise should also be simple and to the point. You will have more than enough chance to elaborate on your premise in the body of the marketing plan.

Next, simply state where the idea came from—what the "basis" was for your having made this premise (e.g., "marketing research identified . . . ," "sales reports, when tabulated showed . . . ").

SITUATIONAL ANALYSIS

The situational analysis is the heart of your analysis and rationale for the new product or the plans you develop for existing products. It is the foundation upon which you can base decisions and provide reasons for those decisions. The situational analysis can be thought of as the section of the marketing plan in which you "make your case." It is an examination of your company's, division's, or department's business objectives and strategies and an evaluation of how your premise or plans fit, support, and help to fulfill them.

BUSINESS OBJECTIVES AND STRATEGIES

This statement of "higher" needs creates the context for your plan and sets the overall parameters within which you must work. If your business objectives are geared towards scaling down the operation, cost cutting, and building on the strength of current profitable products with no new product introduction, you obviously would not want to pursue new technology and products.

First, **BUSINESS OBJECTIVES** are set or reiterated. The ultimate long-term global objective is called the *mission,* and can have a horizon of five to ten years or longer. The mission is usually "pie-in-the-sky," the corporate dream or vision, and doesn't often include real numbers because of its projection into the future. *Short-term* (usually within the next year), *medium-term* (usually one to three years out), and *long-term* (usually three to five years out) business objectives work together toward the common goal of achieving the mission. Of course, the notion of short versus medium versus long term differs from one type of business to another (e.g., a high-tech firm may consider five or six years as medium-term because it takes ten years to develop a project, whereas a novelty manufacturer may view three years as long-term).

Except in the case of nonprofit organizations, business objectives are "bottom line" oriented, which means two things:

1. Everything that is done in the plan is focused on making the business profitable
2. Everything is quantitative, meaning measurable in discrete values such as dollars, percentages, number of markets, etc.

An example of a bottom-line oriented business objective is: "To deliver a minimum of 50 percent increase in revenues, 30 percent increase in profits, and 60 percent increase in dividends to stockholders, over a three-year time frame."

To support and fulfill each business objective, **BUSINESS STRATEGIES** in each business function are developed (the types and number of business functions vary from one corporation to another). For example, in *manufacturing,* one strategy to increase profit might be to reduce the cost of manufacturing or to modernize the plant equipment. In *research and development,* a strategy could be to build expertise in a particular area or to deploy new technologies that were developed overseas. In *finance,* strategies might include improving the accounting system, becoming more aggressive in domestic investments, or investigating the purchase of a complementary business. The business strategy that directs the function of *marketing* usually concentrates on what marketing systems can do to contribute to or fulfill the business objectives— related to products and ways to market products. For example, if the stated business objective is "to deliver a minimum of 50 percent increase in revenue, 30 percent increase in profit, and 60 percent increase in dividends to stockholders over a three-year time frame," the marketing-directed business strategy might be "to introduce new products, to improve existing products, and to upgrade the corporate image in the eyes of consumers and the investment community."

Based on overall strategies for the marketing department, individuals and groups take initiatives, some concerning product development, others addressing distribution, and so on. Along the way, business plans are developed for specific products or projects that affect many products, or even for the company as an entity itself (e.g., new distribution channels for all brands, new public relations program, new corporate identity program, etc.). However all of these plans are geared toward fulfilling the previously established business objectives and strategies. Within each business plan, a marketing plan is developed, complete with its own overall objectives and functional strategies and tactics.

MARKET ANALYSIS

Discussed in more detail in Marketing Research, chapter 2, this is a methodical collection of data and interpretation of the characteristics of a marketplace, so that the marketer has a context within which to plan specific products or programs. Market analysis uses sizing and segmentation (breaking up the market into quantifiable categories with homogeneous characteristics) to identify structure, trends, shares, and relationships within and beyond the market.

SWOT ANALYSIS

SWOT is the acronym for "*strengths, weaknesses, opportunities,* and *threats.*" A SWOT analysis can be performed on a company, a line, or a product, depending upon needs. It is performed to remind the marketer realistically and objectively of the product or the company's capabilities and limitations in the marketplace, before the plan is developed.

The opportunities in the marketplace are identified as they pertain to a premise or business. Is there an opportunity for a new product concept? A new type of packaging? A better distribution channel? A fresh approach to advertising? A blockbuster promotion idea? A way to take advantage of public relations channels? Opportunities are defined as they relate to each of the functional areas in marketing.

Threats to a company's current or desired position in the marketplace are then identified. These may be based upon environmental, legal, competitive, technological, or any other actual or possible issues that could hinder the company's goals. Identifying threats enables the company to take measures necessary to guard against them.

The company's ability to capitalize on opportunities and to defend against threats depends upon its strengths and weaknesses. A marketer may not want to go into a certain business if the company doesn't have or offer the know-how to succeed in that business. This lack of knowledge may be listed as a weakness. Conversely, existing expertise and having the right distribution channels in place to facilitate expansion would be strengths that might be capitalized upon. Sometimes a weakness can be turned into a strength—for example, having excess capacity could be viewed as a weakness, but if expansion is desired, it might become a strength. All in all, a SWOT analysis provides an objective context within which to define objectives and build marketing plans, and should be a required exercise for every strategic effort.

COMPETITIVE ANALYSIS

A marketer should have data on how competitors are performing in the marketplace. It is necessary to determine which competitors are likely to threaten efforts to launch a new product or an existing business. This section of the marketing plan should include a recap of competitive offerings and market share, and could contain information on competitive programs and spending in each functional area. Competitive marketing program analyses are usually conducted in greater detail by each of the functional areas within marketing.

Competitive information may feed into the SWOT analysis (usually in the "threats" section), or separate SWOT analyses of each of the competitors may be done so that their strengths and weaknesses can be better understood and acted upon. The level of analysis required really depends on the competitive environment in that category and a particular brand's position in it.

STRATEGIC DIRECTION

The gathered information is applied to building the plans to support the new or existing products. Several key factors influence the formulation of marketing objectives and strategies:

1. **Overall Direction**: This is translating what has been seen as an opportunity into concrete actions that can be taken. For example, if the opportunity is to market ice cream novelties through sports and recreational facilities, then the overall direction may be to investigate developing products and supporting programs to provide sports stadiums and recreational facilities with ideal products and turnkey programs that will create demand for and facilitate sales of our ice cream.

2. **Target Audience**: A description of the targeted consumers of a product that includes demographics, psychographics, life-style information, etc., should not be limited to clinical statistics. Using the device of describing the target audience as one "typical" consumer presents a clearer picture. This image is

developed from detailed research, to be discussed in
chapter 2, Marketing Research.
3. **Benefits and Positioning**: What are the benefits of
the product or project? What is the desired brand
image? How is the product unique, and what want or
need will it satisfy? Is the product upscale or
downscale? Positioning is based on the key benefits
that are believed are most attractive to the consumer,
in context of competitive offerings. Positioning is
discussed in greater detail later in this chapter and in
chapter 2 as well.
4. **Performance Criteria**: These measurable guidelines, such as minimum sales, profits, etc., during
specific time periods, set the tone for your marketing
objectives.

MARKETING OBJECTIVES

After assembling the required information, *marketing
objectives* for a product or project can be set. These objectives are then provided to other nonmarketing functions (e.g., manufacturing) so that those plans can be
developed to support them.

The statement of marketing objectives for a specific
project or brand should include four elements:

1. Identification of the product *or project;*
2. Description of the *target audience;*
3. Enumeration of the *benefits* to the audience;
4. Establishment of "bottom-line"-oriented measurable goals based on the business objectives and
strategies.

An example of a marketing objective for a new kind of
microwavable frozen dinner for cats could be:

> *To develop and launch a new line of cat food di-
> rected to busy, indulgent (primary) and caring
> (secondary) cat owners, that delivers key ben-
> efits of convenience, multiple courses, and
> microwavability, and generates gross sales of at
> least $15 MM and net margins of at least 14 per-
> cent in the first year.*

MARKETING STRATEGIES

Marketing strategies are the means by which marketing
objectives will be achieved. In the same way that business strategies are written to direct each of the business
functions, such as marketing, manufacturing, and re-

search and development, marketing strategies are aimed at each of the functional areas within marketing. Product development, distribution, packaging, pricing, advertising, promotion, and public relations are each assigned a role and given guidelines for development of their respective plans. Whether the responsibility falls upon the product manager, the functional manager, or an outside agency, functional planning begins with the direction provided by marketing objectives and strategies. From these, functional objectives and strategies are written.

MARKETING FUNCTIONS

Utilizing the example of sale of packaged ice cream novelties in outdoor recreational settings, marketing strategies might be written as follows:

Product:
Role: *Major, as the form is critical for success.*
Strategies: *Evaluate current product lines for application in ballparks and other recreational settings (flavors, sizes, etc.) and investigate opportunities for new products that would appeal to our target audience in the out-of-home recreational setting.*

Packaging:
Role: *Minor, as consumers will order product based on need before packaging is seen.*
Strategy: *Develop single-serve versions of our existing product line that are self-evident and have strong appeal to the target audience.*

Distribution:
Role: *Critical, as we are entering a new channel.*
Strategy: *Penetrate and gain distribution in the concessions of at least sports stadiums, amusement parks, and other outdoor recreation facilities, concessions.*

Promotion:
Role: *Moderate, because purchases are impulse oriented and situationally based.*
Strategy: *Utilize offers that create spontaneous trial of products with targeted consumers that can be delivered in conjunction with trade and consumer point-of-sale advertising efforts.*

Determination of the relative roles of the functions will help the marketing manager to determine the best allocation of budget and resources.

The role of marketing research will be determined by informational needs and anticipated evaluatory requirements. It may be utilized by any and all of the functional areas to help define plausible, measurable objectives.

FUNCTIONAL PLANS

Once direction is provided for each of the functions, their plans can be written. Essentially, it does not matter if a company is set up so that different departments exist for each marketing function or if a general marketing manager is responsible for planning each function (sometimes with the help of outside agencies). The point is, the functions need to be addressed, regardless of the organizational setup.

The rule of thumb is that everything that's done in each marketing function should reflect and support the overall marketing objectives, which in turn should reflect and support the business plan. If the steps just outlined are followed, they should.

Each functional plan begins with a "preplanning" discussion of the research and data that will affect the ultimate conclusions and decisions. If the *product development plan* is being written, the introduction might present the key findings from product research and information on recent competitive introductions. Lessons learned from previous years might also be discussed. The role assigned to the function would also be reiterated and objectives, strategies, and specific tactics set, ideally containing timetables and budgets.

As a rule, each functional plan is not included in its entirety as part of the marketing plan. Rather, the key points, objectives, strategies, and tactics are summarized. However, the functional plan is retained for reference by the functional manager and is usually presented to the marketing manager for approval.

BUDGETING

Perhaps the most controversial subject in any company is budgeting: who gets what share of the money pie. Budgeting plays a critical and timely role in the marketing planning process and should be not an arbitrary but a methodical process. Most often, budgets are set from the top down, and functional managers have to work with what they're given. Also, the functional budgets are often set with no more justification as the "same or a percentage above or below last year." Often there is far too little justification and accountability for allocations of dollars within a brand. This practice encourages functional managers to spend *all* that is allocated to them, instead of arriving at what they feel are appropriate expenditures.

Budgets should be set based on the impact desired (whether short- or long-term) of programs in each functional area, built from the bottom-up in an orderly fashion in the marketing plan—NOT ARBITRARILY. Marketing managers should act as though the money were theirs—and oftentimes the internal incentive structure in a business makes this partially so. In any case, this is our prescription for setting a budget logically and effectively: After the situational analysis has been put together, it is distributed with key roles and guidelines to the functional counterparts. At this point, budgetary guidelines should be provided for each function. This will alleviate the urge to spend up to the limit and yet keep things realistic so that the planners are not "spinning their wheels" to plan programs that cannot realistically be funded. This direction is necessary for the functional planning processes, and is often not provided or is given in an incomplete form.

Then, collectively if possible, or individually, each function puts together its respective plan—distribution plan, pricing plan, advertising plan, etc. The final result of these efforts is the almost complete marketing plan. Each function should then prepare a budget for their plans that allows them to evaluate the cost and impact of each project, both for that function, and across the big picture of the entire marketing plan. Each program should be listed, along with the objective that it was designed to address. If applicable, a short description of the expected impact is provided—whether it be directly to the bottom line (preferable) or more qualitative, such as "build brand name recognition with consumers." Then, the dollar requirement to develop and execute this program should be provided and justified if possible.

Then, it is up to the marketing manager to assess the individual function budget requests, evaluate all programs as they relate to one another, and arrive at the optimal budget mix for the brand. If the total spending requested by the functions exceeds the limit, and the marketing manager believes the spending to be justified, then this is the marketing manager's chance to negotiate for a higher budget based on goals and supporting data. More realistically, however, the marketing manager will come back to some or all of the functions with a request to pare down the budget by certain amounts. The functional manager then determines and recommends the places from which the cuts can least painfully be made and identifies the potential risks to the marketing manager. Final decisions are made by the marketing manager. The advantage of this process is that it makes planners "work" for their budgets, think through projects, assess their value to the business more thoroughly, and ultimately, feel more responsibility and accountability.

SUMMARY

Marketing planning is a fluid process, with information flowing to, from, and between all of the marketing functions and the marketing manager. It is also a lengthy process, often spanning four to five months. Business objectives dictate the overall task of marketing, and the business strategies guide the formulation of marketing objectives. Ideas on how to fulfill these objectives can come from anyone or any function, inside or outside of marketing. Marketing research helps to provide the information necessary for making judgments and testing ideas. The marketing manager determines the optimal use of each marketing function, assigns roles to each, and provides strategic direction. In turn, each of the marketing functions develops its own detailed plan to support the objectives. The critical "action" portions of these plans become integrated into the overall marketing plan. Finally, after implementation, marketing research closes the loop by helping to evaluate the success or failure of the chosen tactics. This information is then utilized in formulating the following year's plans.

POSITIONING
In Plain Language

Positioning is one of the most broadly used and valuable terms in marketing. The success of the product itself depends on the positioning choice, and the successful planning of every marketing function depends upon understanding it.

Positioning is a comparative measurement used to determine where a product is (or will be) situated in the marketplace relative to competitive offerings. It differentiates the product from others, based on a particular attribute or set of attributes (if positive, called *benefits;* if negative, called *detriments*). Attributes can include such characteristics of a product as price, sweetness, speed, brightness, weight, mileage per gallon, etc. Each product has its own set of attributes, which consumers consider when making a purchase decision.

Positioning is determined by how consumers *value* an individual attribute or group of attributes. We can say that positioning of image for a Mercedes is "upscale," but only because consumers perceive it as upscale. We can say that the taste of a particular coffee is "superior," but only because consumers perceive it as superior. Positioning is a subjective measurement: If all coffees tasted exactly the same, none would be superior over another.

Similarly, when attributes are grouped together to produce a "clustered" attribute such as "upscale" (e.g., made up of packaging, price, name and name allure, spokespersons, advertising), the attribute becomes an entity of itself. If we break this attribute up into its components and ask which are most important in creating the perception, we can get some very varied opinions. That is because every individual has a different idea of what "upscale" means.

Positioning is used for many purposes in marketing strategy and planning. Most important, positioning is used to help distinguish how a particular product differs from the other competitive offerings. In this way, it serves to segment the market into subcategories that address different consumer needs. It is used to find and define product benefits so that they can be communicated through advertising and other marketing programs to the right target audience. Positioning helps us to detect product weaknesses so that they can be eliminated. Positioning is also used to locate gaps in the market that new products can fill or that existing products can be adapted to satisfy. The "Great Taste, Less Filling" positioning of Miller Lite beer is a good example of the strategic use of positioning. In this case, whether Miller fulfilled on those promises was secondary to the fact that those were the two reasons why people would prefer light beer to other alternatives. Miller had them both covered.

Many marketers trying to figure out what elements or clusters to strive for with their products feel overwhelmed because there are so many dimensions upon which to compare products. Knowledge of the industry, historical trends, competitive failures and successes, and buying behavior in your product category can help you to construct your own positioning strategies. Keeping up with consumer trends is critical. The ultimate test of important positioning criteria is consumer preference, and marketing researchers conduct intricate studies to determine what that is.

When product categories are broken down into segments, or subcategories, the value of attribute sets can vary widely among those segments. For example, smell might be more important than texture to the average consumer of "perfumed soaps," but texture could be more important to the average consumer of "natural soaps." Product positioning is a fluid, ever-changing process that follows changes in consumer tastes and preferences, and seeks out needs and wants among the consumer segments. New positions for products are constantly being created.

Although we have been talking about using product attributes to establish a product's positioning, we have to remember that creative vehicles (i.e., packaging, advertising, promotions, and public relations) are the means by which we relate and enhance that positioning to the consumer. Product positioning (i.e., image) can be established by creating an illusion of superiority, utilizing advertising, packaging, promotions, and public relations, when significant differences do not exist. That is what makes the marketing game so important and, at times, so unpredictable.

It is critical that the marketer knows how he or she wants consumers to think of the product he or she is attempting to sell. The *positioning statement* should clearly identify a unique product attribute or benefit—the reason why the consumer should buy the product. The want or need for this benefit and the way that consumers perceive this benefit (i.e., its utility and appeal) should be tested through marketing research. The positioning statement format is as follows:

For (target audience), (brand) is the (qualifier such as "only," "leading," etc.) brand/model/ etc. of (category) that (benefits and reason to believe those benefits).

For a new type of ski positioned toward the performance skier who likes to ski both moguls (bumps, requiring flexibility for control) and flat surfaces (requiring stiffness for speed), a good positioning statement might read:

For competitive skiers who love to run moguls, the new XYZ variable stiffness ski is the first and only model of competitive ski that can be switched from flexible for control on mogul terrain, to stiff for speed on flat terrain, at the push of a button.

In contrast, a poorly communicated positioning statement might read:

For skiers, the new XYZ ski is the model of ski that changes from stiff to flexible.

Note how the first statement involves the skiers' feelings and more clearly defines the way the marketer would want consumers to think about the product. A clearly formulated positioning statement is critical, because it is how the product positioning is communicated in the marketing plan and to the functions. It ensures that all of the communication-oriented marketing tools work toward a common goal.

TWO

TOP-LINE

OVERVIEW

All marketing decisions involve some form of marketing research, because all decisions rely on information. Marketing research provides the means of acquiring and processing such information. Marketing research can be as complex as a 200 question survey given to 3,000 people, or as simple as picking up the phone and asking a friend or associate a question. It allows you to measure and evaluate *all* marketing premises and programs in all marketing functions, including advertising, promotion, product development, and distribution.

Understanding marketing research and its components can become very complicated for the layman, because of the wide variety of marketing research classifications.

Here's a look at marketing research and its subcategories:

Marketing research is the gathering of information needed and used in any and all kinds of decision making in marketing. Marketing research comprises two subtypes of research: (1) market research (often confused and wrongly interchanged with "marketing research"); and (2) consumer research.

Market research is the investigation of the world in which the product will be sold and will compete. It includes the study and measurement of anything that influences the performance of a product. All too often, marketers forget to look beyond their own businesses to see how things going on in the world can affect their products.

Market research has four layers or levels: (1) world; (2) industry; (3) business/category; and (4) product. At the "world" level, macro issues (like the economy, social structure, the water supply, environmentalism, etc.) can influence a product's performance (e.g., the effects of the environmental movement on marketing of plastic products).

Narrowing its focus, market research goes on to study the "industry" level (e.g., consumer packaged goods, industrial machinery, transportation, etc.) where trends, innovations, and events in other types of industries influence a product's performance (such as the effects of microwave technology on the food industry).

After surveying this industry level, market research delves into the "business/category" layer (e.g., frozen food, cosmetics, automobiles, etc.), where trends and events across categories affect a product's performance or determine opportunities (e.g., the effects of low-fat and cholesterol-free trends on an ice cream business). The category level can also be reviewed in greater detail at sublevels or category *segments* (e.g., frozen dinners for children versus those for adults; full-course versus entree only and/or extra helping frozen dinners; upscale versus mainstream frozen dinners).

Finally, market research is refined at the "brand" level, where specific research is performed on a product and competitive products within a category.

Consumer research is a far simpler concept. This is the investigation of how people perceive, influence purchase, purchase, and use a product.

There are three key ways to distinguish different types of research and research designs:

SOURCES OF INFORMATION: There are two ways of gathering information or "sources" for both market and consumer research: (1) *primary research,* where the researcher directly studies, tests, and measures actual events or people's reactions to things (e.g., surveys, interviews, observation); and (2) *secondary research,* where the researcher relies on the research information others have gathered or their interpretation of others' information (e.g., reading books, reports, and articles, buying *Nielsen* data).

As a general rule the marketer will probably draw most *market* research information from secondary sources, and *consumer* research information from a mix of primary and secondary sources.

Most of what is to be learned in marketing research is the result of primary consumer research and drawn from consumer reactions to products, whether the consumer is a brother, child, parent, friend, purchasing manager, or buying committee. (The "consumer" is the person or groups of people who either buy or influence the purchase of your product. The importance of each "consumer" is determined by how much influence he has.)

TYPES OF MEASUREMENT: There are two types of information gathering: (1) *qualitative research,* involving nonnumeric measurements (e.g., feelings and emotions about product characteristics); and (2) *quantitative research,* involving numerical measurements (e.g., sales data, ratings).

In general, *qualitative* research is directional, telling marketers where they should focus their research efforts, while *quantitative* research is more definitive, giving marketers comparative "hard-number" measurements like rankings, ratings, and so on. However, note that there's sometimes a fuzzy line dividing these two, as qualities of something can be measured (i.e., rated, ranked) and quantities can be judged (i.e., two things together make a different impression than each alone).

TYPES OF RESEARCH DESIGN: Research is said to be *syndicated* or generic if it is conducted for no specific single customer and is sold to a number of customers (e.g., Nielsen Scantrack). Research is said to be *customized* if it is tailored to the needs of one or more specific clients.

Syndicated research includes volume and performance tracking studies (e.g., Nielsen Scantrack, which determines the size and makeup of a TV audience); events tracking studies (e.g., couponing, special pricing, display usage and impact); and market and consumer information and dynamics studies (e.g., demographics, household usage, and indices that measure how well a category or brand is developed in a particular geographic market as compared with the rest of the nation).

While syndicated data does not often answer specific research questions, especially those that are qualitative, it does provide raw data from which many other relationships can be observed and questions developed. As well, marketers often pay syndicators fees to conduct studies drawing upon the syndicated data to provide answers to specific questions from the marketer.

THE ROLE OF MARKETING RESEARCH

As discussed in chapter 1, marketing research plays a vital role in building a marketing plan, especially in supplying data for the situational analysis and other subsequent marketing functional plans (i.e., product, packaging, advertising, promotions, public relations, pricing, and distribution plans).

The product of marketing research is information, which is fuel for all decision making. Marketing research is the most valuable resource to a marketer but is often not utilized to its fullest potential. Most people think that marketing research plays its most important role early on in the new product development process. However, marketing research should be used throughout the life of any product or business to monitor its performance, identify new opportunities, and alert marketers to potential threats.

MARKETING RESEARCH PLANNING

While the other marketing functions have a single grand charter or plan (e.g., advertising plan), marketing research has lots of little plans, usually built around questions that arise during the development of each of the other functional plans. As such, marketing research plans can be said to be "information gathering and evaluation" plans for the other functions. A marketing research expert also can and should *initiate* a research project if he/she believes it to be important.

Ideally, if one had all the information in the world at one's fingertips, one would be able to make every decision without using judgment or intuition—pure logic would drive decisions. But this is not realistic. The ability to make decisions with only partial information is what gives a marketer the opportunity to prove his/her value—because he or she must always make decisions based on incomplete or imperfect information. Utilizing the proper channels to get the *right* information gives the marketer the edge. The reason we use marketing research is to minimize the incompleteness and imperfection in the decision-making process.

When it comes right down to it, "strategic thinking" is simply the ability to organize known information and to decide upon and prioritize what else needs to be known. And strategic planning is like a chain, using one long series of questions, finding answers that lead to subsequent questions, finding answers to them and so on. However, determining what questions to ask and in what order to ask them is a lot more difficult than it sounds. Mastery of the "questioning process" may be the single most important and most frequently neglected job of any marketer.

The average marketer cannot always depend upon the marketing research manager or analyst to tell him what questions he should be asking. This is because the researcher is often given a problem in a vacuum and the research department works on a priority basis. It is up to the marketer to: (1) formulate an effective, prioritized *questioning* regimen; (2) provide the researcher with all of the known facts surrounding the issue; or (3) both of the above. The best way to optimize marketing research is to *talk* to the functional experts about where you want to be with your product and what you want to know to get you there.

Questioning strategies differ somewhat depending upon objectives and timing. The most common lines of questioning in the marketing world stem from day-to-day requests, where information is needed to make smaller or more isolated decisions. Sometimes these questions are very simple, such as, "What is my market share in the Raleigh/Durham market this week?" Questions like these can be answered by reviewing syndicated data.

However, other questions are more complicated and much broader, involving a series of supporting questions, especially when you want to know *why* something has happened. For example, let's say you work for a snack company and your division's sales of its canned nuts took a big drop last year. You are asked to find out why and make recommendations on what to do about it. This is a very broad problem, and there are likely many factors contributing to its cause. You need to know what questions to ask—and in what order—to find answers to a complex problem.

Since shortage of time and money are often the major constraints for the researcher in today's highly competitive, low-budget, fast-changing business environment, the marketer can make the most of the dollars and minutes available by planning his/her research well. The most valuable single practice a marketer can learn is how to organize and prioritize his/her questions.

Here is PM's simple prescription to help marketers identify key or "major" questions, figure out what "supporting" questions must be answered in order to discern the answer to the major questions, and how to go about developing the proper research tools to do so.

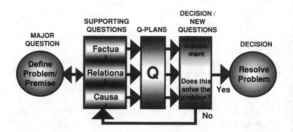

MAJOR QUESTION: We begin with defining the problem or asking the *major question* (the "premise" if this is a marketing plan), identifying the specific *knowledge* needed to be obtained to make the right final decision. Questions can be broad or narrow, from "How do I grow my product's share?" to "Does our advertising work?"

Major questions often reflect business and marketing objectives and strategies. You may ask, "How can I increase sales of my cookies brand by 50 percent over the next two years?" because it is one of your division's marketing objectives. But if you find out the following week that your company is getting out of the cookies category in six months and wants to maximize the value of the business, this major question changes to "How can I increase profitability of my cookies brand over the next six months to make it more attractive to prospective buyers?" The two questions have very different answers. Understanding exactly what your major questions are will help you to focus rather than fragment your research efforts.

SUPPORTING QUESTIONS: Supporting questions are those that are asked to obtain information to help answer the major question. A supporting question can be *factual* if it seeks information from which you can obtain a measurable answer (e.g., "How much did my share drop in March, April, and May of last year?"). A supporting question can also be *correlational*, if it asks about two or more things that occur or vary together. And, a supporting question can be *causal,* if it asks the "reason" or source of the event.

Sometimes answers to supporting questions help us to realize that what we thought was a major question is actually a supporting question in disguise and that there are more basic questions that need be asked.

PRIORITIZING QUESTIONS: Questions unfold like a pyramid, from the point at the top, representing a major question, down through all of its supporting questions, that will eventually provide the key information to answer the major question. If you have difficulty prioritizing your questions, you can use another tool called the *question tree*. The tree is a physical way of organizing questions so that the answer to simpler questions helps to answer questions higher up on the hierarchical ladder.

A tree can get very full very quickly, so think through and select questions carefully. A PM Tools form for a question tree is included at the back of this chapter for your use.

Once the questions are organized in the proper hierarchy, we are ready to develop *research plans,* or *Q-Plans,* for each question, beginning on the lowest branch of the tree and working our way upward. Here is an example of a typical question tree:

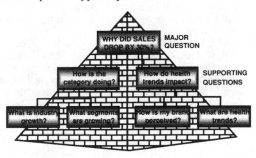

THE Q-PLAN

The *Q-Plan* (short for "Question Plan") is the nuts and bolts of research. It is adapted from the basic research-planning format used by most companies— the three major steps in conducting research: (1) questions/hypotheses; (2) methodology; and (3) results analysis.

QUESTION/HYPOTHESIS: State the question or *hypothesis* (an assumption that you want to prove, such as "If I remove the scent from Irish Spring soap, loyal consumers will switch brands"), and the situation surrounding the issue being researched—the snapshot or the current predicament or insight, how it came to be, and where you want to go from there. Describe the situation and things and events affecting the situation, including the "what you know" that pertains to the situation. Discuss what you will do with the information once you get it. Discuss the situation from as many angles as you can. Many call this process "defining the problem." Have fun with this—tell the story. In this way, you will understand where the particular question you are researching fits into the grand scheme of things, or along your question tree if you are using a hierarchy.

METHODOLOGY: Once the question or hypothesis has been determined, figure out the best way of obtaining the information that answers your question or proves the hypothesis (i.e., determine the best marketing research tool to use and how to best use it).

Application, or what decisions the information will help to make, usually dictates the most appropriate research technique to use. This section is the "game plan": what research techniques will be used and how they will be used to answer a question or test a hypothesis. It has three sections:

RESEARCH APPLICATION AND TECHNIQUE: Describes the application for which information is sought and the technique or method best suited to obtain this information, as well as an overall discussion of how the technique will be used. There are literally hundreds of research techniques/methods/studies that can be selected to answer a particular question or prove a particular hypothesis. Selection is dependent upon the *application* to which the information will be applied and the type of information sought. Will it be used to obtain: (1) situational analysis or "strategic marketing" information (e.g., positioning, segmentation, consumer behavior); or will it be used to find answers to questions concerning specific marketing functions (e.g., product development, advertising, distribution)?

PREPARATION AND FIELDWORK: Describes how a sample will be selected, how data will be collected, and how responses will be measured, using the selected technique. This includes scheduling and conducting interviews, using the library, etc. The *validity* should be verified (i.e., whether your research design measures the data correctly and accurately), and its *reliability* assured (whether your research design can be replicated in another place and yield the same or similar results).

PROCESSING, TABULATION AND REPORTING: Describes how the data will be recorded (e.g., computer program), organized (e.g., measurement criteria), and reported (as either a written or oral presentation).

RESULTS ANALYSIS: This is the final and most important part of the research process. The first step in *analysis* is to determine which data will be used and how it will be organized and used to the researcher's best advantage. So many varying conclusions can be drawn from even small packets of *raw data* that one must not only select the information itself, but also the most valuable ways of using it.

Some marketing research analysts begin this process by looking through all the data for *anomalies,* or information that really stands out as different from the rest. Sometimes this is a good place to begin, other times one needs to survey the results as a whole to draw a conclusion or see a pattern.

The second step in analysis is to interpret the results of the study and apply them to the original question or hypothesis. Analysts often present the conclusions of the study and attach the raw data, so that others can draw their own conclusions and insights, as well as formulate newer or more refined questions based on the results of the study. There is no "cut-and-dried" formula for analysis—it depends entirely upon personal style. The results should then be evaluated to see if major questions are answered or if, given new information, paths on the question tree change.

SITUATIONAL ANALYSIS RESEARCH

If your questions or hypotheses involve general market information sought for the situational analysis of your marketing plan or for strategic use during the normal course of business (e.g., how the market is broken up, who competes in each "portion" of the market, how your product stacks up against others, etc.), your application is "strategic marketing" knowledge. Research methods for strategic marketing applications include:

SEGMENTATION STUDIES: This type of research is performed or should be performed for every product. *Segmentation* is the division of a general market into smaller portions of the market, each of which is defined by a particular criterion (e.g., geography, age, sex, affinity for product benefits) and has an audience that is fairly consistent within that definition. For example, the automobile market can be broken down by the class of car, including "luxury," "compact," "sports," and "economy."

Segmentation is used in all marketing functions to help us understand the variability and dynamics in consumer need and behavior, so that we can compare our products with those of competitors, identify opportunities, and map out plans of action to position and market our products. The following are the most frequently used bases upon which to segment a market:

GEOGRAPHIC SEGMENTATION: Breaking down a market by specific selling areas. This is done by companies in ways related to their specific needs, but standards also exist. Major markets and subcategorizations that are used by the media are often adopted by product groups as their segmentation categories also.

DEMOGRAPHIC SEGMENTATION: Breaking down a market by characteristics of the consumer, including age, sex, household size, income, educational level, and so on. This type of segmentation, called a user profile, helps marketers determine who is using their products and what candidates can be targeted with additional or modified marketing efforts.

PSYCHOGRAPHIC SEGMENTATION: Breaking down a market by behavioral characteristics of consumers, including opinions, attitudes, beliefs, activities, and interests. Identifying a portion of the consumers as "health conscious" is an example of a psychographic segmentation.

PRODUCT BENEFIT SEGMENTATION: Breaking down a market for a product by consumer perception of benefits and fulfillment of them. Examples of a product's benefits include: "cleans effectively," "smells good," "tastes great." Marketers of Lite Beer from Miller understood that the light beer market, when segmented by benefit, was divided into two key attributes sought by its consumers: "great taste" and "doesn't fill you up." They attempted to satisfy both segments by touting their slogan "tastes great, less filling."

Attribute studies are often used to determine the relative importance that consumers place on specific product characteristics/benefits. For example, one might want to examine the attributes of hand soap, which could include "scent," "texture," "cleaning power," and "deodorant properties." Attribute studies, if done properly, identify: (1) what is important to the consumer; and (2) how well a specific product fulfills the demands for those attributes or benefits. Consumers are often asked to rate or rank these attributes; this provides marketers with critical information on the positioning of their products with respect to consumer needs, preferences, and competitive offerings. Attribute studies are the heart and soul of benefit segmentation and positioning analysis. The PM Tools section of this chapter contains a template for designing your own attribute studies.

PRODUCT APPLICATION SEGMENTATION: Breaking out a market by how a product is used (application) and how often (usage occasion). Application segmentations include specifications such as "indoors and outdoors," "at night," and "in recipes." Usage occasion includes both frequency of purchase qualifiers such as "frequent buyers" versus "occasional buyers," and frequency of usage qualifiers such as "heavy users" versus "light users."

Often, several types of segmentations are combined into one *cross-segmentation,* rendering specific or *pinpoint* segments (e.g. "active people over age 40 living in the Northeast" and "sedentary people over age 40 living in the Northeast"). Pursuing a specific market segment is called **niche marketing,** and pursuing groups of segments that make up a large proportion of a total market's composition is called **broad-based marketing**.

Effective segmentation is not always achieved, as there are so many options or qualifiers that may be used to divide up segments. So, how do we know whether we have selected the best ones? This can be decided by identifying where the most (or most important for your brand) purchasing power lies in the market, what are the most important consumer needs (fulfilled or unfulfilled), who the competition is, and where the opportunities occur. Segments should be evaluated for sales and growth potential as well as for the anticipated ability to capture a percentage of that segment, based on the company's or product's strengths and weaknesses.

POSITIONING STUDIES AND OPPORTUNITY ANALYSES: Once

we've determined what's important to the consumers and what their ideal preferences are, and where our company's and competitors' products are situated with respect to those preferences, we can conduct an opportunity analysis. There are many tools at the marketer's disposal for identifying opportunities in the marketplace for the company, existing products, and new products.

Positioning maps are a popular method of visually presenting the results of attitudinal and positioning studies. Using at least two major segments of the market, we draw a grid. Then we plot our company or products, competitors, and even the "ideal" consumer point for reference. This is also a good method for defining niches, where we see concentrations of consumer interest or competitive activity. Here is a sample positioning map for a product called Bongo Bubble in the bubble gum market:

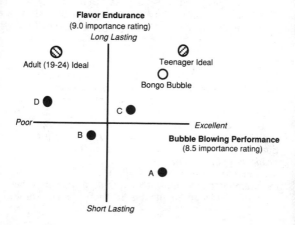

In this example, let's say that we identified the two key attributes of importance to the consumer: (l) how long the flavor lasts; and (2) how well the consumer can blow bubbles with the gum. This diagram lets us see that Bongo Bubble is perceived as being the leader along those two dimensions.

Of course, there are usually many more than two attributes that distinguish a product, and *multivariate attribute analyses* can be conducted along more than two dimensions. It is often easiest and most fruitful to work with two at a time and try different permutations. When these maps are used to identify unfulfilled needs or gaps of opportunity in the marketplace, this is called *gap analysis*.

The same chart, identifying pockets of consumers in different "age" segments, shows that older consumers like the flavor-lasting quality of bubble gum but don't really care much whether it blows good bubbles.

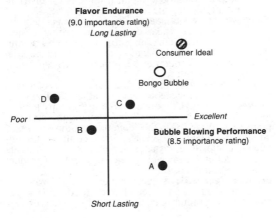

Perhaps this signifies that there is a gap (no competition or insufficient competition) in this segment of the market, and the need for an "adult"-oriented, "semibubble" gum with long flavor-lasting qualities could be capitalized upon. This is a simple example of an enormously powerful opportunity assessment device. A template for a positioning map is provided in the PM Tools section at the back of this chapter.

FUNCTIONAL RESEARCH

Each marketing function has unique research requirements and methods of testing and evaluation. Rather than present them here out of context, we have included them in their respective chapters.

MARKETING RESEARCH GLOSSARY

A/B Split Method: A way of measuring the effectiveness of various offers by splitting two or more offers into different geographical regions for distribution, and monitoring the results.

Adoption Process: The progressive steps by which consumers make decisions regarding a new product or innovation. The initial response is awareness, then interest, evaluation and comparison, trial purchase, and rejection or adoption (evidenced by repeat purchase) follow.

Aggregation: Viewing various portions of a market as one homogeneous entity, rather than as *segmented* sections. Corporate marketing groups tend to aggregate their businesses when developing strategic plans (e.g., AT&T is in the "communications business" comprising telephones, central office equipment, computers, cable, long-distance service, etc.) to provide clear direction for managing diverse yet related product areas as a single portfolio.

Aided Recall: A questioning technique whereby consumers are asked to recollect a brand name, logo, commercial, product, etc., with the help of clues or suggestions.

Analysis of Variance (ANOVA): A statistical method used to determine the relationship between different groups, using the averages of an attribute that all groups have in common.

Area of Dominant Influence (ADI): A breakdown of geographic markets by county based on high percentages of television viewing.

Attitude: An attraction or repulsion response to a specific stimulus, and the tendency for a consumer to react to those emotions with action.

Attribute: A distinct quality or set of characteristics that facilitates description and comparison of a product, audience, or program, such as "brightness," "taste," "maturity."

Brainstorming: An ideation technique, where a finite group of participants (usually five to ten) is given a specifically defined problem or objective to discuss. Freewheeling, unlimited offering of ideas is encouraged; nothing is rejected. This method is based on the principle that the subconscious will produce flashes of creative brilliance when highly stimulated and unconstrained. It is used to generate a long list of ideas, good or bad, to be later evaluated and narrowed.

Brand Development Index (BDI): This is an indication of how well a brand is performing in a specific geographic area, relative to its average performance in the whole country. It is determined by measuring the percentage of a brand's sales in a geographic area then relating the percentage of population in that area to that of the whole country to produce an index number. For example, if Brand A has a 4 percent share of sales in Detroit, and Detroit's population is 5 percent of the entire U.S. population, the BDI in Detroit is 80. BDIs are used to help determine the stronger versus weaker markets in which a brand competes.

Buddy Interview: A type of *qualitative* research in which two people are interviewed at once, typically two who are friends or family members. It is thought that this raises the comfort level of both participants and makes them more open, honest, and apt to disclose more detailed information.

Buying Center: Everyone who is involved in the decision to purchase a product.

Case Study: A single project or situation that has been observed and documented for an extended period of time. Used to simulate decision-making environments in business courses, where students are presented with a problem and enough information from which to draw conclusions and make decisions.

Causal Question: A question whose answer will identify the "reason" why something happened.

Causal Relationship: A situation in which changes in one variable directly effect a change on another. An example is a rumor of a merger causing the stock of the parent company to rise.

Census Data: Demographic data collected by the United States Bureau of the Census, used in many types of research studies.

Cleancepts™: A method of preparing and testing *concept boards*, where the marketing elements (e.g., product ingredients, packaging, pricing, advertising, and so on) are separated and individually added to the consumer's view. In this manner, when readings are taken on the appeal of a concept, the effect of each element (positively or negatively) on the appeal of a concept can be cleanly identified. This process was invented by Brian Scott Sockin.

Closed-Ended Question: Also called a "multiple choice" question, where *respondents* are restricted in their answers by a selection of predetermined responses. This method allows for ease of tabulation and comparison of results.

Cluster Analyses: Research methods that group objects and events, based on the relationships of specific *attributes* for those objects or events.

Coding: Categorizing data for computer entry, cataloging, or manual manipulation.

Cognitive Dissonance: The psychological theory suggesting that when people have beliefs that conflict with their behavior, they justify their behavior by changing their beliefs. For example, if a normally frugal consumer buys a luxury item on the spur of the moment, that consumer will justify the purchase by saying that the item was a bargain "too good to pass up" or that it would be a necessity in the future.

Competitive Analysis: A comparison or series of comparisons made between competitive products, using specific attributes (e.g., "cleaning power"), groups of attributes (e.g., "image"), or performance (e.g., market share). This may be done at the manufacturer level as well, to determine relative volume, share, and spending levels.

Concept Test: Evaluation of the potential of a new product, innovation, or other idea. The concept test usually involves exposing consumers to verbal and visual stimulation and soliciting feedback from them.

Confidence Level: A statistical measurement that states in percentage the accuracy arrived at in repeated tests. For example, if a test had a 90 percent confidence level, it could be said to produce the same results ninety times if repeated a hundred times.

Construct: A concept that is not directly observable, such as attitudes and needs.

Consumer Research: The investigation of how people perceive, influence purchase, purchase, and use a product.

Correlation Analysis: A statistical method used to measure the strength of the relationship between two variables—to what degree changes in one variable can predict the changes in another variable.

Cross-Sectional Study: Research performed on a variety of selected events or subjects, at a specific point in time. Much more commonly used than the *longitudinal study*, in which a single event or subject is followed for a long time.

Cross-Tabulation: The statistical measurement in which two or more variables are cross-referenced and tallied to determine specific attributes present simultaneously in both.

Cue: A stimulus that generates responses to satisfy a consumer motive to do something.

Data Base: A computerized list of names, companies, and entities and information associated with them, used to target or track marketing activities. A company may construct its own data base, or may purchase data bases already in existence.

Delphi Method: A group judgment technique where expert opinions from outside the company are initially solicited, pooled together, and provided to all of the experts. The experts within the company then have a chance to reevaluate and evolve their opinions, based on the inputs of their counterparts. New opinions are then pooled and distributed. The process continues until a desired solution is reached.

Demographic Segmentation: Way of breaking down a market by consumer statistics of socioeconomic factors such as age, income, sex, occupation, education, family size, and the like. An example of demographics breakdown might read as follows:

CHARACTERISTIC BREAKDOWN:

Age: Preschool; 6–11; 12–17; 18–34; 35–44; 50–64; 65+

Income: Under $10,000; $10,000–$14,999; $15,000–$24,999; $25,000–$34,999

Education: Grade school or less; high school; high school graduate; college; college grad

Family Size: 1–2; 3–4; 5+

Sex: Female; male

Depth Interview: A personal interview technique in which consumers are spoken with individually in an attempt to get them to open up and express their true feelings about the subject matter.

Diary: A method of collecting consumer behavior with regard to product and/or media (e.g., readers, viewers, and listeners of primarily television, radio, and print) usage. Consumers are asked to keep a daily record of their habits (and sometimes feelings) with regard to the item being investigated. This is a type of *longitudinal* testing method.

Differential Advantage: Also called Competitive Advantage or Point-of-Difference. An edge for a product, as perceived by the consumer, within a designated market. The advantage can take the form of a physical attribute, price, image, shelf space, advertising, etc.

Exit Interview: A personal interview conducted with consumers at the place of sale after a product purchase has either been made or considered. Researchers stop people as they leave the store, asking either for oral responses to questions or for them to fill out a questionnaire.

Exploratory Research: Studies focused on ideas, used most often to get a directional feel for the next steps to use in solving a problem or gaining insight into it.

External Validity: The extent to which research findings can be generalized to other situations.

Factual Question: A question from which you get a measurable answer, such as "How much did my share drop last quarter?" or "How much did the overall market grow last quarter?"

Field Experiment: A research study that is conducted in a realistic setting, in which one or more variables are manipulated by the experimenter under controlled conditions.

Focus Group: An interview method where eight to twelve people are brought together for a "group interview," under the guidance of a trained interviewer, to focus on a specific concept, product, or subject. Focus groups are good for generating lots of ideas but are not very reliable measurements of opinions, partially because it is difficult to get a representative, unbiased group of people and, second, because people in the group fall victim to group dynamics and are influenced by others in the room.

Gap Analysis: A research technique in which *positioning maps* are used to identify unfulfilled needs or "gaps" of opportunity in the marketplace.

Geographic Segmentation: Dividing a population or marketplace into homogeneous groups based on physical location (Northeast, West Coast, etc.).

Halo Effect: Two different definitions: (1) Ideally, a consumer should be able to evaluate each attribute of a brand. However, when a consumer does not like a brand, he/she will naturally tend to exaggerate his/her feelings toward all of the attributes of the brand. Similarly, if a consumer likes a brand, he/she will tend to like the attributes of that brand more than if they were evaluated individually; and (2) The spillover of good or bad impressions of one brand to another when the two are associated together (either through actual cooperative marketing programs, use of a common name or trademark such as the company name, or association through usage). A nuclear waste disposal company that decides to produce a line of microwavable entrees could expect to see a bad halo effect from their core business transferred to the food line.

Hypothesis: A statement that makes an assumption regarding the answer to a problem. Hypotheses are stated and then proved or disproved through research.

Instrumentation Effect: The degree to which experimental results are influenced by changes in the measuring instruments.

Interval Scale: A measurement scale that uses units with the same value throughout the scale (e.g., mail scale).

Interviewer Error: Research errors derived from: (1) consumer impression of the interviewer's appearance, style, and actions; (2) poorly or incompletely asked or followed-up questions; and (3) poorly or incompletely recorded responses.

Leading Question: A question framed to sway the *respondents* answers in one direction or another, or one that provides a clue as to how he/she should answer.

Longitudinal Study: Long-term study in which a fixed sample of attributes are measured over time. A case history is an example of a longitudinal study.

Mail Survey: A questionnaire sent and returned through the mail to selected individuals. Typical response is 1/4 to 1/2 of a percent, however incentives such as free merchandise, a report on the results, etc., can boost response.

Major Question: In questioning strategy, a question that identifies the specific *knowledge* needed to be obtained to make the right final decision. In the marketing plan, often called the "premise."

Mall Intercept Interview: One administered in a shopping mall in which consumers are stopped and asked to participate, often for a small incentive.

Market Research: The investigation of the environments in which a product is marketed and the influences on the sales performance of the product. Market research has four layers or levels: (1) world; (2) industry; (3) business/category; and (4) product.

Market Segmentation: Dividing a market into subgroups with homogeneous characteristics (see *demographic, geographic,* and *psychographic segmentations*).

Marketing Research: The gathering of information needed and used in any and all kinds of decision making in marketing. Comprising marketing research are two subtypes of research: (1) market research (often confused and wrongly interchanged with "marketing research"); and (2) consumer research.

Mean: The average number, obtained by adding all elements in a group and dividing by the number of elements.

Minimarket Test: A miniature version of the *market test* conducted in one specific location, sometimes even in one retail account. This test has the advantage of keeping a launch more secret than a full-scale market test but is less reliable in predicting the rest of the target market than a larger sampling.

Moderator: One who leads a *focus group* or other type of group interview.

Morphological Analysis: A study that begins with the listing of the most important elements of a challenge and developing unique combinations based on those attributes.

Mortality Effect: An experiment error that occurs when multiple groups are used and some groups lose subjects who are fundamentally different from those subjects lost by other groups. This error is not an inevitable result when a group loses a member.

Multiattribute Studies: Ones with models that link attribute judgments with overall liking or effect.

Nonresponse Bias: A type of research error that occurs when portions of a research sample do not respond or respond incompletely or improperly.

Observation Method: Research technique in which a situation is watched over a period of time and relevant information is recorded.

Omission: A research error resulting from *respondents* to questions leaving out information by not answering or incompletely answering questions.

Open-Ended Question: A question that allows the *respondent* to answer freely without being limited to a set of predetermined choices.

Order Bias: The misleading effect of the order of questions, in general, and the cumulative effect that previous questions have on later questions and on responses. This can be avoided by varying the order among different individuals or groups.

Panel: A sample of consumers used to evaluate and provide opinions on products, packaging, and other marketing programs, often as a group situated in one place. (Panels are also utilized through teleconferencing, etc.)

Penetration: The degree to which a product or message has reached the targeted audience, expressed as a percentage of a population or geographical area.

Physical Attribute Analysis: Listing of key "visible, touchable, smellable, audible, and/or tastable" product attributes and modifying them to create new combinations that help to develop a new product.

Pilot Study: A "trial" research study done with a relatively small group of people or limited circumstances, designed to determine the potential of a larger and more in-depth study of the same topic.

Population: All individuals or subjects that make up a finite group of people, conforming to specifically set criteria (e.g., U.S. males ages twenty-four to forty-five).

Positioning: A relative measurement used to indicate where a product is situated in the marketplace relative to competitive offerings, based upon a particular attribute or set of attributes. Positioning is discussed in detail in chapter 1 because of its critical role in all aspects of marketing. The diagramming of positioning elements and ratings is called a *positioning map*.

Preference: The appeal of one product, attribute, or message over another to the consumer.

Pretest: A sample survey undertaken to troubleshoot or determine the effectiveness of the survey for use on a larger scale. Pretests often include more than one version of a survey.

Price Elasticity: The degree to which demand for a product or service will change as a result of the change in price. A price elasticity of 1.0 means that demand will vary exactly and inversely with a change in price. For example, if the price goes up 10 percent, sales go down 10 percent.

Primary Research: Direct, personal study of events or consumers (e.g., surveys, interviews, observation).

Product Application Segmentation: Breaking down a market by how a product is used (application) and how often (usage occasion).

Product Benefit Segmentation: Breaking down a market for products by perception and fulfillment of benefits to the consumer.

Projectability: The degree to which the results of a study can be said accurately to reflect larger groups or *populations*.

Projective Technique: A questioning method whereby *respondents* are asked to elaborate on or interpret vague information or images.

Psychographic Segmentation: Breaking down a market by behavioral characteristics of consumers, including opinions, attitudes, beliefs, activities, and interests.

Purchase Intent: The degree to which an individual has made a mental decision to buy a product. Usually measured on a scale (e.g., from 1 to 5; 1 being "definitely would not buy" to 5 being "definitely would buy").

Q-Plan: A format for using and evaluating research including three key steps: (1) formulating questions and/or hypotheses; (2) establishing and utilizing the appropriate methodology for answering those questions and/or hypotheses; and (3) identifying and utilizing the most appropriate method to analyze and communicate the results of a study.

Q-Sort: A psychographic method of organizing values, beliefs, and opinions, where participants are asked to group statements on a subject into groups, ranking them in order of importance. From Q-sorting, *cluster analysis* and *market aggregation* can be derived.

Qualitative Research: Research involving nonnumeric measurements such as feelings and emotions about product characteristics.

Quantitative Research: Research involving numerical measurements, such as sales data, ratings, etc.

Questionnaire: A research tool used to elicit answers to questions from *respondents*. Questions may be *open-ended* (*respondents* answer in their own words) or *close-ended* (answered by checking one of the several predetermined answers). The former is the more difficult to record and analyze because of lack of standardization.

Question Tree: A physical way of organizing questions so that the answer to simpler questions help to answer questions higher up on the hierarchical ladder.

Random Error: Normally expected error in a research study, occurring because of variations in the testing situation or individuals being tested.

Random Sample: A collection of individuals to be used for a test, selected so that each and every member of the contextual *population* has an equal chance of being included.

Raw Data: Data collected from a study that has yet to be organized, tabulated, or analyzed.

Recall Research: A research technique used to determine the "memorability" and subsequently (although sometimes falsely) the success of delivery of a message. Recall testing is either a*ided* or *unaided* by the tester.

Recognition Test: Similar to *recall research,* except that consumers are shown stimuli and asked if they remember having seen them before.

Regression Analysis: A statistical research technique used to determine the effect of each variable in an equation on the final outcome and to predict changes in effect based on manipulation of any or all of the variables.

Relational Question: A question that deals with observations about "coincidental" events that occur in a market—relationships that have occurred together, but whose cause is undetermined.

Reliability: The degree to which a research study can be replicated under similar conditions in different places and times.

Repeat Purchase: Purchases of a product that are made after the first *trial* purchase. Often measured in research studies by consumer intent to buy the product again after trying it.

Representative Sample: A sample of a population that approximates the results that would be obtained from measuring the entire population, ideally covering all factions and segments of the population fairly.

Response Bias: A research error that occurs because individuals tend to distort their answers for many reasons, usually psychological in character, such as defense mechanisms, desire for social acceptability, etc. An example is a mom saying that she doesn't believe in giving her children sugar when they ask, when in reality she may. She has given an answer that she believes to be right or acceptable rather than being truthful.

Role Playing: A type of *projective* research technique in which individuals assume and play out roles of other individuals to gain perspective on those individuals' thoughts and behaviors.

Sample: A group of individuals or elements selected from a larger group of people or elements.

Scanner: A computer-driven device that automatically reads printed *universal product codes* from products to pick up price information, track volume, and perform various research functions such as consumer *panel* research.

Secondary Research: Research that is "secondhand," gathered from others' *primary* research or their interpretation of others' information. Examples include reading books, reports, and articles.

Stratified Sample: A sample that is derived by dividing a population into homogeneous subsets and taking a random sample of each of those subsets.

Syndicated Data: Information collected on a regular basis, for no specific single customer, and sold to or used by a number of customers.

Telephone Interview: A survey technique in which questions are asked of *respondents* over the phone, usually as part of a standardized script.

Test Market: Selling a product or marketing program in a selected small area or areas that is representative of a larger ultimate market. Test markets allow the marketer to evaluate performance on a small scale, from which broader plans can be determined or refined (if performance shows promise).

Token Economy Study: A type of simulation in which research participants are given a form of currency with which actually to purchase products to take home (i.e., for free, but only up to a certain dollar or package number value). These studies force the consumer to make real purchase decisions, in a very inexpensive manner, and often are considered to be more *projectable* than far more elaborate concept and market tests.

Trend Analysis: A sales forecasting method that uses historical data to predict the future.

Trial Purchase: Initial purchase of a product, often measured as percentage of intention to "try" a product for the first time.

Unaided Recall: A questioning method in *recall research,* in which the respondent is asked to remember an object or event without any prompting or hints from the researcher.

Use Test: A method used in product development research where consumers are given a product to try and asked to provide feedback. Sometimes called a Home Use Test (HUT).

Utility: The value of a product, product attribute, or set of attributes to the consumer.

Validity: The degree to which a research technique accurately measures or predicts an outcome.

PM TOOLS™
RESEARCH AND PLANNING

- Market Sizing and Segmentation Worksheet
- Market Leaders and Market Characteristics
- Attribute Analysis
- Positioning Map
- Question Tree
- SWOT Analysis
- Positioning Statement

MARKET SIZING AND SEGMENTATION WORKSHEET

Category: _____

Market Segments:	Your Presence	19___	19___	19___	19___	19___
1 _____	☐	$ ___	$ ___	$ ___	$ ___	$ ___
2 _____	☐	$ ___	$ ___	$ ___	$ ___	$ ___
3 _____	☐	$ ___	$ ___	$ ___	$ ___	$ ___
4 _____	☐	$ ___	$ ___	$ ___	$ ___	$ ___
5 _____	☐	$ ___	$ ___	$ ___	$ ___	$ ___
6 _____	☐	$ ___	$ ___	$ ___	$ ___	$ ___
7 _____	☐	$ ___	$ ___	$ ___	$ ___	$ ___
8 _____	☐	$ ___	$ ___	$ ___	$ ___	$ ___
Total Market:		$ ___	$ ___	$ ___	$ ___	$ ___

MARKET LEADERS

TOP FIVE COMPETITORS

	$ Share	Vol. Share
1	_____ %	_____ %
2	_____ %	_____ %
3	_____ %	_____ %
4	_____ %	_____ %
5	_____ %	_____ %

TOP FIVE PRODUCTS

	$ Share	Vol. Share
1	_____ %	_____ %
2	_____ %	_____ %
3	_____ %	_____ %
4	_____ %	_____ %
5	_____ %	_____ %

MARKET CHARACTERISTICS

LIFE CYCLE ☐ New/Undevel. ☐ Growing ☐ Mature ☐ Declining

SEASONALITY ☐ No Skew ☐ Winter Skew ☐ Spring Skew ☐ Summer Skew ☐ Fall Skew

STRUCTURE ☐ Monopoly ☐ Oligopoly ☐ Healthy ☐ Fragmented

ATTRIBUTE ANALYSIS
INSTRUCTIONS

This is used to evaluate how strong your brand is along key attributes versus the competition.

Key Attribute Listing: List the attributes that you believe to be most important to the average consumer when he/she makes a decision to purchase yours or competitors' products. Take a reading on how important they are on a scale of 1 to 10, 1 being "not at all important" to 10 being "extremely important." This reading is to be taken with potential or current consumers of your brand, but can be taken by your own staff to see if your own perceptions of your brand match those of consumers. There is room for 9 attributes, but it can be as few or as many as you determine.

Attribute Fulfillment: Rewrite the key attributes in the left-hand column designated. Write in the competitive brands in the row beneath the grid as indicated. Then perform the same rating exercise as with the listing, except that the ratings will be made for HOW WELL a product fulfills or delivers that attribute or benefit. The ratings will be on a scale of 1 to 10, 1 being "not at all fulfills" to 10 being "fulfills extremely well."

Brand Strength: This is the final analysis, where the brand's strengths and weaknesses will be determined, relative to competitors', along each of the attributes and as a whole. Multiply the rating of the attribute from the attribute list by the rating in each box to yield the total strength. For example, if the attribute of "good taste" is rated as an "8" in importance and product "C" is rated as a "10" in having good taste, the total brand strength score is 18 for that attribute. Remember, just because a brand is rated high on fulfilling a particular attribute doesn't mean that that attribute is important to them.

Finally, tally up the scores for each product to see who wins.

ATTRIBUTE ANALYSIS
Attribute Listing

Key Attributes:	Rating:
1. _____	_____
2. _____	_____
3. _____	_____
4. _____	_____
5. _____	_____
6. _____	_____
7. _____	_____
8. _____	_____
9. _____	_____

Attribute Fulfillment

Attributes

Competitors

Brand Strength

Attributes

Totals:

Competitors

POSITIONING MAP

```
                    Y
                    | High
                    |
                    |
                    |
                    |
                    |
 _____|_____ X
 Low                |              High
                    |
                    |
                    |
                    | Low
```

KEY:

A _____   X = _____

B _____   Y = _____

C _____

D _____   SEGMENT:

E _____

F _____   _____

G _____

INSTRUCTIONS: Pick two product attributes or benefits that you wish to use to judge your brand. Make one the "X" axis and the second the "Y" axis. Write what segment you are evaluating (e.g., geographic, demographic, psychographic, etc.). List your product in the "A" spot on the key and each competitive with a subsequent letter.

Map each product from low to high on the map, using either actual numbers derived from an *attribute analysis*, or your own estimations or perceptions.

QUESTION TREE

Major Question

Question	Answer
Question	Answer
Question	Answer

Question	Answer
Question	Answer
Question	Answer

Question	Answer
Question	Answer
Question	Answer

SWOT ANALYSIS

STRENGTHS	WEAKNESSES	OPPORTUNITIES	THREATS

POSITIONING STATEMENT

For _____ (target audience),

_____ (brand) is the _____

(qualifier, e.g., "only," "first," "leading," etc.) _____

(category) that _____

_____ (benefits).

THREE

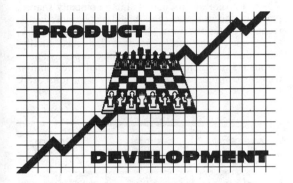

TOP-LINE

OVERVIEW

The "consumer universe" is in a constant state of flux. Thirty-something years ago, supermarkets were new and the wife did all the shopping and cooking for her family. The husband decided about the big ticket items, such as cars or TV sets, and the wife made most of the household purchase decisions. Advertisers generally targeted only the white Anglo-Saxon family.

Today purchase decisions are made or influenced by various members of the household. The smart marketer has recognized the growing consumer base that can be reached by segmented marketing. The aging population, the growth of single-parent households, and the dual working household have made a difference in consumers' needs and preferences for products. Product offerings and marketing programs ideally adapt and evolve accordingly.

What exactly is a ***product?*** It is a *single* salable or tradable physical entity or service. Anything that can be planned, developed, and marketed to anyone is a product. Nestlé Crunch is a product. Grey Advertising's creative service is a product. If a child wants to trade baseball cards for completed homework assignments, cards are the child's product; and the completed homework assignments are the other child's barter product. The definition extends beyond the physical tangible thing on the shelf in supermarkets. When a group of products within a company share a major common thread (e.g., brand name, ingredients, technology, application, target consumer, trademark, logo), they constitute a ***product line***. And finally, when this concept is extended to the competitive marketplace, in which other products that offer similar benefits compete, a ***product category*** is the term used.

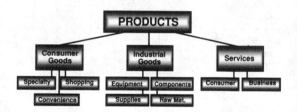

There are different types of products: (1) consumer goods; (2) industrial goods; and (3) services. Consumer goods can be divided into three major categories: convenience, shopping, and specialty goods.

Convenience goods include: ***staple goods*** (items that are replenished often, such as milk and eggs); ***impulse goods*** (low-priced products, such as an auto air freshener at a car wash, purchased "on a whim" with very little decision consideration); and ***emergency goods*** (products, such as motor oil, purchased out of immediate and usually unexpected need). Convenience goods seldom involve much decision making or preplanning. ***Shopping goods*** are products whose purchase requires at least some comparative evaluation of product attributes, such as price, quality, appearance, etc. (e.g., foods, apparel, toys, appliances, carpeting). ***Specialty goods*** are products (often high-priced or "big-ticket" items) that involve considerable evaluation and commitment by the purchaser. Consumers must often make a special effort to buy them and will go to great lengths to find and evaluate them (e.g., Godiva chocolates, cars, boats, bicycles).

Consumer goods packaged by manufacturers for retail sale and that have a relatively short useful life, such as packaged food, cigarettes, etc., are called *packaged goods*. On the other hand, such products are considered *consumer durables* if they have a long useful life, such as sports equipment and appliances.

Industrial goods include: (1) equipment (e.g., telephone switches, computers, manufacturing machines); (2) accessories (e.g., power tools, moving carts, office furniture); (3) supplies (fuel, office supplies, etc.); and (4) raw materials (e.g., land, fruit, vegetables, metals).

Services are personal and business actions of value, such as advertising, hairdressing, automobile repair, and travel consultation, performed with or without the exchange of physical products.

The word *brand* is used interchangeably with "product" when the product has a trade name assigned to it. This includes the majority of packaged and durable goods. *Private label brands* are brands "owned" by the wholesaler or retailer, often produced and packaged under a special name by major manufacturers and sold at a lower cost than the branded counterparts. Goods produced by other manufacturers are called *co-packed goods* and the manufacturer is called a co-packer. The company that produces a product that uses your product as an ingredient or component under their name, or packages your product under their own label, is said to *OEM* your product—you are the OEM (Original Equipment Manufacturer). Finally, a *product portfolio* is a diversified group of products that are planned together, often balanced against one another with respect to long-term financial planning (e.g., until recently, Quaker's portfolio included food, beverages, and toys among others).

BRAND NAME AND EQUITY

Most products are branded, meaning that they have been given a name, logo, or other identifying symbol or title to distinguish them from other similar products. Coca-Cola is a brand. The DMS-100 digital switch is a brand. Goodyear tires is a brand. The Goodyear All-Season Radial is a brand. Bugs Bunny is a brand.

Brand equity is the value of the brand to the consumer base and has five major components:

1. **BRAND AWARENESS** (also called "brand recognition"): The degree to which a brand is recognized. Brand awareness can be considered "high" or "low" and "positive" or "negative." People can also be aware of the brand name or specific

elements associated with a brand, such as logo, packaging, advertising, and so on. Within the process from learning about a product through purchasing the product, building *awareness* is usually the first objective of a manufacturer. While some purchase decisions for "impulse" items are made without prior awareness or its predecessor *knowledge,* most products must build this awareness before they can move the potential buyer toward the ultimate objective of purchase.

2. **BRAND LOYALTY**: The degree to which a brand has a constituency of "regular" users. Developing brand loyalty is very important to brands in all markets, and the establishment of this constituency is called the *consumer base.* Brand loyalty inhibits *brand switching* to competitive brands despite the use of a variety of marketing tactics, including pricing, promotion, advertising, and so on. The sales from the loyal consumer base, or the sales that a brand can come to count on, are called the *base volume.* The total of sales from additional users who try the brand because of a marketing action is called *incremental volume,* and this includes more frequent purchases from a loyal base, and purchases by non-users or competitive users.

Brand loyalty has two different levels: (l) *brand preference,* where, all things being equal, the consumer will choose one brand over others; and (2) *brand insistence,* where the consumer will accept no product other than the usual one, and will go to great lengths to acquire it.

Brand loyalty develops from familiarity, satisfaction, and family lineage experience with a brand ("it's the one my parents used"). Attitudinal elements that inspire repeat purchase of the brand include such qualitative things as image, comfort, and the company name.

3. **DIFFERENTIAL ADVANTAGE** (also called "competitive advantage" and "point of difference"): The single attribute or combination of attributes that consumers cannot find in competitive offerings and that they value enough to discourage them from switching brands or trying other brands. The advantage can be tangibly or only perceptually different from all available competitors.

The key to advantage is consumer perception (or business customer perception in the case of industrial marketing). Too often marketing managers become enamored of what they think is a differential advantage, only to learn later that the benefit for that particular product either had no influence on consumers or was even a negative attribute. There are also varying degrees of perception of advantage by different groups of people who buy products. Before an alleged "differential advantage" is infused into a product at inception or in its evolution, it should be tested against its key consumer base, *or* its new target users. The advantage also does not necessarily have to be a physical attribute or price of the product; it can also take the form of image, shelf space, advertising, etc.

The differential advantage often becomes the platform for positioning, advertising, and promoting of the brand, providing consumers with a reason to buy one product over other offerings.

4. **PERCEIVED QUALITY/VALUE**: The degree to which a brand has an image of quality or value, relative to its price and what a consumer must go through to obtain the product. In industrial markets, this is measured by *performance/price,* the ratio of how well a product delivers on its benefits based on the price.

5. **BRAND ASSOCIATIONS**: The memories and other connections that are made with a brand, both positive and negative. The Teenage Mutant Ninja Turtles kids property has a certain image; if a preschool targeted product ties in with the property for a promotion, that product becomes associated with the Turtles and "borrows" or internalizes some of its equity through association. When parents or children watch the television cartoon, they may think of the product with which it was linked. When one brand has an effect on the perception of another, this is called a *halo effect* and can be positive or negative.

The psychological connection that is made between a brand and any other product, person, event, or thing is called *linkage,* and can be exemplified by Mr. Whipple as a spokesperson for Charmin bathroom tissue, Kool-Aid Man as a spokescharacter for Kool-Aid drink mix, and beautiful beaches and relaxation associated with Club Med.

Developing and managing brand equity is one of the major "unwritten" objectives of every product marketer. Staying attuned to the status of a brand's equity relative to consumer and competitive trends will result in more effective marketing plans for your products.

THE PRODUCT LIFE CYCLE

The ***product life cycle*** (also called the PLC) defines the phases that a product goes through from introduction through its decline over time. Product life cycle follows four stages: (1) *introduction;* (2) *growth;* (3) *maturity;* and (4) *decline.* Many marketing managers determine functional marketing strategies based on where the product is in its life cycle.

The product is presented to the consumer during the ***introduction*** phase. Usually this is a period of high investment and spending to generate awareness and trial. Because more than 90 percent of the two thousand new products introduced each year fail, marketers are growing more cautious with introductions. Sales during this phase are typically low but climb steadily. Categories and industries can also be viewed in life cycle terms. An example of a category in the introduction phase is high-definition TV. An example of a product in the introduction phase is Pop Secret Pop Quiz™ colored microwave popcorn.

The introduction of a product is also called ***commercialization*** or ***trade release,*** when the product is made available to the wholesalers, retailers, and ultimately consumers. Release is *national* if it's made to all major geographical areas of the nation; *regional,* if specific portions of the nation are selected and others excluded; and *local* or pinpoint, if only very specific markets are selected. The word ***rollout*** refers to the progression into the markets (i.e., a national rollout means that the product is released simultaneously across the nation, whereas a market-by-market rollout means that a product is released step-by-step from market to market).

The ***growth*** phase is characterized by sharp inclines in sales, as the product gains regular users and begins to build equity in the consumer's mind. A typical strategy that accompanies the growth phase is full marketing support and relatively high spending to build the business. An example of a category now in a growth phase is high SPF sunscreens.

The ***maturity*** phase is the time when sales peak and level as the novelty of a product wears off, its utility becomes maximized, or as competitors begin taking share away and saturating or crowding the category. Profits usually drop as competition gets fierce. A typical strategy applied during this phase is either maintenance (if the category is not saturated), or heavy promotional spending if it is. Of course, these are general prescriptions and should only be viewed as "average" responses on the part of America's marketers—not gospel—and their applications differ from one prod-uct's situation to another. An example of a mature category is cola.

The *decline* phase is characterized by a loss in consumer interest and reduced sales of the product or category, low or negative profits because of loss of economics of scale, and competitive dropouts or relaunches with improvements. A typical strategy followed in this phase is to cut spending and take as much profit as possible until the product disappears, or to put the product on a very low maintenance schedule and keep it in the portfolio if it has at least a small loyal consumer base that can support it. An example of a category in decline is typewriters.

Some product categories, usually those that are entertainment, fashion-driven, and/or faddish typically have very short life cycles. Interest wanes very quickly in these categories, as innovations are constant. Toys and high-style apparel are good examples of these.

Life cycles should be used only to take a snapshot of how the product is doing, a signal to indicate which strategy should be pursued. Many other factors, such as competitive activity and consumer trends, also have to be examined in determining strategies. A product can die suddenly, as Red Dye #2 did. And a life cycle can *scallop* or begin a new climb, just when you think it's declining. This is especially true with nostalgia products like the Lava Lamp, which had long ago surpassed its maturity phase and been in the declining mode until recently.

It is the job of the marketer to avoid being pushed into taking a cookie cutter approach to divesting products. Every opportunity should be explored to develop or to breathe new life into all products in the portfolio. Even when opportunities are exhausted, efforts should be made to look for new ones periodically—the jet stream of consumer interest and preference shifts all the time.

PRODUCT ADOPTION

Product adoption is the decision-making process that influencers or buyers go through when approached with a product offer. There are several models of adoption, but the most popular and accurate is the following:

1. **AWARENESS:** Potential consumers are made aware of the product offer.
2. **INTEREST:** Consumers become interested in the offer.
3. **EVALUATION:** Consumers seek information about a product and competitive products and determine how each satisfies their needs based on product benefits.
4. **TRIAL:** The consumer tries the product for the first time, whether by purchase or sampling. The consumer decides at this point whether the product fulfills his/her needs and whether to buy it again.
5. **ADOPTION:** The consumer decides that the product is worthy of future purchase. At this point, the consumer has adopted the product.

The adoption process is the same for different types of products, but the length and amount of consideration at each stage varies. For example, a *convenience* product requires a very short period of consideration on the part of the consumer and little comparison with other products, whereas a *shopping* product requires a significant effort.

Consumers can also be categorized by their tendency to try a product for the first time. Innovators lead the pack in trying a product. They tend to be young and affluent, and ready to make purchase decisions with little outside influence. Early adopters have similar traits as innovators, but they are less ready to try a product without at least some degree of evaluation of others' opinions, and tend to be opinion leaders in their social circles. The early majority is the portion of the population that adopts a product just before the "average" consumer does, typically relying on significant information and opinions before doing so. The late majority is the average consumer, somewhat skeptical and cautious in trying a new product. Before trying it, a member of the late majority will wait until a sizable percentage of consumers has already tried a product and is happy with it. They will wait until improvements have been made and costs have come down. The laggards are the last group to try a new product, typically bound by strong patterns of conservatism or constraint. They usually adopt new products just prior to or when they are being made obsolete by newer products.

THE PRODUCT DEVELOPMENT PLAN

Before embarking on the product development process, general research should be conducted on competitive offerings by physical attribute and benefit (this breakdown may already have been completed in the situational analysis). If it is an existing product, a review of the prior year's product plans and results should be conducted and lessons learned should be stated. All of this should be articulated at the beginning of the plan. Once complete, the product development plan follows these steps:

1. Set product development *objectives* based on marketing objectives.
2. Conduct extensive product *research*.
3. Determine product development *strategies* that support and fulfill product objectives.
4. Determine product development *tactics* that put product strategies into action.

PRODUCT DEVELOPMENT OBJECTIVES

Product development objectives, as with all other functional objectives, should flow from the marketing strategies established for the project. First, unfulfilled needs or opportunities in the marketplace should be considered, as well as what *type* of product should be developed to address them. When we think of product *development* as a function of marketing, we have to be careful to avoid relating it only to "new products"; it is any type of innovation in a product, new or existing. Product development objectives include at least one of the following:

1. **NEW PRODUCT (OR LINE) IN EXISTING CATEGORY**: One which competes with other products and is usually differentiated from them by one or more distinguishing features or *competitive advantages*—benefits of the product that are perceived by consumers as superior to competitive offerings. An example of a new product in an existing category is the Apple Macintosh computer.
2. **NEW PRODUCT (OR LINE) INITIATING A NEW CATEGORY**: One that forges the way with a flash of brilliance, that does not compete directly with other products, and is usually considered a

breakthrough if it succeeds. An example of a new product creating a new category is the *wine cooler*.

3. **PRODUCT (OR LINE) EXTENSION**: New variation on an existing product (e.g., flavor, "lite") that makes it a type of new product but under the same trademark or brand name. An example of a line extension is Bud Dry beer, extended from the Budweiser brand.

4. **PRODUCT (OR LINE) SPIN-OFF**: One that begins as part of one product and emerges as a whole new line under a trademark or brand name different from its parent. This normally happens when the benefit conveyed by the product's name becomes more important or more recognizable than the original trademark. An example of a line spin-off is Light n' Lively brand of dairy products, spun off from Sealtest, and now becoming its own independent trademark. Spin-offs often occur in the entertainment industry, especially in television situation comedies, where one character is spun off of the original show and gets his/her own program (e.g., Rhoda, originally a character on "The Mary Tyler Moore Show").

5. **PRODUCT (OR LINE) VITALIZATION**: Also called product or line revitalization. Existing products or lines are made more appealing or compelling to consumers through enhancement of the product's physical or marketing attributes. Marketers often say that such efforts "breathe new life into the product" if successful. An example of a product revitalization is the Hula Hoop now being cross-marketed with Mattel's Barbie doll.

Vitalization can take the form of a brand or line *modernization* or *contemporization,* in which existing products or lines are brought up to date or into the future through product, packaging, advertising, promotion, and image. When the revitalization attempts to change people's perception of how a product or line stacks up against others, it is called a *repositioning*.

We believe it is wrong to "wait and see," as so many organizations do, and that product development should take place each and every year with each and every product! A marketer who researches and recognizes emerging trends and acts on them will have the first crack at the share of market. For example, recognizing the trend for low-fat products before they became mainstream would have given the marketer the impetus to line extend his brand before the trend took full shape and before a competitor could act first. Marketers should do their homework and treat their brands as havens for new opportunities on an ongoing basis. Each and every product manager should be a product development manager.

Product development objectives simply state what type of product (from the five categories above) is sought to be developed, for whom (rough target audience, which will be further defined after research), and the desired outcome of such development. For example, let's say that the marketing plan's situational analysis came up with an opportunity to make adhesive bandages that appeal to kids. The product development objective for this line might be:

> "To develop a *new line* of adhesive bandages designed especially to answer the needs of *kids, six to twelve,* that they will *love* and *use.*"

PRODUCT DEVELOPMENT RESEARCH

Research in this domain is predominantly used for product development but can be valuable for other marketing functions as well. Because product development is a specialty in itself, well-defined paths and well-developed techniques abound. To simplify, we divide product development research into six major steps, each with its own arsenal of research techniques: (1) concept ideation; (2) concept prescreening and screening; (3) concept testing and evaluation; (4) final screening; (5) concept development; and (6) product testing.

1. **CONCEPT IDEATION**: The generation of ideas. New products or new ideas for existing products can be benefit-based (e.g., prevents tooth decay), form-based (e.g., better tasting), or technology-based (e.g., more advanced). Ideas for new and existing products come from a wide variety of places, beginning with INTERNAL SOURCES: scientists, your own department, marketing task teams, functional business counterparts, employee suggestion programs, customer service center, social relationships, and top management.

   Product ideas also come from a wide variety of EXTERNAL SOURCES: exploratory marketing research studies, customers and consumers, events in your own category, competitors, events in other categories, technology, service agencies, universities, government, journalistic writing, and other global markets.

Although we're sure that many of the world's best product ideas have come "naturally" to people during the course of a normal workday, or during a round of golf, there are a number of sophisticated methods and technologies for inspiring them.

Ideation methods fall into one of three categories: (l) *problem analysis;* (2) *relationship analysis;* and (3) strategic marketing studies (discussed earlier).

Problem analysis techniques focus on identifying problems or challenges within product categories or products themselves, and solving them. Problem analysis can also pose problems already identified to users and probe for solutions. Techniques include *brainstorming* (a finite group of participants, usually five to ten, is given a specifically defined problem or objective to discuss); and *synectics* (broadly outlining a problem to a group to inspire ideas, without defining the problem specifics and thereby preventing bias).

Relationship analysis focuses on the interaction between different elements. *Forced relationship analysis* uncovers relationships between various products or materials, such as a car and a library, from which new ideas can emerge, such as the electronic computer atlas. *Morphological analysis* itemizes the most important attributes of a problem and then combines them in new ways to produce new ideas.

2. **CONCEPT PRESCREENING AND SCREENING**: Because the ideation phase often produces an extraordinary number of ideas, prescreening and screening are employed to weed out the bad ideas from the pool and keep those that are worthy of further exploration and testing. *Prescreening* refers to the internal first-stage narrowing of ideas, often by the initiator of the product development process. Frequently there is much overlap among ideas. The prescreener tries to isolate and separate *core ideas* or central themes from *build ideas* or overlays. In doing so, the number of ideas usually shrinks considerably, often without discounting any of them at this stage.

Next, *screening* occurs, which is usually a more scientific way of weeding out ideas, based on specific "minimal requirements" set by the screener or screening group. Criteria can be "market potential," "ease of manufacture," "financial potential," and so on. More criteria, specific to the category or target consumer, are also added in this rating process. For example, if we are developing a children's product and the parent is a critical decision maker, we might like to include "parent appeal" as one of the criteria. A *Concept Screening Form* can be found in the PM Tools section at the back of this chapter.

At this stage of the game, the marketer must be aware of and take care not to commit either of two types of errors: (1) **go-errors,** where poor ideas that should have been screened out are pursued; and (2) **drop-errors,** where good ideas were eliminated prematurely, because of inadequate or overly rigid screening criteria.

3. **CONCEPT TESTING AND EVALUATION**: Once a few good ideas survive the prescreening and screening processes, ideas are evaluated and enlarged into **concepts,** which are more defined ideas that include physical attributes, rough positioning, and identification of rough consumer target. **Concept boards**, art boards that present a concept in visual form, are used to encourage new ideas to grow from a core concept or to gauge consumer appeal, purchase intent, and other consumer behavior.

Concepts can also be **prototyped,** actually constructed or built as mock-ups at this stage for testing viability both with consumers and the manufacturer. Simple products, such as food products, are often prototyped in many forms, ingredients, and flavors early on in the development process, but products that are more complex and expensive to develop are prototyped in later stages. Products are not the only things that can be developed and tested. Elements like packaging and promotions, that help to reposition or vitalize a product, can be prototyped and tested as well.

Consumer response to presentation of concepts or products can also be gauged through a variety of methods and evaluation of results by marketers. A **focus group** of eight to twelve people can be brought together under the guidance of a trained interviewer or **moderator** to consider a specific concept, product, or subject. Participants are selected on the basis of specific criteria (consumption of product being tested, frequent category users, males, females, etc.). The **personal interview** or **depth interview** queries an individual directly. (Sometimes it is found that two friends or family members interviewed together are more likely to open up or be honest, and this is called a *buddy interview*.) The *mall intercept interview* is an interview conducted by stopping shoppers in a mall and often offering a small reward for their participation. An *exit interview* is one that is performed with consumers at the place of sale, after a product purchase has either been made or considered.

Both *telephone interviews* (with scripted introductions and standardized questions) and *mail surveys* are good for targeting many people inexpensively, compared to the above methods. However, they are limited in the quantity and quality of participation because there is no significant reward for the participant. You can expect a 3- to 5-percent response rate for a mail survey under excellent conditions (i.e., reward for participation, interesting and pertinent content, and simplicity to fill out and mail back with business reply). In addition, strategic marketing studies, such as attribute tests, described in the last section, are also productive methods of testing the appeal of concepts.

Finally, there is the concept of *Cleancepts*™, where the marketing elements of a product (e.g., product ingredients, packaging, pricing, advertising, and so on) are separated and layered onto a concept board, a graphic layout of a concept shown to a group, and tested individually. In this manner, when readings are taken on the appeal of a concept, it can be more cleanly measured what on that board is adding to and taking away from the overall appeal of a concept. Cleancepts is a good method to deploy in later stages of concept testing, once the basic premises and elements have been refined to some extent. Cleancepts is an invention of the authors, and a sample of the Cleancepts concept board can be found in the "PM Tools" section of this chapter.

4. **FINAL SCREENING (OPTIONAL)**: If there are still a number of candidates to choose from that have been tested in the last phase of development, they are put through a more rigid evaluation called the *final screen*, which focuses on the test results and business analysis criteria of the other business functions, such as operations, manufacturing, and finance. The final screening process usually produces one or more "final candidates." If further concept development, refinement, and testing need

to be done, the remaining competitors battle it out in a second round of Concept Development and Testing.

5. **CONCEPT/PRODUCT DEVELOPMENT**: Based on what has already been learned, a decision is made to build a real business proposition for concepts likely to be pursued and a physical translation of all that knowledge is made into a workable prototype of the product or service.

6. **PRODUCT TESTING**: The physical testing of the product under laboratory and actual "field" conditions, as well as with potential users during subsequent consumer research (e.g., new focus groups to discuss the physical product).

PRODUCT DEVELOPMENT STRATEGIES

To refine marketing objectives and functional direction and guidelines, we integrate learning from product development research into the marketing plan's situational analysis, if needed. Then we set product development strategies for the physical properties of the product:

1. **FORM AND APPEARANCE**: The shape or model of the product and visible characteristics.
2. **INGREDIENT BASE**: The material the product is made of and in what quantities.
3. **DELIVERY VEHICLE**: The ways the product is applied or used.

Because new product ideas can come from anyplace in the entire marketing system, the emphasis for a new product may have developed from its physical attributes or from attributes outside the physical product domain (e.g., distribution, image, packaging, etc.). Packaging is often tested simultaneously with the product. To the majority of consumers, packaging is perceived as part of the product itself (as in Jiffy Pop popcorn).

To expand on the bandages example used earlier, in which a product was being projected to satisfy a need by children six to twelve for bandages with easy, no-pain removal, appealing "nonembarrassing" graphics, shapes that are easy for little fingers to open and apply, and adhesive quality that keeps the bandage on until taken off, strategies could read like this:

1. **FORM:** Utilize shapes and graphics attractive to kids that will make the product fun to use and encourage wear.
2. **INGREDIENT BASE:** Utilize an adhesive that will not come off easily in daily wear but will not cause pain when the bandage is removed.
3. **DELIVERY VEHICLE:** Utilize a pull strip for easy opening and include a small "first aid kit" portable carrying case for easy transportation.

PRODUCT DEVELOPMENT TACTICS

These are specific measures taken to achieve the strategies and are not generic, as some of the other functions (e.g., advertising) are. They are also specific to the product. Using the bandages example, if we want to utilize graphics that children six to twelve will love, tactics (developed from continued research) could be popular cartoon characters with broadbased boy/girl split and appeal or graphics that appeal to one specific gender (e.g., Hot Wheels cars for boys; Barbie dolls for girls). Or the graphics might be targeted to specific age groups within the six to twelve category.

If we want to fulfill the need for easy, painless removal, tactics are the specific types of adhesives and plastic strip materials that hold the adhesive, etc.

Some tactics will be purely marketing based, and others will involve R&D and manufacturing input and decisions. However, it is the marketer's responsibility to present the consumer needs and benefits in priority order to these other factions and to work closely with them to that end.

CANNIBALIZATION

Before we close this chapter, it is important to discuss the one danger of product development efforts—*cannibalization,* which occurs when one or more new products "steal" sales away from another product or group of products in one manufacturer's portfolio. It is usually expressed as a percentage. Cannibalization is one of the major pitfalls of new product development, and the marketer has to be able accurately to project its effect on total sales.

An example of cannibalization is a company's introduction of a LITE version of their existing brand. The negative effect of the LITE product's sales on the *base brand*'s sales will give the cannibalization rate:

Before	After
LITE Introduction:	LITE Introduction:
Base Brand Sales =	Base Brand Sales =
$100 MM	$70 MM

LITE Sales = $50 MM

In this simplified example, $30 MM of LITE's $50 MM sales was estimated to have come from consumers switching from the base brand, or 30 percent cannibalization of the base brand: $30 MM /$100 MM = 30 percent. Of course, this assumes that no other factors were responsible for a reduction in base brand sales besides consumer switching to LITE. In reality, when predicting or tracking cannibalization rates, many other factors must be considered that affect sales of the base brand, such as changes in market conditions, competitive activities, marketing programs, and/or distribution.

Cannibalization is tolerated when the total line sales and income will exceed the projected original sales, had the new product not been introduced. The fact that, in the absence of the company's own new product, a competitive entry could steal share from the base business anyway also makes a case for tolerating cannibalization. The only time it is okay for a new brand to cannibalize a base brand without incremental volume or profit is when trends indicate that demand for the original brand will die anyway. But in any case, the cannibalization must be justified by the total health of the business.

PRODUCT DEVELOPMENT GLOSSARY

Base Brand: The original form(s) of the product or brand, from which line extensions are later developed, usually the core of the business and the largest volume and share generator.

Brand: An individual product defined and separated from other similar products in a category by a unique, protected identifying brand name, symbol, logo, or combination thereof.

Brand Awareness: The knowledge of a particular brand's existence. This definition should be expanded to "the *accurate* knowledge of a particular brand's existence," because the brand should be (and is not always) associated with the proper category. Awareness is often a primary objective of advertising, particularly with a new product introduction. It can be measured with marketing research techniques.

Brand Development: Penetration measure of a product's sales, usually per thousand population. If 100 people in 1,000 buy a product, the product has a brand development of 10.

Brand Development Index: The comparative measure of brand development over a variety of market areas (usually geographical). Indices vary around an average index of 100.

Brand Equity: Any cues that the target audience associates with a brand, including the brand name itself, logo, symbols, images.

Brand Extension: Addition of a new but related product to an already established line of products under the same brand name. This allows the new product to capitalize on the positive brand image or equities established by the parent brand, while addressing a different consumer need or want. For example, Jell-O brand pudding pops were developed as a brand extension to Jell-O brand pudding mixes.

Brand Image: The sum total of the qualities that consumers associate with a brand. These qualities may include physical elements, such as price and packaging, and also emotional cues, such as "rugged" or "feminine." All functions of marketing should work together to communicate and enhance a particular desirable brand image, once it is established.

Brand Loyalty: Degree to which a consumer will continue to purchase a particular brand as opposed to switching brands within the same category. A product that has a low degree of brand loyalty will be very sensitive to price promotions, and vice versa. Generally, the more unique the benefit offered by a particular product (or the more "uniqueness" a product is *perceived* to have by consumers), the greater will be the degree of brand loyalty. With many food products, loyalty is very much related to taste. Peers and family also have a great influence on brand loyalty. Advertising has the task of communicating the reason why consumers should be loyal to a particular product.

Brand Manager: Person who directs and coordinates all the marketing activities and the related functional input needed to achieve marketing objectives established for a particular brand. Usually the "team leader" on the business.

Brand Name: The identifying, proprietary trademark belonging to the manufacturer that produces the brand, which cannot be used by other manufacturers.

Brand Share: Also called *market share*. The percentage of total category sales (in dollars or in units) that one brand has relative to all other competitors in the category. Share grows or declines at someone else's expense or to someone else's benefit. What share means in terms of volume for a brand depends on the total category sales, growth, or decline.

Brand Switching: The purchase by a consumer of a brand in a category that is not the consumer's usually purchased brand. Promotions often prompt brand switching, particularly in low brand loyalty or commodity categories.

Cannibalization: A negative effect or loss of sales and share on the base of other existing product(s), due to consumer switching to a newly introduced line extension by the same manufacturer. For example, this happens to a full-fat/calorie food product when a manufacturer puts out a "light" version of the product. When new products are introduced, a projection of cannibalization of existing products must be taken into account when calling volume in the marketing plans. While the first product loses, the gains associated with the second product should outweigh these losses. Also, the "do it yourself before a competitor steals your share" principle applies here.

Category: Generic classification of similar products or services. For example, competing brands of cereals fall into the cereal category. Total category sales are used as a base to determine *brand share*. If total sales volume in a category is declining, all brands within the category will suffer—and the brand leaders (who will suffer most) in the category will probably beef up advertising and promotion efforts to bring the category back to life.

Commercialization: The introductory phase when a product is released to the trade for sale.

Commodity Product: A product within a category in which brands are not or are not perceived to be very different from one another. Examples are coffee, sugar, and eggs.

Concept Board: An art board used for consumer interviews, presenting a concept in visual form. Used to encourage new ideas to grow from a core concept or to gauge consumer appeal, purchase intent, and other consumer behavior.

Consumer Goods: Products made for and purchased by the ultimate consumer rather than for manufacturing or industrial use.

Consumption: Consumer purchases of the product. Measured by scanner data and provided to manufacturers.

Convenience Goods: Frequently purchased products, such as milk, bread, and eggs, that the consumer wants to buy with a minimum of effort.

Co-Packer: A manufacturer that supplies empty plant capacity for other manufacturers' use.

Decline Phase: The stage in the product life cycle where sales start to diminish due to "wear out." The decline phase is characterized by a loss in consumer interest and purchase of the product or category, low or negative profits because of loss of economies of scale, and replacement by new products that better satisfy needs.

Depth Interview: A personal interview technique in which consumers are spoken to individually, and the researcher attempts to get them to express freely their true feelings about the subject matter.

Drop-Error: A good concept that was mistakenly eliminated during the screening process.

Durables: Consumer goods that have a relatively long useful life, such as sports equipment, appliances, etc.

Emergency Goods: Products purchased out of immediate and usually unexpected need (such as a new muffler).

Extension: (Brand or Line) The addition of related varieties of an existing product under the same brand name.

Fad: Trendy product, usually with a short life cycle that peaks and dies very quickly (pet rocks).

Flanker Brands: Additional brands made by the same company that are secondary in importance to the core or main brand.

Fragmented Category: A product category in which the market has been overly segmented, resulting in many small *niches* and very few moderate- to high-volume segments. Many competitors, products with minor differentiating points and small shares, such as 1 to 2 percent, are characteristic of fragmented categories (e.g., the ready-to-eat cereals category).

Generic Brand: A product that does not carry a proprietary name and is known by a descriptive term (e.g., raisin bran).

Go Error: A type of mistake made in new product concept development, where a bad idea is mistakenly selected, pursued, and subsequently fails.

Growth Phase: The stage in the product life cycle that is characterized by sharp inclines in sales, as the product gains regular users and is still building equity in the consumer's mind. A typical strategy employed in the growth phase is full marketing support and relatively high spending to build the business.

Halo Effect: The phenomenon whereby perceptions of one brand have a positive or a negative effect on other related brands or products, or on other products that the company manufactures.

Heavy Users: The percentage of a product's users, usually small, that accounts for a large proportion of a product's sales. This is known in marketing circles as the 80/20 rule—i.e., 80 percent of the product's sales are attributable to 20 percent of its consumers.

Ideation: The first stage in the product development process, in which new concepts for products are generated.

Impulse Goods: Low-priced products purchased without prior consideration or planning. These goods are normally found close to the checkout counter.

Incremental Volume: Sales gained from additional users (other than the normal consumer base) who try the brand, or additional purchases of the product (above the norm) by the normal consumer base. Incremental volume is the objective when the product is promoted.

Industrial Goods: Products sold to industry customers for use in the manufacturing of other goods.

Introduction Phase: The first phase in the *product life cycle,* in which the product is introduced to the consumer. Typically this is a period of high investment and spending to generate awareness and trial of the product. Sales are normally low but will climb steadily during this phase if the product is successful.

Line Extension: See *extension.*

Linkage: The psychological connections that are made between a brand and any other product, event, or thing in the world.

Mail Survey: A request for information using questionnaires sent and returned through the mail to selected individuals. Typical response is 1/4 to 1/2 of a percent, however incentives such as offering free merchandise or a report on the results can boost response.

Marketing Mix: Combination of functional marketing elements, including product, packaging, price, distribution, advertising, promotion, and public relations, that is used to maximize sales of a product. An essential part of marketing planning and strategy is determination and development of the most effective marketing mix.

Maturity Phase: The phase in the product life cycle in which sales have peaked and begin to decline as the novelty or utility of a product wears off or as competitors begin to crowd the category to the point where too many products are vying for too small a consumer purchasing pie. Shares begin to erode, profits usually drop, and competition intensifies. A typical strategy assumed during this phase is either maintenance if the category is not saturated, or heavy promotional spending if it is.

Modernization: A process whereby existing products or lines are brought up to date or into the future through changes in product, packaging, advertising, promotion, and image. When the revitalization attempts to change people's perception of how a product or line stacks up against others, it is called a *repositioning.*

Original Equipment Manufacturer (OEM): The company that produces a product for sale as part of another company's product or to be marketed by another company under a different name.

Planned Obsolescence: The planned useful life of a product and time that it takes to become obsolete.

Premium Product: A particular brand or product in a category that has a perceived higher image and is usually higher priced than most of the competition. Premium products are successful if the consumer agrees that the quality exceeds the other offerings available.

Prescreening: The internal first-stage narrowing of new ideas, often done by the initiator of the product development process.

Price/Performance: The ratio of how well a product delivers on its benefits based on the price.

Private Label Brand: A brand that is sponsored by a member of the distribution trade, as distinguished from a brand bearing the name of a manufacturer or producer. Manufacturers of their own products often *co-pack* private label brands for a price. Private label brands are typically priced at the lowest end of the scale in the category, since they are not supported by expensive marketing programs and are usually made as cheaply as possible. More and more, however, private label brands have been increasing quality in an effort to gain more consumer dollars.

Problem Analysis: A group of ideation methods that focus on identifying problems or challenges within product categories or products themselves and solving them. Problem analysis can also pose an already identified problem to users and probe for solutions. Problem analysis techniques include *brainstorming* and *synectics,* among others.

Product: A single salable or tradable entity or service. Anything that can be planned, developed, and marketed to anyone is a product.

Product Category: A group of products that offer similar benefits (e.g., cereals, ice-cream).

Product Development: The marketing process by which a product is planned and developed.

Product Line: A group of related products, produced by the same manufacturer. The line usually carries the same brand name, but with different flavors, sizes, ingredient lines, etc., that appeal to slightly different target audiences or provide variety for the core audience.

Product Mix: All of the products or product lines offered by a firm, constrained by the manufacturer's capabilities, and designed to fulfill a full range of consumer needs.

Product Portfolio: A group of products that are planned together, often diversified and balancing one another with respect to long-term financial planning.

Prototype: A physical sample or rendering of a proposed new product or concept, tested externally, for appeal and utility with consumers, and internally, for manufacturing capability and financial solvency.

Repositioning: The act of changing a product's image among the current target audience, or to a new target audience. This is normally done during a product's maturity or decline phase, or when marketing research has determined that there are negative perceptions about a product, its image or attributes, or when a new opportunity is defined.

Rollout: The progression of the release of a product into the markets. (A national rollout means that the product is released simultaneously across the nation, whereas a market-by-market rollout means that a product is released step-by-step from market to market.)

Saturated Category: An overcrowded product category in which product offerings exceed consumer demand.

Screening: The stage in the product development process where a large number of ideas are refined down to a few "best candidates," based on selected criteria (e.g., ease of manufacture, profitability, consumer appeal).

Seasonality: Sales pattern of a particular product, characterized by peaks and valleys in consumption influenced by seasons of the year. For example, some products perform better in the summer, while others perform better around holidays. Seasonality is an important consideration when planning marketing strategy and when planning for production requirements.

Service Mark: Unique name or symbol registered and used to represent a service company or service provided by a company. Like a trademark used to identify manufactured products, use of a service mark is exclusive to the holder.

Shopping Goods: Products that consumers buy after doing some comparison shopping (apparel, toys, carpet, appliances).

Specialty Goods: Products (often high-priced or "big-ticket" items) that involve considerable consumer evaluation and commitment in the adoption decision making process. Specialty goods require the consumer to make a special effort to buy them, and consumers will go to great lengths to find and evaluate them (e.g., cars, boats, bicycles).

Spin-Off: A new product that begins as part of one product and emerges as a whole new line under a trademark or brand name different from its parent.

Standard Industrial Classification (SIC): The numerical system used to subdivide the industrial community into specific market segments.

Stock Keeping Unit (SKU): Every form, flavor, size, variety, etc., for every product that is manufactured. If a product comes in four flavors and there are two sizes for every flavor, there are eight product SKUs. Each SKU carries a separate *bar code* and is usually subject to a separate trade handling allowance.

Synectics: An ideation technique in which the problem is masked and facts or layers of the problem are slowly inserted into the conversation. For example, if the problem is to invent a new type of shampoo that incorporates a conditioner, the discussion could open up with "How can people wash and condition their hair more easily?" Ideas such as a special dispenser on the wall that could contain shampoo on the left side and conditioner on the right could spring up. In this fashion, the synectic method tries to build ideas from the ground up, rather than by attacking the question at random, as with *brainstorming*.

Synergy: The combined action of two or more elements. For example, if a cereal brand engages in a cooperative marketing program with a fruit brand, their synergy may produce benefits for each.

Think Tank: A group of people organized for research on general or specific topics, usually for extended periods of time.

Trade Release: To make the product available for purchase by the trade for resale.

Trademark: A unique registered identification symbol used exclusively by a manufacturer of a particular product for that product. No other manufacturers may use anything that is a registered trademark of someone else.

Utility: The ability of a product to satisfy a need or want in the marketplace.

Vitalization: The process by which existing, mature, or declining products or lines are made more appealing or relevant to consumers through enhancement of the product's physical or marketing attributes.

PM TOOLS™
PRODUCT
DEVELOPMENT

- Ideation Checklist
- New Product Concept Screening, Part I and Part II
- Competitive Brand Analysis
- Cannibalization Worksheet
- BDI / CDI Worksheet
- Cleancepts™ Modular Concept Board Sample

IDEATION CHECKLIST

INTERNAL SOURCES:

Scientists ☐
Your own department ☐
Marketing task team ☐
Functional bus. counterparts ☐
Employee suggestion program ☐
Customer service center ☐
Social relationships ☐
Top management ☐
Other_____ ☐
Other_____ ☐
Other_____ ☐

EXTERNAL SOURCES

Exploratory research studies ☐
Customers / consumers ☐
Events in your own category ☐
Competitors ☐
Events in other categories ☐
Technological advancements ☐
Inventors / engineers ☐
Service agencies ☐
Other_____ ☐
Other_____ ☐
Other_____ ☐

INSTRUCTIONS: Ideas for new products can come from a multitude of sources. This is a checklist that you can use if you've exhausted your traditional sources or just want additional ideas.

NEW PRODUCT CONCEPT SCREENING Part I

CONCEPT:_____

	1	2	3	4	5
_____ (low to high)	1	2	3	4	5
_____ (low to high)	1	2	3	4	5
_____ (low to high)	1	2	3	4	5
_____ (low to high)	1	2	3	4	5
_____ (low to high)	1	2	3	4	5
_____ (low to high)	1	2	3	4	5
_____ (low to high)	1	2	3	4	5
_____ (low to high)	1	2	3	4	5
_____ (low to high)	1	2	3	4	5

INSTRUCTIONS: List the criteria that you or the "concept screening group" believe to be important in screening concepts. Examples include "ease of manufacture," "fit with the brand image" (if a line extension), "potential profitability," "gut feel," and any other criteria that address marketing or other business objectives. Try to group criteria together whenever possible into single headings (e.g., you can use the criterion "appeal" to cover the many individual criteria that make up "appeal"). Note that "low to high" is used as a generic qualifier for all ranges, such as "poor to excellent," "not at all attractive to extremely attractive," etc.

Distribute these forms to all involved in the concept screening process and have each person rate the concept for how well it fulfills each criteria.

NEW PRODUCT CONCEPT SCREENING - Part II

Criteria	Importance Rating (1 - 5)		Average Criteria Rating (from Part I)		Score
_____	_____	X	_____	=	|
_____	_____	X	_____	=	|
_____	_____	X	_____	=	|
_____	_____	X	_____	=	|
_____	_____	X	_____	=	|
_____	_____	X	_____	=	|
_____	_____	X	_____	=	|
_____	_____	X	_____	=	|
_____	_____		_____	=	|
_____			**Total Score**		|

INSTRUCTIONS: List the criteria again, as you did in Part I. In the next column, rate each criterion for importance to the project. For example, if "ease of manufacture" is a criterion, is it a "1" (not at all important) or a "5" (extremely important). These ratings should be *relative to the other criteria listed*. Next, average all of the ratings from the form used in Part I and list them. Multiply both scores in each row to get a score for each criterion. Add them up to get the total concept score.

COMPETITIVE BRAND ANALYSIS

Brand Awareness H M L

_____ ☐ ☐ ☐
_____ ☐ ☐ ☐
_____ ☐ ☐ ☐
_____ ☐ ☐ ☐

Brand Loyalty H M L

_____ ☐ ☐ ☐
_____ ☐ ☐ ☐
_____ ☐ ☐ ☐
_____ ☐ ☐ ☐

Perceived Value H M L

_____ ☐ ☐ ☐
_____ ☐ ☐ ☐
_____ ☐ ☐ ☐
_____ ☐ ☐ ☐

Differential Advantages

_____ _____
_____ _____
_____ _____
_____ _____

Brand Associations

_____ _____
_____ _____
_____ _____
_____ _____

INSTRUCTIONS: Put your brand's name on the first line of each category and the names of up to four major competitors on the lines that follow. Rate Brand Awareness, Brand Loyalty, and the Perceived Value of the product to consumers as "High," "Medium," or "Low." Next list the key advantages each product has. List associations that each brand has that can be to the brand's benefit or detriment (e.g., U.S. Postal Service may be affected by consumer's association with the U.S. government, positive or negative).

CANNIBALIZATION WORKSHEET

INSTRUCTIONS: List all SKU's or packs in your line. Next, select a period with which you are going to compare line performance with and without the introduction of the new product. At least three months should be used, since introduction of the new product, and compared with the same period just prior to introduction if sales are relatively stable, or sales from the same period a year ago if sales are seasonal. The column with "A" totals are for the previous period and the column with "B" totals are for the more recent period including the new product. Follow the calculations and make your own judgement in the final analysis as to the volume attributable to cannibalization vs. other rationales.

Line SKU	SKU Unit Volume (to)	SKU Unit Volume (to)	Percent Inc. / Dec.
_____	_____	_____	_____
_____	_____	_____	_____
_____	_____	_____	_____
_____	_____	_____	_____
_____	_____	_____	_____
_____	_____	_____	_____
_____	_____	_____	_____
_____	_____	_____	_____
_____	_____	_____	_____
Tot: _____ (A)	**Tot:** _____ (B)	

New Product

New Product Volume / Total Volume Change _____ (C)

Volume attributable to Cannibalization _____ (C)/(B-A)

Volume attributable to new users, inc. usage, etc. _____

BDI/CDI WORKSHEET

INSTRUCTIONS: The Business & Category Development Indices are used to help the marketer gauge the performance of a product (BDI) or the category (CDI) in a particular geographical market relative to the rest of the country. First list the market, then the share of market in that geographical region (A). Then list the percent of the total U.S. population that lives in that region. To get the BDI/CDI, divide B by A. A score over 1.0 indicates a potentially strong or well-developed market, and under 1.0 indicates a potentially weak or underdeveloped market. Sometimes BDIs and CDIs are given in percents as well (e.g., 1.0 = 100%; 1.1 = 110%) or just stated without the percent (e.g., 1.0 = 100; 1.1 = 110).

Geographic Market	Market Share (%)	U.S. Pop. (%)	BDI / CDI
_____	_____(A)	_____ (B)	_____(A/B)
_____	_____(A)	_____ (B)	_____(A/B)
_____	_____(A)	_____ (B)	_____(A/B)
_____	_____(A)	_____ (B)	_____(A/B)
_____	_____(A)	_____ (B)	_____(A/B)
_____	_____(A)	_____ (B)	_____(A/B)
_____	_____(A)	_____ (B)	_____(A/B)
_____	_____(A)	_____ (B)	_____(A/B)
_____	_____(A)	_____ (B)	_____(A/B)
_____	_____(A)	_____ (B)	_____(A/B)
_____	_____(A)	_____ (B)	_____(A/B)
_____	_____(A)	_____ (B)	_____(A/B)
_____	_____(A)	_____ (B)	_____(A/B)
_____	_____(A)	_____ (B)	_____(A/B)
_____	_____(A)	_____ (B)	_____(A/B)

CLEANCEPTS™ MODULAR CONCEPT BOARD SAMPLE

PACKAGING

ADVERTISING/ PROMOTION

NAME

TRADEMARK

PRICING

PRODUCT

Line/Flavor Extension

Line/Flavor Extension

Line/Flavor Extension

FOUR

PACKAGING DEVELOPMENT

TOP-LINE

OVERVIEW

Only a few books and resources are devoted to packaging. This lack of focus on the subject is also apparent in many marketing departments in major corporations. While the larger companies do have separate *package design* and research areas, it is rare to find a packaging *department* that plans and develops integrated packaging strategies and works proactively with all the pertinent functions that must have input into packaging decisions. The marketing manager usually takes on control of packaging strategy development, while the technology people develop the form, and the design area plans the graphics. And, in so far as the marketing manager must be a generalist, development of sound packaging strategies may not be getting the attention that it should.

This situation takes on even more meaning when you realize that the package may be *the single most impor-*

tant factor in generating sales. In fact, around 80 percent of purchase decisions are made in the store.[1] The package itself is the final salesman—*it closes the deal*. Of course, if the actual product is found to be unsatisfactory, the consumer will not repeat the purchase—but the package is critical in distinguishing a brand from its competitors and may make the difference in the initial brand choice or in causing a brand switch. If intelligent marketers believe this to be so, then why is package design or redesign often undertaken with less strategic thought than is advertising? Marketers are beginning to address that question and to realize the importance of the package in today's environment.

A *package* is defined as a container in which the manufacturer's product is presented for sale. The *primary package* contains the actual goods. The *secondary packages* are those used to carton or *case* given amounts of the primary packages for distribution. Most references to the "package" in this section will be to the primary package.

The package has three main functions: (1) to encase the product in set weights or units for ease of transportation, sale, and purchase; (2) to protect the product from damage, tampering, or spoilage; and (3) to assist in the marketing of the product through graphics and functional *utility* or usage. Packaging typically is developed simultaneously with the physical product in new product launches or existing product relaunches because the majority of consumers do not separate the two when considering a product purchase.

PACKAGING STRUCTURE AND UTILITY

Functional *utility* of the package is the value that it brings to the consumer for physical transport, storage, and use of the product. Utility is more important with some products than with others. For example, it is critical with sprays, aerosols, microwavable containers, and other products where the package itself plays a critical role in the ability to use the product. In those cases, the package is as much "the product" as what it contains.

A functional package that doesn't perform properly will turn the consumer off to the product. By the

---

[1] "Romancing the Package," *Adweek's Marketing Week*, 32:4, January 21, 1991, p. 14.

same token, a package that presents an innovative, more convenient way to dispense the product is viewed by the consumer as a product improvement and can really drive brand switching. In a large company, the packaging research and technology department normally is responsible for development of functional packaging.

A package that can be used for something after the product is consumed can have a high degree of added value to the consumer, and thus can drive increased purchases. Jelly and jam jars imprinted with kid-targeted graphics are often reusable as drinking glasses. Cool Whip Whipped Topping has been packaged in a bonus "measuring cup" bowl from time to time. In this way, packaging is related to consumer promotion in that the package *itself* becomes the promotion if its bonus utility is communicated. If the utility is incidental and not communicated by the marketer (but rather discovered by the consumer on his/her own) then it is not a promotion. However, a popular utility that has been discovered by the consumer can be communicated in future advertising or promotions if marketing research shows it to be important to other consumers.

PACKAGING GRAPHICS, COLOR, AND COPY

Graphics and color are extremely important in the supermarket environment, where a product and its package must compete for the consumer's attention with several other branded or store-label competitors. It is critical that **brand registration** or any perceived **brand equities** come through clearly in the package graphics, so that the consumer who wants to purchase a particular brand can find and identify it easily. Advertising and packaging are related in that the advertising message should clearly identify what the package looks like.

The dominant color used in the package can have an effect on brand image—black connotes an "upscale" feel, while blue connotes "clean and cool," and white connotes "light" or "pure." In the cigarette industry, the color green is pretty much a standard to indicate a menthol flavor because it is associated with refreshment. A marketer who has several line extensions for a brand may elect to use changes in color in some fashion to communicate the differences, while maintaining the core brand package equities. It is important to note that if a product is to be sold internationally, different sets of dos and don'ts regarding use of particular colors exist in particular countries. A marketer who intends to export his product should consult with retailing experts from each locality before making packaging decisions.

The marketer faces the challenge of balancing the current consumer's recognition of the package with the need for new packaging. Packaging changes are usually not drastic—sometimes a marketer will decide to take an interim step in package redesign that will not confuse current consumers and will move closer to where the marketer wants to be. The danger is that a drastic change may cause brand-loyal consumers to think that the product inside is somehow different. However, package lines should be updated as the brand image changes or as the target audience and its needs change.

Unfortunately, packaging economics and retailer demand for structurally similar or identical packages within a category often limit the ability of marketers to differentiate their product from others in a structured way. Also, an accepted structural innovation is likely to be structurally copied. Therefore package graphics must take on an important role in product differentiation. When it comes to words, the fewer the better. Choose one, two, or a few highly targeted words that convey the message to the desired consumer. The brand name or logo on the package should itself give off a targeted message.

If package photography or other artwork is used, it should depict the product inside in its most appealing form or final usage—whether it is a deliciously prepared food, a model with gorgeously colored hair, or a whole collection of baseball cards. Illustration is generally less appealing and effective than photography, unless the illustration is a recognizable brand character or other equity. Remember, the package closes the sale. It must communicate the benefit, loudly and clearly.

THE CONSUMER AND PACKAGING

Through its written message and graphics, packaging attracts the consumer to the brand. Besides the brand name, it uses any strong brand equities that might influence the consumer in a positive way. So the first step in planning the package is to determine what the brand equities are.

A brand equity is a feature that a consumer associates with a particular brand. This may be a symbol, like the Texaco Star; a character, like the Pillsbury Doughboy or Tony the Tiger; or even a color, like the red of the Coca-Cola can. An equity may be the brand name itself, or any quality that the consumer links to the brand, such as "purity" and Ivory Soap. Marketers strive to develop positive brand equities, or those that add perceived value to the brand. Negative brand equities are normally changed as soon as they are discovered.

The marketer's job is to develop and communicate positive brand equities, and as times change to maintain and update them as necessary. For example, while use of the Pillsbury Doughboy has increased over the years, the character's form has been slimmed down to keep up with the current emphasis on looking lean.

Marketing research can help determine what the strongest brand equities are and identify their positive and negative associations. Packaging strategy must take these brand equities into account and determine how best to communicate them via the package.

As consumer needs change, so do packaging needs; and as consumer segments with differing needs emerge, packaging must be adapted if the marketer wishes to reach each segment effectively.

Differences in household size are one major reason to create different sized packages for the same brand. A single-person household would be less likely to buy an economy-sized packaged product than would a family of six. And while a heavy user of the product might purchase multipacks or larger sizes, a light user would be more attracted to single or smaller sizes. The marketer must be in tune not only with the frequency of purchase of his product but also with the amount generally purchased in a single shopping trip. This will affect both the size and quantity offerings of the product in the packaging mix.

Consumers basically want convenient, easy-to-open (but tamper-proof), resealable (if applicable), quality packaging, but they don't want to pay more for it. If a package design looks like an extravagance without related utility value, the consumer may react negatively. Therefore, it is critical to research consumer feelings about any packaging alternatives under consideration.

THE RETAILER AND PACKAGING

Acceptance by the retailer is a critical consideration in packaging development. An unusual, eye-catching structural design may not be acceptable on the retail shelves, although consumers may tell you they'd love it and would definitely buy it. If the marketer produced a package based on the consumer research alone, he might be stuck with a product that consumers would buy, but find no place to sell it to them.

While research findings on positive consumer acceptance are important to the retailer and can be a major selling point for the manufacturer, research also needs to be done to determine retailer needs and preferences. The retailer is concerned with the following basic questions:

1. **IS IT MANAGEABLE ON THE SHELF** currently being used to hold that product category? The last thing that a retailer wants to do is to have to create separate space in a different location because the package's configuration does not allow it to be placed in its usual position. The retailer does not want a package to take up more space than is necessary to display it in a fashion that is customary for the category. Trying to get a "packaging breakthrough" that does not conform to retailer expectations into distribution may take more money than it is worth, or finally may be impossible. This is not to say that packaging breakthroughs should never be pursued—just that retailers' reactions should be sought so that all possible issues can surface.

2. **DOES THE PACKAGE HOLD UP IN THE HANDLING PROCESS?** No retailer wants to place crushed, broken, or leaking packages on the shelves. The store will bear the brunt of consumer complaints, *not* the manufacturer. Make sure the package travels well from the line to the case to the warehouse to the retailer, and then onto the shelves.

3. **IS IT EASY FOR THE CHECKOUT PERSON TO HANDLE?** It should have a scannable *bar code* that is in a clear, easy-to-find place. The bar code gives the retailer the price and item information. And the information on the bar code must be correct, because more and more retailers will be is-

suing fines to manufacturers if it isn't. It pays to invest in a portable scanner to check all the bar codes on the outgoing mechanicals before the package is printed.

4. **ARE THE CASE QUANTITIES ACCEPTABLE**, in terms of realistic sales turnaround and the handling ability of store personnel? If sales do not keep up with the quantities that the retailer must purchase in a case, the retailer faces storage problems and also problems with a product that might go out of date. While the manufacturer usually takes back these "unsalables," the space that they take up and the paperwork that must be done to return them could pose difficulties. The manufacturer must balance the retailer preferences with regard to case load with the possibility of "out of stock" situations if the product sells faster than the retailer orders it.

The question of where the retailer is likely to place the package in the store is important to packaging strategy. Is the product opening up a whole new category, or will it compete in an existing one? How many *facings* (shelf space) is it likely to get?

Sales departments usually utilize shelf management research to persuade the retailer to place the product in a particular place or to give a particular brand or product the largest number of facings possible. This will increase sales because the potential for out of stocks is reduced, and more consumer attention will be gained. Generally, the amount of shelf space one product is given versus that given a competitor or even over a neighboring category depends on its sales performance and profitability. For this reason, shelf management studies focus not only on the product category in which the key product competes but also on other products within the *form* (such as frozen, refrigerated, or dry). These may not deserve as much shelf space because of lower velocity and/or lower profit per unit.

Finally, the manufacturer must be sensitive to the types and sizes of stores that will sell the product. Small convenience stores usually require smaller versions of the package, while discount club stores prefer the largest sizes.

The retailer is a source of valuable information—information that could prevent a manufacturer from making a costly packaging mistake. Marketers need only ask for retailer input and cooperation early in the packaging planning process.

THE COMPANY AND PACKAGING

In developing packaging strategy, several key players and concerns within a company or business unit should be considered, although their level of involvement will vary according to the extent of the packaging assignment. The highest level of involvement is necessary with a new product/new package introduction.

A new product introduction will require research into the product's protection needs, consumer convenience/functional issues, and distribution concerns. A new package introduction of an existing product will also need input from operations, technology, and purchasing personnel. Even package redesign that does not alter package structure will still involve some operations and purchasing issues.

The internal considerations in packaging strategy are:

1. Market Research
     Understanding of the target consumers and their packaging preferences and motivations to purchase the product.
          Understanding of the competitive environment.
          Evaluating the effect of design options on consumer and retailers.
2. Packaging Research and Technology
     Product protection needs.
     Functional alternative development.
3. Operations
     Plant/manufacturing capabilities.
     Logistic decisions.
4. Purchasing and Finance
     Materials and capital (machinery) costs.
5. Sales
     Retailer considerations.
     Timing of introduction.
6. Marketing
     Overall strategy coordination and decision making.
     Graphic and functional design choices.

As you can see, this is ultimately a team effort. Just as it is important that marketing include all the functions at an early stage, each function must be sensitive to the fact that the others are depending on its expertise and ability to stick to timetables.

THE PACKAGING PLAN

Prior to embarking on the packaging development process, general research should be conducted on previous product packages and other competitive offerings with reference to physical attribute and benefit. (This breakout may already be complete in the situational analysis.) Also, previous packaging successes and failures for the brand should be reviewed, and "lessons learned" stated with their implications. All of this should be articulated at the beginning of your plan. The packaging development plan follows these steps:

1. Set packaging *objectives* based on marketing objectives (and often in concert with product development objectives).
2. Conduct packaging *research*.
3. Determine packaging *strategies* that support and fulfill packaging objectives.
4. Determine packaging *tactics* that put product strategies into action.

PACKAGING OBJECTIVES

Packaging objectives flow naturally from overall marketing objectives for the project. Objectives include:

1. The APPLICATION for the packaging we are going to develop. (Is it for a relaunch of an existing product? For a new product? For a line extension?)
2. The taRGET AUDIENCE to whom we are marketing this product.
3. The DESIRED OUTCOME or fulfillment of benefits that the packaging will accomplish. These outcomes should include both physical utility and visible communications objectives.

Let's say that we came up with an opportunity to make a new line of cereals, Morning Mates, in which "base" ingredients came in one set of boxes (flakes, puffs, crispies, etc.) and "mix-ins" come in other boxes (dried fruits, marshmallows, nuts, etc.). The audience for this product line was found to be split between adult and child segments, as was the rest of the category. A packaging objective for this product might be:

> *Develop packages that will clearly communicate to mainstream consumers that Morning Mates can be mixed and matched in a variety of combinations, offer a superior way to close the package and maintain freshness because of their longer anticipated shelf usage life, and allow consumers to create their own breakfasts exactly to their liking every day.*

Typically, broad objectives like these will be set for the entire line if more than one product package is involved. Following the specific objectives for each product *stock keeping unit* (SKU) or distinct package will be set as well. For example, in this case, objectives could be set for the child and adult lines (and each product design in those lines), as well as for the base versus mix-in SKUs. In multi-SKU lines, objectives first establish a common thread across all products, then across smaller groups of products, eventually getting into specifics for each product SKU itself.

PACKAGING RESEARCH

Packaging research is often conducted during or as part of product development, because consumer response to name, logo, and/or package functional and graphic design are integral to the product's appeal itself. In such cases, various product development techniques are used (focus groups, personal interviews, etc.).

The following outlines the research steps that should be taken in developing packaging strategy. Remember, all of these steps may not be necessary when you are executing a simple design change (for example, updating package graphics for a line of products, or redesigning separately designed sublines so that they look like a line of products).

1. **IDENTIFY CONSUMER TARGET SEGMENTS**: This should have been done in the situational analysis research. Here we apply that knowledge or research in further depth. Get to know why consumers want your product, what they will usually do with it, and how often they are likely to use it. What about their lives makes them interested in your product? Are they too busy to cook? Then design a quick, convenient package that minimizes

cooking time. Do they watch a lot of television? Then design a package that can be carried comfortably into the living room. Are the consumers cost conscious, or do they go for quality? This will affect the materials and the structural aspects of the package. Do the users work out at a gym? Then design a package that stresses low fat content.

2. **CHECK OUT THE RETAIL ENVIRONMENT**: Retail dynamics will influence your product and its packaging, both primary and secondary. Where will your product be sold? In what section of the store? What's the competition for attention like on the shelf itself? What type of packaging does the competition have with respect to graphics, size, and structure? How does the retailer expect your product to be transported and delivered to the stores? Are there any other retailer requirements?

3. **APPLY PRODUCT RESEARCH**: Reiterate the product's equities, strengths and weaknesses, opportunities and threats. How can packaging help to reinforce strengths and minimize weaknesses? Can the package provide any added value? What equities should the packaging convey to the buyer? Also, determine how, when, why, and how much the product is or will be used by your target consumer(s). Lastly, determine the product's protection requirements.

4. **RESEARCH MANUFACTURING AND DISTRIBUTION ABILITIES, NEEDS, AND LIMITATIONS:** You may want to eliminate certain designs from consideration if they require extensive plant changes or if they are cost prohibitive. However, if you are looking for a breakthrough and can reasonably pay the price, you may want to leave the field open to explore every option. Remember that the research and technology, purchasing, and the operations functions should be included in discussions at a very early stage in packaging strategy development and given adequate time to test the selected options.

5. **DETERMINE THE LEGAL REQUIREMENTS INVOLVED**: With your legal department's help, determine and understand legislation and government requirements for labeling and use that will affect package graphics and copy.

6. **SET THE TESTING PARAMETERS**: Work with marketing research to develop the test for the structural and design ideas to give your target con-

sumers before doing any further development or purchasing. Designs should be consumer tested at the earliest possible stage, usually after all pertinent players within the company have selected and approved a couple of favorite options. Testing methods include many of the same methods used in product development research, including interviews, quantitative rating of attributes for fulfillment of desired utilities, and relationship to competitive offerings.

PACKAGING STRATEGIES

The packaging strategy is the action plan for fulfilling the packaging objectives; it outlines and considers the needs, functions, and activities of all the players involved in creation or acceptance of the packaging of a product. It takes into account the previous discussions on consumer, retailer, and company considerations. Packaging research should have fleshed out consumer needs and preferences with regard to product benefits, which could be translated into a physical package to deliver those benefits.

There are two types of packaging strategies: (1) structural and utility strategies related to form and function; and (2) creative strategies involving communication of benefits, image, etc.

1. **STRUCTURAL STRATEGY**: Simply state the means and methods that will be applied to achieve objectives. If one of the objectives is to keep a product fresh on the shelf without refrigeration, a structural strategy could be to utilize an aseptically sealed package.

   In the case of our cereal example, a structural strategy to deliver freshness and longer shelf life once opened (arising from the assumption that consumers who mix and match will take longer to finish one particular box) could be to use a resealable closure.

   Complex structural strategies should be worked out directly with technical and manufacturing counterparts, and in many cases, the answers will come exclusively from those areas.

2. **CREATIVE STRATEGY**: The creative strategy is that part of the packaging plan that establishes how product benefits will be communicated through the package.

A package exists in an environment of clutter and direct category competition. Therefore, package graphics and copy must work even harder than advertising to gain attention quickly and effectively and must do this better than the brand that is literally next door. A creative strategy or "brief" includes:

- Product positioning (target market, key benefit).
- Benefits translation. What do you want the consumer to think when he/she sees this package? Why should the consumer want to purchase it? What main benefits do you want them to remember in priority order?
- Brand name, product category, and subline(s), and their relative order of importance as copy points.
- Brand equities, prioritized as to inclusion in the design.
- Artwork requirements, such as product photography.
- Tone and manner (for color and/or graphic choice).
- Ingredient line, nutritional information, and any legal requirements.
- Other mandatory or desired communication features, such as recipes, flags, bursts, coupons, romance copy, etc.
- Package size(s) and configuration(s).
- Competitive considerations.
- Timetable.

If a structural option has already been selected, then a prototype should accompany the creative brief. If there are a few structural options, viewing the graphics on each of these options may play a role in determining the winner. The other items or information that should accompany the creative brief are photographs of the shelf that will become the new home for the package, actual competitors' packages, and *your* current and past packages.

In the case of our cereal example, a creative strategy to communicate the benefit of "variety and personalization," where cereals are created each and every morning exactly to the consumer's liking in just the quantity desired, could be to utilize copy and graphics on all package faces that show someone mixing and matching or to use color coding.

Remember, for product lines, each step must be completed for each layer, beginning with the full line and continuing down to the individual product. Strategies may differ as changes occur in the layer being considered.

PACKAGING TACTICS

Tactics for packaging, like product development, are the physical translation of each of the packaging strategies into visible and touchable results, such as package shapes, colors, graphics, etc. Packaging tactics, like packaging strategies, come in two varieties: (1) structural; and (2) creative.

In our cereals example, *structural* tactics to make a resealable closure could include the use of plastic interlocking strips (similar to those used with plastic storage bags), clips, glue strips with reusable tack or plastic packaging. *Creative* tactics to communicate variety and personalization of mix 'n' match could include the use of spokespeople or spokes-characters.

Like packaging strategies, when more than one product package is being developed in a line, sets of tactics should be developed beginning with the entire line, working our way down to executional elements for individual SKUs.

OTHER PACKAGING CONSIDERATIONS

Basically, the planning steps represent the ideal procedure. In reality, enough time is rarely available to go through each of them in the optimal fashion. Unfortunately, the most important area—new product development—usually is short of the time it requires. The launch often cannot be delayed to allow for optimal strategy development time. The key here is to *make sure that packaging strategy development gets under way **as soon as a decision is made** to launch a new product or line extension.*

Finally, several other items should be considered when developing packaging plans: (1) legal issues; (2) environmental uses; and (3) promotional applications.

LEGAL ISSUES: There are strict rules that govern what may be claimed on the package, and a mistake could cause havoc—especially in the extreme case of having to remove a product from the shelves. Packaging designed with a look that is too close to a competitor may subject the marketer to trademark infringement lawsuits and injunctions. The FDA is considering banning all labeling that it deems to be misleading, such as the use of the word "fresh" and percent fat content claims. This will have *major* implications for food manufacturers in the future.

The legal department must therefore take extra care in approving new package designs and the wording on them. Legal should approve the copy that is given to the design firm to ensure that all mandated information is included, and that there are no trademark violations or unsubstantiated or misleading claims. Then they should approve the final mechanicals *in writing*.

ENVIRONMENTAL ISSUES: Packaging is very strongly affected by concerns about the environment. Use of nonbiodegradable plastics and other materials can have an adverse effect on the way consumers perceive a product. Fluorocarbons used in aerosol containers were under strong consumer scrutiny in the last decade. Although the situational analysis in the marketing plan should cover macro issues like the environment for the product as a whole, world and industry issues should always be considered when developing packaging.

PROMOTIONAL APPLICATIONS: Whenever possible, the package should be shown *in use* in the advertising. An opened package indicates action. Feature the package in the main visual, or use it as an accessory to the action in the main visual. The package creates and reinforces brand identity—an attention-getting, likable advertisement is of little value when the brand cannot be identified or recalled. For greater attention in print, tilt the package so that it is not parallel with the borders of the ad.[2]

---

[2] Stanley Sacharow, *The Package as a Marketing Tool*, Chilton Book Company: Radnor, PA, 1982, p. 64.

PACKAGING DEVELOPMENT GLOSSARY

Bar Code: A series of lines that form a code that can be read by a scanner. Bar coding contains price and product information and is used on packages (also called a *UPC code*) so that the supermarket checkout person does not have to enter the information manually. Scanner data is also used by research companies to provide information to marketers about consumption. Bar codes are also found on coupons (for product, value, and redemption offer number) and on envelopes and business reply cards for automated postal sorting.

Blister Pack: A type of package that consists of a solid, sturdy backing and a plastic dome. The product itself is normally encased under the plastic dome. Usually, small items that may be easily pilfered or that do not conform to a standard, stackable size are packaged this way. Common examples of products that are blister packed are cosmetics, batteries, and multiple packs of cigarettes packaged with a *bonus* premium.

Bonus Pack: Packaging that contains a greater quantity of the product at the same price as the original lesser amount: e.g., two of the same item packaged together to sell for the price of one, a free related item packaged with the original item, or a taller box of cereal offering 33 percent more free. Bonus packs are used in consumer promotion to add value for the consumer without buying down the price with a coupon, or to gain trial of a companion item by the same manufacturer (like a sample fabric softener with purchase of detergent).

Brand Registration: Identification of the brand by the consumer at the sight of a package or advertisement. The objective is normally to achieve high levels of brand registration.

Die Cut: A piece of cardboard or other material that is cut by a sharp plate (the die) in the size and shape of the final printed piece. Die cuts are used by the design firm to create a mechanical that is sure to fit the final cut and printed structure.

Facing: A packaging unit in a front (on the shelf) or a top (in the well) position that a consumer can see without moving anything around. Products or brands are normally assigned a particular number of facings in the retail store.

Flag: Graphic design used on packages and other promotional pieces to highlight a special message such as "coupon inside."

Generic Name: The name of the product category in which the brand competes. For example, Dannon is a brand name for the category of yogurt. Yogurt is the generic name.

Grade Label: The identification of a product's quality, based on set government standards (e.g., Grade A beef).

Header Card: A portion of a special package display shipper that rises up from the back side and contains copy and graphics that communicate a selling message.

Label: A separate printed item that is applied to a package in place of imprinting the package itself. This contains copy and graphics that the manufacturer chooses or is bound by law to include. According to the Fair Packaging and Labeling Act of 1966, the package label (or printed matter on the package if there is no separate label) must contain sufficient information to enable the consumer to identify product contents and make value comparisons with other brands. A label usually contains the brand name or *logo,* the name and address of the manufacturer or distributor, the product's *generic name,* product composition and size, and nutritional information if nutrients have been added or a nutrition claim is being made.

Logo: A symbol that is used in conjunction with the brand name to achieve brand recognition.

Mandatory Copy: Copy that by law must be included on the packaging or in the advertising of a particular product or product category. For example, the Surgeon General's Warning is mandatory copy on packages and advertisements for cigarettes. All mandatory copy should accompany the creative or design brief when it goes to the package design firm or the advertising agency.

Mock-up: A prototype of the package, die cut and assembled to its final form, for use in creative presentation or testing.

Package: A container in which the manufacturer's product is presented for sale. The package has three main functions: (1) to encase the product in set weights or units for ease of transportation, sale, and purchase; (2) to protect the product from damage, tampering, or spoilage; and (3) to assist in the marketing of the product.

Package Band: Advertisements, announcements, or special price offers printed on a strip of paper that forms a band around the package.

Package Burst: Graphic device in an attention-getting shape and/or color that contains a special advertising or promotion message. On packaging, it usually signifies a new product, a product improvement, or a promotional offer inside.

Package Design: The process of planning and creating the structure and the graphics and copy of the package. This is a strategic process that involves many different players within and outside the company: e.g., marketing, manufacturing, operations and distribution, retailers, and consumers.

Package Flat: A printed package before it has been dimensionally assembled and filled with product.

Package Insert: Promotional or informational material that is placed inside the package, either by machinery or by hand. This includes coupons, recipes, or usage ideas, instructions, a premium, a sample, etc.

Package Registration: A communication priority directed at advertising or promotional agencies indicating that the visual of the package must be apparent in the ad. The strength of this priority relative to other creative considerations will vary according to the desired message or objective.

Panel: A package *facing,* or the outer side that faces you from any perspective when the package is assembled. The panels on the other side are called inside panels.

Primary Package: The package that contains the actual goods.

Proof of Purchase: Evidence that a product has actually been bought. What constitutes this evidence is usually dictated by the manufacturer, usually right on or in the package itself or in promotional communications. A box top, label, or a bar code from a package are all typically used as proofs of purchase. Promotional offers designed to build continuity can use the technique of having consumers collect proofs of purchase to redeem for a refund or premium.

Romance Copy: Copy that says or implies good things about the product without making any refutable claims.

Sample: A free or low-cost, trial-sized package (or regular size, if a smaller unit is not feasible) that is delivered either in the store or via direct mail to induce trial of the product.

Scanner: A computer-driven device that automatically reads printed *universal product codes* from products, used to determine price, track volume, and perform various research functions.

Secondary Package: Cartons or cases that contain specific numbers of *primary packages* for distribution.

Shrink Wrap: Clear, plastic protective covering used on product packages that can be shrunk by heat to fit tightly around the package.

Stock Keeping Unit (SKU): Every form, flavor, size, variety, etc., for every product that is manufactured. For example, if a product comes in four flavors and there are two sizes for every flavor, there are eight product SKUs. Each SKU carries a separate *bar code* and is usually subject to a separate trade handling allowance.

Trial Size: Smaller than usual size of a package, delivered either free or at a very low cost to induce trial of the product.

Trademark: A registered brand name, *logo*, symbol, or copy line that a manufacturer owns and that cannot be copied by any other manufacturer. A manufacturer must apply for a trademark, and it will be granted only if the name, symbol, or copy appears on the package or on permanent signage at retail around the package, and if the package is for sale or is intended for sale at an outlet.

Twin Pack: Retail product package made up of two containers of the same product together under a secondary outer wrapping or band. A twin pack is usually offered at a discount price that is less than the price of the two containers purchased individually.

UPC Code: Acronym for "universal product code" —see *bar code*.

PM TOOLS™
PACKAGING
DEVELOPMENT

- Creative Guidelines Packaging
- Packaging Planner

CREATIVE
GUIDELINES
PACKAGING

BRAND POSITIONING:

For _____ (target audience),
_____ (brand) is the _____
(qualifier, e.g., "only," "first," "leading," etc.)
_____ (category) that _____
_____ (benefits).

OBJECTIVES:

_____
_____
_____
_____

STRATEGY:

_____
_____
_____
_____

COMMUNICATION PRIORITIES:
(e.g., taste, usage, value, brand registration, etc.)

_____
_____
_____
_____

TONE AND MANNER:

_____
_____
_____
_____

OTHER:

_____
_____
_____
_____

PACKAGING PLANNER

**PRODUCT
NAME:**_____

**PRIMARY/SECONDARY PACKAGE
FORM AND SHAPE:**

_____

_____

DIMENSIONS:_____

_____

CONTENTS:_____

_____

MATERIALS:_____

_____

PANEL COPY:

  Front:

  Side:

  Back:

  Top:

  Bottom:

  Other (e.g., labeling):

OTHER:

_____

_____

_____

FIVE

TOP-LINE

OVERVIEW

Between the manufacturer or service provider and the ultimate consumer are layers of *intermediaries* or *middlemen* who are responsible for the product's distribution. Distribution is the means by which a product gets from the manufacturer to the ultimate consumer, and the paths from the product provider to the consumer are called the *channels of distribution*. Distribution can involve a physical product, the title or ownership to a product, a service, payment or cash flow, or even informational flow.

Combinations of intermediaries and their roles make up hundreds of different channels, many of which are extremely specialized.

Among the intermediaries involved in moving goods or services from manufacturer to the consumer, the *agent* is the party who brings the buyer (wholesaler, retailer, or consumer) and seller (manufacturer/service provider) together. Agents do not take title to goods, rarely take possession of them for any length of time, and usually offer limited services to the manufacturer. Agents usually represent many companies and cover specific product categories or distribution channels (e.g., health and beauty aid [HBA] products, food products, college stores).

Wholesalers actually take title to goods, buying and reselling them for a profit, sometimes directly to consumers and other times to retailers, who in turn sell them to consumers. Today, wholesalers are more hesitant to take on large inventories and are utilizing inventory systems that permit them to keep just enough product on hand for sale without undue financial risk and responsibility.

Retailers are entities that sell products directly to the consumer and always assume ownership and possession of goods. When goods are placed in a retail establishment on the condition that the manufacturer will be paid only if they sell, we say that the products have been *consigned*.

DISTRIBUTION CHANNELS

Channels are "paths" by which goods flow from the manufacturer to the consumer, and they are differentiated by what kind and how many intermediaries are in between them. A *zero-level* channel has no intermediaries, it is also called *direct marketing* because the manufacturer sells directly to the consumer. Avon is a good example of a direct marketer. Direct marketing includes such efforts as *personal selling* (direct interaction with the customer), *telemarketing* (telephone used to solicit sales), and *mail order selling* (orders received by mail and solicited through an assortment of media).

A *one-level* channel has one intermediary, such as a retail store. A two-level channel has two intermediaries, and so on. There can be four, five, and even higher level channels, but because everybody takes a share of the profit along the way, products distributed through more than three channels often end up with prices too high to compete with other products. *Multichannel distribution* refers to situations in which more than one channel are used to reach the same consumer, such as companies that sell products through stores and mail order catalogs simultaneously.

An interesting form of one-level channel distribution that has emerged in recent years is *network marketing*, in which there is essentially only one intermediary between the manufacturer and the customer, but up to thousands of subintermediaries act as agents, wholesalers, and retailers at the same time, creating a pyramid. Many large companies have begun to explore and use network marketing because it puts them in touch with many "personal networks" of target consumers that would otherwise elude them.

As an overlay to the channel layout, there are *facilitators* who assist in working with the channels of distribution but don't buy or sell. These functionaries include advertising and promotion agencies, banks, insurance companies, transportation companies, and so on.

When goods and services make their way back from the consumer to the manufacturer or service provider, such as in recycling, this is called a *reverse channel* and can have zero to several intermediaries, sometimes including government or not-for-profit interests.

Finally, *vertical channels* are marketing channels in which the manufacturer integrates channel intermediaries into its own operations (e.g., retail stores such as Firestone). Vertical channels afford greater control and sometimes result in lower costs, albeit greater overhead and risk.

CHANNEL INTERMEDIARIES

There are many different types of marketing intermediaries for each channel category. Below is a summary of the most common:

AGENTS: Agents negotiate purchases, sales, or both for a client but rarely take possession of goods and never take official title to goods. Agents include the following parties:

1. **COMMISSION MERCHANT**: Acts on behalf of the product or service provider to negotiate and sell products, receiving a preset fee when the sale is complete. The commission merchant will often take possession of the goods and pay the provider sales receipts minus his commission. Commission

merchants are most often used for agricultural products.

2. **AUCTION HOUSE**: Acts as an intermediary, bringing sellers and buyers of products together and mediating the sale. The auction house provides the place for the exchange of goods as well. Auction houses are used as negotiators for products such as livestock and agricultural products.

3. **BROKER**: Acts as a negotiator for the exchange of ownership of goods, typically on a one-time basis. Brokers are awarded fees for facilitating or finding either the buyer or seller in the sale. Brokers can be very specialized and are useful in "unloading" merchandise in an unusual situation (e.g., excess inventory of a failed product). Brokers who are hired for the long term are called *manufacturer's reps* (see following).

4. **SELLING AGENT**: Acts as an out-of-house marketing department for a manufacturer, with full authority to act on behalf of the manufacturer in the channels.

5. **MANUFACTURER'S REPRESENTATIVE**: An independent salesperson or brokerage house that represents a number of companies and products in a specific industry (e.g., college market reps or chain account food brokers). They typically take orders for clients and receive a predetermined commission.

6. **LICENSING AGENT**: Acts as a negotiator for the sale of licensed properties, such as cartoon characters, trade names, and personalities. The licensing agent arranges for goods to be produced or services performed with permission for use of a particular trademark. In the entertainment world, people are considered products and are licensed by personal agents of many types.

WHOLESALERS: Wholesalers assume ownership of the goods that they represent and serve as the middlemen between the manufacturer or service provider and the retailer or consumer. Wholesalers share the financial burden of marketing a product with the manufacturer by taking the title to goods, thus assuming part of the risk. Wholesalers can sell directly to retailers or consumers or to buyers at *trade shows* (temporary industry-specific exhibits) or *merchandise marts* (permanent industry specific exhibits). These are the various types of wholesalers and their functions:

1. **FULL-SERVICE WHOLESALER**: Provides a full array of sales support functions for the manufacturer including, but not exclusively, sourcing, warehousing and storage, transportation, research, and financing. *Rack jobbers* are full-service wholesalers that specialize in a specific type of goods and provide the in-store display and merchandising means to service a product in a particular category, such as cosmetics, on a regular basis.

2. **PARTIAL-SERVICE WHOLESALER**: Provides limited or specific wholesaling functions to manufacturers. There are four types of partial service wholesalers:
   - CASH AND CARRY WHOLESALERS do everything that a full-service wholesaler would do except share in financing and transportation of products. This type of wholesaling works well for small chain stores.
   - TRUCK WHOLESALERS sell products directly to the store from trucks, typically perishable goods like dairy products, but also beverages.
   - DROP SHIPPERS take orders for products to retailers and consumers and have them directly shipped by the manufacturer or their agent rather than transporting and warehousing the goods themselves.
   - MAIL ORDER WHOLESALERS use the catalog, television, and other media to sell directly to retailers and consumers. Today, mail order houses maintain limited inventories yet shorten turnaround time for items. This is possible through computer tracking and forecasting controls for each product, technology not available years ago.

RETAILERS: Over two million retail outlets sell goods to the public. There are different types of retail establishments, based on the types of products sold:

1. **GENERAL MERCHANDISERS**: These retailers sell a large range of merchandise:
   - DEPARTMENT STORES, very large establishments that sell a large assortment of merchandise across product and price categories.
   - VARIETY STORES that sell a large assortment of low-priced items.
   - MASS MERCHANDISERS, similar to department stores in that they offer a wide range of products

but do not usually provide the same depth of assortment that a department store offers. These include *discount houses* and *club stores,* which offer low prices but limited store services, *off-price retailers,* and *outlet malls* which offer brand name discount clothing and merchandise at warehouse prices, often directly serving as an outlet for specific manufacturers, *hypermarkets* or supersized "everything under one roof" stores, which sell both food and merchandise, and *catalog/showroom retailers,* which display limited merchandise in a store and discount sales of department store merchandise through a catalog.

2. **SUPERMARKETS**: These retailers sell a wide variety of food products as their primary lines. Hypermarkets can also be grouped into this category if food is a substantial portion of their lines. *Convenience stores,* also called "c-stores," are minisupermarkets, carrying limited merchandise, usually that which is purchased frequently, immediately, and with minimum thought (e.g., milk, newspapers, cat food, etc.).

3. **SPECIALTY RETAILER**: This retailer typically sells a specific type of product, such as fabrics, hats, delicatessen.

4. **LIMITED-LINE RETAILER**: This retailer usually sells a wide array of products in a limited category, such as toys or electronics.

Chain stores are owned and managed by a single group, under the banner of a single trade name, such as McDonald's. Chains are said to be "voluntary" when stores are independently owned (sometimes under different names) but belong to an organization that gives them cooperative power in the channel. When chains sell the rights and support to individuals to open up a chain outlet of their own, those are called *franchises*. Franchisees deliver fees, royalties, advertising contributions, or a combination of all of these to the franchiser, in return for the right to use the franchise name, store blueprints, suppliers, etc.

CHANNEL SUPPORT AND DEALING

Manufacturers are increasingly having to pump budget dollars into a "trade budget." In fact, today, approximately a third of the advertising and promotion budget is allocated to trade discounts and programs.

Support of the trade occurs in three ways: (1) through materials and data; (2) through promotions; and (3) through *deals* (really a form of trade promotion, but arranging cash discounts rather than programs).

TRADE SUPPORT MATERIALS AND DATA: These include selling sheets, brochures, and *sales kits*, which highlight key marketing programs for the products being distributed. The trade wants these informational materials because they want to give the proper exposure to products that are being marketed well, and order enough product to keep up with consumer demand that will be generated from those programs.

Sales support data include volume tracking, price analysis, and many other kinds of information that help the channel members manage the flow and retailing of goods. Sales planning and forecasting with all types of accounts is extremely important to them, as it helps them manage their own inventories and shelf movement.

If *base sales forecasts*, predictions based on the way business was conducted this year, have not been set for the project, projections should be developed prior to writing the distribution plan.

Various measurements are derived from such forecasts, including *dollar volume* (the value of goods sold, either at wholesale or retail levels); *unit volume* (the number of units of goods sold, either at wholesale or retail levels); *ACV* ("all commodity volume," the percentage of total distribution of a product, based on the percentage of volume moved in those outlets that carry it); and *velocity* (the unit volume of goods sold per single point of distribution—unit volume/ACV).

TRADE PROMOTIONS: Trade promotions come in many shapes and forms, including items and programs for the retailer (e.g., displays, shelf-talkers, trade sweepstakes, sales games), and items and programs for the consumer (e.g., bonus packs, premiums, contests). A detailed discussion of these can be found in chapter 8, Promotion.

TRADE DEALING: Trade deals are distribution discounts offered to channel members to perform many different functions. Also called *trade allowances,* deals are used to gain distribution, increase distribution, secure better shelf space locations, special merchandising of displays in the store, and so on. In essence, the retailers charge the manufacturer for these *favors* because there is a high demand for them.

Years ago when categories were growing and not overcrowded as they are today, retailers were hungry for good products. Today, with so many products and versions of products in categories that are saturated and fragmenting, the battle for sales has, in many cases, come down to what manufacturers will pay to garner the special edge retailers can provide. On the retailer side, costs are high to stock and destock, track, and control this proliferation of products. As a result, manufacturer dealing has become a lucrative profit center for retailers, supplementing income from sales of the products themselves.

CHANNEL LEADERSHIP AND POWER

Who's in control of the distribution channels? The *channel captain* is the entity in the distribution channel that exercises the most power or control, or the *channel leadership*. Years ago, the power lay predominantly within the realm of the manufacturer or wholesaler. Today, as brands proliferate, categories become saturated, and retailing institutions consolidate, retailers have more choice and therefore have accumulated more power and channel leadership roles. There are two major types of power:

1. **REWARD POWER**: Derived from the granting of privileges for performing certain actions. (A manufacturer or service provider can grant exclusivity to a wholesaler; a retailer grants end-aisle displays to their best customers.)
2. **COERCIVE POWER**: Derived from threats to cut off or curtail use of a channel. (A retailer can refuse to carry a manufacturer's goods unless the manufacturer pays for the shelf space; a manufacturer can threaten to go to another wholesaler unless a better selling job is done.)

These powers are discerned and executed based on three different derivatives:

1. **LEGITIMATE POWER**: That derived from legal binding, such as contracts.
2. **REFERENT POWER**: That derived from a consensus of influential parties, such as the Grower's Cooperative in the grape juice industry, which bestows power to parties that they feel operate in the best interest of the industry.
3. **EXPERT POWER**: That derived from recognized expertise on a given subject.

As retailing institutions consolidate, retailers have more choice and therefore have accumulated more power and leadership roles. As manufacturers merge into megacorporations, they have more leverage with retailers.

PHYSICAL DISTRIBUTION SYSTEMS

As physical distribution of products eats up an enormous portion of a product's marketing budget, and as transportation costs continue to climb, good strategic management of physical distribution resources can effect economies and free funds earmarked for distribution so that other marketing functions can use them. Poor management of physical distribution, on the other hand, can surprise marketing managers with budget "black holes" that suck away cash from other programs.

Physical distribution of products, also called *logistics,* has earned itself entire departments in many organizations, which facilitate the movement of products from manufacture to the trade. Logistics are concerned with fulfilling the needs of the trade and ultimate consumer—making them happy and delivering product in an efficient manner while being responsive to their recommendations, questions, and complaints.

At the trade level, this means making product available to middlemen and retailers within a specified time and supporting them when they need it. At the consumer level, this means responding to consumer questions and complaints and following through. Companies set standards for logistics that can be organized into five major categories: (1) transportation of goods; (2) warehousing and inventory management; (3) means of product fulfillment; (4) order processing; and (5) issue response.

1. **TRANSPORTATION**: Transportation often takes the largest bite of the logistics budget. Specialized transportation systems are deployed depending upon whether a product is perishable, fragile, locally or nationally marketed, etc.

   There are three types of rates for the transportation of goods: (1) *class rate,* determined by the class of goods and the weight or amount; (2) *commodity rate,* which include discounts for large or bulk shipments; (3) *negotiated rate,* which is determined per customer job.

   There are three types of transporters or carriers: (1) *common carriers,* which are government-regulated conveyors of many different types of goods and that can be used by anyone (e.g., United Parcel Service, Federal Express, U.S. Postal Service); (2) *contract carriers,* who work within specific industries to carry specific types of products (e.g., frozen food) under individual arrangements with companies; and (3) *private carriers,* whose services are dedicated to specific companies, without government intervention or regulation.

   Each of the many modes of transport (including railroads, trucks, ships, and airplanes) has its advantages and problems. Shipping a *container* or standardized physically contained load by boat from Asia to New York, for example, is relatively inexpensive. However, the trip can take six to twelve weeks or more. Air is the choice of transport for products such as plants and flowers because of their perishability. The product's individual needs must be considered first, and then the most cost-effective mode of transportation can be determined.

   Finally, there are also intermediaries in the transportation business, including those that consolidate small shipments to obtain "truck load" or "car load" rates, which are based on a full vehicle. LTL (less than truck load) and LTC (less than carload) intermediaries offer special rates to customers for assembling truck- and carloads, which are less than companies would have paid to standard common carriers.

2. **WAREHOUSING AND INVENTORY MANAGEMENT**: Warehouses of all shapes and forms, from full-service to self-storage, supply space for the storage and/or distribution of goods. *Make-bulk* warehouses consolidate smaller into larger

loads. Break-bulk warehouses divide larger into smaller loads.

Inventory management is the control of the flow of goods from the manufacturer into the distribution channels and within the channels themselves. It makes products available to the trade and consumer. Because product sitting in a warehouse costs the marketer money to produce but has not yet generated income, many manufacturers are moving toward a system of sharpening sales forecasts and preordering in order to be able to utilize a *just-in-time* inventory system. Just-in-time makes just enough product available to meet demand by closely following order trends. While the marketer is in danger of *stockout,* not having enough product on hand to meet demand, he minimizes the risk or *monetary exposure* of carrying obsolete products in inventory.

3. **PRODUCT FULFILLMENT**: A *fulfillment house* is a center that not only stores and ships goods but also assembles, packages, and/or arranges for transportation. The mail order industry is a major patron of fulfillment houses, where many small packages are sent to many locations. Fulfillment houses are typically better suited for labor-intensive distribution of goods. They are also used for fulfillment of consumer promotion offers.

4. **ORDER PROCESSING**: The order-processing part of logistics is critical and sets the pace for the remaining steps in distribution. Today, electronic scanning systems and sophisticated order tracking systems dovetail with traditional methods, enabling marketers to keep inventories low yet keep up with demand.

5. **ISSUE RESPONSE**: Issue response is often used interchangeably with the notion "customer service." In reality, all of the above are considered forms of customer service. Issue response centers are more concerned with direct interraction with trade and consumer factions and the management of inquiries, recommendations, and the problems that arise from them. Large consumer products companies go to great lengths and expense to create such centers, both to serve loyal customers and to foster the image of the company as being consumer-minded. Some companies have even set up internal issue response centers for their sales forces to facilitate cooperation and responsiveness to field needs.

SALES FORECASTING

Sales forecasting is the projection of anticipated product sales, based on all of the elements of the marketing mix and a necessity for building effective distribution plans. There are many different qualitative (opinion driven) and quantitative (numbers driven) forecasting methods used in industry today. These are the major qualitative methods and their advantages and disadvantages:

- **CONSENSUS TECHNIQUE**: Forecasting opinions of company executives (often those with many years of experience or history with the product) are pooled together and averaged. This is very simple, often costless, and probably the most popular forecasting method used, also called "guesstimating." It is most effective when the forecasters are provided with as much up-to-date information as possible. The drawback of the consensus method is the wide variety and inaccuracy of predictions.
- **DELPHI CONSENSUS TECHNIQUE**: Forecast opinions from experts outside the company are pooled together and reevaluated several times, giving the experts the chance to evolve their opinions based on input from the other experts. This method is used principally for broad categories or industry forecasts and technological development, and can become expensive and time consuming, depending upon the topic and the range of experts.
- **CHANNEL FORECASTING TECHNIQUE**: Soliciting opinions from sales planners, wholesalers, accounts, etc., based on "day-to-day" experience in the field, it is also called "bottom-up" or "distribution" forecasting. Positives include the fact that the channel people have the most direct experience with the sale of the product and consumer, and are often physically in the channels surrounded by competitive products, retailers, etc., where they can discover changes occurring in the marketplace early on. The drawback of the channel technique is that forecasts are often quota driven and end up being "top-down" rather than "bottom-up," as intended. Channel forecasting is best utilized as a contributor to other methods

for "check and balance" rather than as a "stand alone" method.

- **PURCHASE-INTENT TECHNIQUE**: This method bases forecasts on the intent to buy that a consumer, retailer, or middleman expresses. Often companies go out to market with a "presell" to determine wholesaler and retailer interest before committing production schedules and advertising dollars to a product. This method is good for getting a "directional" sense for forecasting.

These are the most popular quantitative methods and their advantages and disadvantages:

- **TREND ANALYSIS**: A method that extrapolates or predicts the future based upon experience with similar events from the past. For example, plotting the trend of "high fat content" in foods can help predict where high- versus low-fat products will shake out the following year. Or, if a competitor ran a promotion three years earlier that is similar to the one you plan to run next quarter, information on the success of that promotion can help to forecast its performance for you.

  Trend analysis can be very simple, employing one or two elements, as shown in earlier examples. However, "real" trend analysis involves studying the track record of your brand and competitive brands over many years, looking for anomalies or significant "bumps and declines" in the entire category or specific products, and figuring out probable causes. This is no easy task but perhaps is the best use of time and money of any forecasting method. While not entirely accurate, it still allows for decision making based on real data.

- **MARKET TEST**: An actual selling test of a product or marketing program in a selected market that is representative of ultimate markets in which the product will be sold. *Test markets'* accuracy of predictability can be very high but is limited in effectiveness by how representative of the rest of the ultimate target the market is. (If a product tests well in New York City, it may not necessarily sell well in Kohler, Wisconsin.) Generally this problem is solved by testing in more than one market.

  A market test is the most expensive type of forecasting and is very time-consuming. Also, market tests let competitors in on your plans, giving them time to launch defense plans that can change the whole complexion of your forecast.

The miniature version of the market test (i.e., in one isolated town) is called a **mini-market test**. This test has the advantage of keeping the launch more secret than a full-scale market test but is a less reliable predictor of the rest of the target market.

- **SIMULATIONS**: There are two types: computer and physical. Computer models simulate the performance of a product based on hypothetical conditions in the marketplace that can be set and controlled by the researcher, often programmed with data obtained in numerous trend analysis studies. Simulations are much less expensive and far quicker than physical tests, but they do not deal directly with the consumer in any way and are therefore one step removed from the market.

  A physical simulation (e.g., a fake cereal aisle) lets consumers make relative purchase decisions in as real a purchasing environment as possible. If the consumer is given a type of currency with which actually to purchase products to take home (i.e., for free, but only up to a certain dollar or package number value), it is called a **token economy study**. Token economies work well in many situations because the consumer must make a purchase decision with "new money" that possesses real value to them. To make accurate predictions for the rest of the country or a particular target market, a large sample is needed.

- **REGRESSION ANALYSIS**: Computerized model that uses calculus and advanced mathematics to attempt to assign values of causality to various elements that may affect sales (e.g., advertising, economy, etc.). This method is quite cumbersome and is seldom used outside of business schools.

- **DIARY PANELS**: A selected group of consumers who record their product buying behavior over a period of time. This information is usually syndicated and sold to many companies. Panel research is good for identifying trends and emerging opportunities not yet exploited in the marketplace. New technology allows the research company to supply consumers with scanners, so that all purchases are scanned upon arrival home from the store and automatically computed. Household information is overlaid upon purchase behavior.

THE DISTRIBUTION PLAN

The distribution plan is often simpler to compose than other functional marketing plans because it deals with physical movement of products rather than concepts. Prior to the writing of the distribution plan, however, you should conduct several cursory analyses. First is the competitive rack-up. How are your competitors' products being distributed? What types of trade deals or incentive programs are they running? What accounts are they in? What is their ACV (all commodity volume) of distribution? Which are their strong or weak markets?

Equally important is the channel review. What distribution channels are available that can be exploited for your products? Are there ways of saving money using alternative distribution channels? Understanding the changing dynamics of the distribution channels will keep you attuned to opportunities, threats, and optimal adaptation.

Finally, look at the prior year's distribution plan and results, if yours is an existing business, and state lessons learned and their implications. Articulate all of this at the beginning of your plan. The distribution plan follows these steps:

1. Set distribution *objectives* based on marketing objectives.
2. Set distribution *strategies* for channel structure, usage of intermediaries, support programs, and physical product distribution that support and fulfill distribution objectives.
3. Set distribution *tactics* to complement strategies and support and fulfill distribution objectives.

DISTRIBUTION OBJECTIVES

Distribution objectives support the marketing objectives for the project. They establish goals for distribution in measurable terms and are similar to advertising and promotion objectives. Distribution objectives address both the physical channels and movement of products plus the motivation and support of the trade. Objectives include:

1. The *target audience* (e.g., males twenty-five to forty-four, etc.).
2. *Geographic market* (e.g. Northeast, West, key metro markets) goals.
3. *Channel market* (e.g., grocers, drugstores, concessions, c-stores) goals.
4. *Physical distribution* (e.g., inventory, warehousing, shipping) goals.
5. "Bottom-line"-oriented *measurable goals* (e.g., reach, penetration, ACV, savings) if possible. (You may not be focused enough to determine these until strategies are developed.)

If our marketing objective was to expand a liquid plant food business by 15 percent over the next year, distribution objectives could read as follows:

Generate an additional 15 percent sales volume through expanded geographical distribution in markets with a high density of caring house plant owners and through new channels that reach this audience in existing and new key markets, while lowering cost per point of distribution by 10 percent.

DISTRIBUTION STRATEGIES

These actions taken to achieve the distribution objectives differ with reference to geographical distribution, channel selection, channel support, and physical product movement.

1. **GEOGRAPHICAL SELECTION STRATEGIES** are either *broad-based,* where distribution of product is sought in all geographical areas (e.g. national or an entire region such as "Northeast") or *targeted,* where distribution is sought in specific markets (e.g., high BDI cities). An example of a geographical distribution strategy based on the plant food objective might be:

To target all urban markets where high concentrations of indoor plant growers live.

2. **CHANNEL SELECTION STRATEGIES** include selection of the best channels for marketing the products (e.g., supermarkets, drugstores, concessions, mass merchandisers, department stores, airport stores). An example of a channel distribution strategy based on the plant food objective might be:

To penetrate and sell through at least 20 percent of regional plant wholesalers and gain at least 50 percent ACV in supermarkets in targeted geographical markets.

3. **CHANNEL SUPPORT STRATEGIES** include materials, information exchange, and programs that will be developed to support sales efforts. An example of a channel support strategy based on the plant food objective might be:

To develop valuable trade incentives and strong point-of-sale materials, trade deals, and comprehensive sales kits, highlighting key brand events and support for the year.

4. **PHYSICAL DISTRIBUTION STRATEGIES** include general means of transport, warehousing, inventory management, fulfillment, order placing, and issue response. An example of a physical distribution strategy based on the plant food objective might be:

To improve order response time by 10 percent and utilize a central warehousing and fulfillment operation in the Midwest to reduce shipping and fulfillment costs.

DISTRIBUTION TACTICS

Distribution tactics are the specific programs developed to realize each distribution strategy. They include the choices of intermediaries for channel selection, the means of transportation, types of warehouses, etc., for physical product distribution and control. They include every type of trade deal, incentive, and support program that will be used to gain distribution and trade support at the wholesale and retail levels.

As an example, a distribution tactic for plant food sales channel support might be:

To offer a 2 percent display allowance to set up our products on end-caps and a lenient buy-back allowance for fourth quarter.

DISTRIBUTION GLOSSARY

Affiliated Chain: A cooperative arrangement between retail stores, whereby they take advantage of efficiencies that can be gained by doing things together.

Agent: A middleman who negotiates purchases, sales, or both for a client but does not take official title to goods.

All Commodity Volume (ACV): The percentage of total distribution of a product, based on the percentage of volume moved in those outlets that carry it.

Allocation: Offer to *retailers* in which promotional product or offers are provided on a limited basis (e.g., two cases per store) for a limited time (e.g., "while supplies last").

Allowance: Also called a *deal*. A discount offered by a manufacturer or wholesaler to the retailer that is contingent upon certain conditions. *Advertising allowances, promotional allowances,* and *display allowances* are several types.

Auction House: Establishment that brings buyers and sellers together in one location for the purpose of permitting buyers to examine merchandise before purchase.

Break-Bulk Warehouse: A warehouse that breaks up larger into smaller loads, usually used for small orders (e.g., mail order) to save on shipping costs to a central warehousing location.

Broker: An *agent* who represents either a buyer or seller of goods but doesn't have direct physical control of the goods. A broker's powers of negotiation are usually limited by the broker's client.

Buyback Allowance: A discount given to a *wholesaler* or *retailer* based upon the amount of product remaining from a previous purchase. These allowances serve as limited assurances to the retailer that the product will sell.

Car Load Rate: The rate for shipping a full car load of goods (e.g., Railroad Car Load).

Case Allowance: Discount offered to a retailer by a wholesaler or manufacturer when merchandise is purchased by the case; the greater the number of cases, the greater the discount.

Cash and Carry Wholesaler: Type of *wholesaling* operation where retailers drive to a warehouse location, select the goods they want, pay, load, and go on their way.

Catalog: A type of *retailer* who produces a catalog or list of items for sale, with a description and price of each item. Orders are normally placed by mail or phone.

Chain Store: A group of retail stores, usually of the same type, centrally owned and operated.

Channel Captain: Dominant and controlling member of a *channel of distribution* with the most clout and power.

Channel Marketing: Method of organization of distribution talent and resources that puts specific people in charge of specific *channels of distribution*.

Channel of Distribution: Means and delivery system used to move products from the manufacturer to the end-user of those products. A channel includes the manufacturer and end-user, and can include one or more intermediaries, each of which facilitates or provides physical means of accomplishment.

Closing: The point in *personal selling* at which the salesperson attempts to move the customer to make a purchase decision.

Club Store: Low-cost "no frills" store where goods are often sold directly from packing cases at discount and often in bulk. Also called a warehouse store.

Coercive Power: Power derived from the ability of someone in a *marketing channel* to cut off or curtail another's participation in the channel. (A retailer can refuse to carry a manufacturer's goods unless the manufacturer pays for the shelf space.)

Cold Call: An unsolicited personal sales call on a potential customer.

Collection Period: The average number of days it takes to collect on all accounts.

Commissary Store (Company Store): A retail store owned and operated by a company or governmental entity, established to sell goods to its employees, usually at a discount and often with the company's products.

Commission: Compensation paid to an *agent* or internal salesperson for the sale of goods, usually given as a percentage of the sales.

Commission Agent: An *agent* who negotiates the sale of goods for a client, usually operating under his own name. The commission agent usually enjoys more power regarding prices, methods, and terms of sale than does a broker, although the commission merchant must follow the rules of its client. The commission agency often arranges delivery, credit, and collection of monies, deducting its fees and remitting the balance to the client.

Common Carrier: Government-regulated transporters that can be used by anyone (e.g., United Parcel Service, Federal Express, U.S. Postal Service) and that convey many kinds of goods.

Consignment: Goods that are provided to a *retailer,* in which payment to the manufacturer or middleman is contingent on the sale being made to the consumer. This is a way for a retailer to carry goods without incurring expense and cost-of-inventory, and an expensive way for manufacturers to get distribution. It is more likely to be arranged when a product is unproved and/or a manufacturer is unknown, or when a manufacturer wants presence in an unusual channel outlet.

Consumption Exercise: An endeavor, usually conducted on a computer, that seeks to find the balance between actual product movement out of the manufacturer's inventories and the reported store sales, thus helping the marketer understand what quantity of goods is "in the pipeline" or in the channel. Often misused as a means of forecasting and as a substitute for unavailable information.

Containerization: Method by which large quantities of product can be combined into a single compact unit for storage and transportation. Special discount rates apply to containers, especially for overseas shipping.

Contract Carrier: Transporters typically working within specific industries with specific types of products (e.g., frozen food) under written agreement with the companies.

Convenience Store (C-Store): A small version of a *supermarket* that carries consumer goods that are purchased frequently, immediately, and with the minimum of thought (e.g., milk, newspapers, cigarettes, cat food).

Dating: A type of trade *deal* in which payments for goods are deferred to a specific date, as a purchase incentive. Or, in labeling, a package notation indicating the last date that this product should be sold.

Deal: Also called an *allowance*. A trade discount for the purchase of goods, in one of many forms, including promotional, advertising, display, *case,* etc.

Dealer: A retailer.

Dealer Loader: Extra incentives given to *retailers* to help them sell products, awarded at certain levels of retailer purchases (i.e., display with 1,000 units or more).

Dealer Loading: Buying products in excess of needs to take advantage of special discounts. Also called *forward buying*.

Department Store: A retail store that handles a wide variety of lines of goods, organized into distinct and separate departments. Examples of department stores include Macy's, Sears, JC Penney, and Lord & Taylor.

Direct Mail Marketing: A type of *direct response marketing*, where offers are made directly to consumers via the mail.

Direct Marketing: Efforts addressed directly to the end-user or consumer of a product (e.g., by mail, telephone, personal selling) that require a direct action or order from them. Middlemen are not usually included in this *channel of distribution*. (Sometimes *fulfillment houses* are used.)

Direct Store Delivery: Product is delivered by the manufacturer to *retail* stores without the use of a *wholesaler* or without going to retailers' warehouses.

Display Allowance: Payment or discount given to a *retailer* for displaying products in a special manner (e.g., end-of-aisle displays).

Distribution Allowances: Discounts offered by manufacturer to a distributor, retail chain, or wholesaler to provide incentive for distributing their products. Often used with new products to build as much distribution as possible within a short time. Also called *slotting allowances*.

Distributor: A firm that handles most key aspects of selling products for a manufacturer, including *warehousing, direct sales,* shipping, billing, legal transfer of goods, and promotional activities.

Drop Ship: A type of wholesaler that does not physically handle the products it sells. The manufacturer typically ships products directly to the *retailer* and invoices the drop shipper, who in turn invoices the customer.

Ex: This commonly used prefix in physical distribution indicates that a specific location is the point of origin of a shipment (e.g., "Ex Factory," "Ex Warehouse," etc.).

Exclusivity: A legal arrangement made between a manufacturer and sellers of products whereby they are granted the sole right to sell within a given area (e.g., territory) or time, or by a particular means.

Expert Power: Power derived from being a recognized expert on a given subject matter in a *channel of distribution*.

Facilitator: A company or individual that helps in the distribution of a product but does not take title ownership (e.g., insurance agencies, shipping companies, and, in most cases, bankers).

Facing: The physical appearance of a product on the shelf to the consumer, based on the dimensions of its front packaging or "face." If twenty boxes of cereal were stocked five deep (one behind another), there would be four facings—the consumer sees four boxes up front.

Factor: A type of commission agent who pays for products up front, accepting a large commission for assuming the risk (i.e., 15 percent to 25 percent or more). Banks often act as factors, and factor arrangements are often used for international purchases because of the higher risk involved.

Failure Fee: Also called a "restocking fee." A manufacturer or wholesaler is required to pay a *retailer* that carries their product a set fee for the removal of the product from the shelf should the product be withdrawn from the market. This fee usually applies to new product launches because of the frequency of failures (over 90 percent) and the expense to stock and destock those failures. Although thought to be excessive by most manufacturers, these fees are helping to keep down the proliferation of new products in an environment of overcrowded and oversaturated categories.

Forward Buying: Buying products in advance of need to obtain special discounts. Also called *dealer loading*.

Franchise: Permission granted to a *retailer* to market a company's name, products, or services under a common brand or method of operation.

Free on Board (FOB): A physical distribution term used to indicate to where goods will be provided for "inland" or domestic shipping. From there, the buyer must pay for transportation to their desired destination.

Freight Absorption: A means of providing buyers with the opportunity to deduct shipping costs from the cost of goods.

Fulfillment House: A center that not only stores and ships products but also assembles, packages, and/or arranges for transportation.

Full-Service Wholesaler: A *wholesaler* that offers a full array of sales support functions for the manufacturer including, but not exclusively, sourcing, warehousing and storage, transportation, research, and financing.

General Store: A retail store that carries a wide variety of nonrelated products but that differs from a *department store* in that products are not arranged by departments.

Grading: Grading is the process of sorting individual units of a product according to predetermined standards or classes.

Handling Allowance: A trade *deal* in which discounts or payments are made for the special handling or stocking of a product.

Home TV Shopping: An increasingly popular *direct selling* method in which products are showcased and sold through television advertising and direct telephone order response from consumers.

Hypermarket: A very large mass *retailer* that sells at lower prices a wide array of products, including groceries and everyday goods.

Independent Store: An individually owned and managed *retail* store.

In-Home Retailing: A method of *direct selling* in which products are sold directly to the consumer through home presentation and demonstration, either through personal selling, television, or computer. Includes *party selling* (e.g., Tupperware) and *home TV shopping* methods.

Inventory: The supply of raw materials, material in process, and finished products on hand.

Invoice: The bill sent to a buyer for products purchased.

Jobber: In today's channels, a slang synonym for *wholesaler*. Sometimes used to designate a special type of wholesaler that deals in odd lots or commodities.

Just-in-Time Inventory: Making just enough product available to meet demand and monitoring it closely, to minimize inventory need and storage at the plant or warehouse and reduce the financial exposure and responsibility of the company.

Key Account: One that brings in large revenues or has influence. These are sometimes handled directly by a company, even if intermediaries are customarily used to sell products.

Legitimate Power: That which is derived in a business relationship from actual legal binding, such as a contract.

Less Than Truck Load (LTL): Less than the quantity required to fill a truck for overland shipment. LTL intermediaries offer lower rates to customers by assembling these into combined truck loads.

Letter of Credit (LOC): A document of promised payment, usually issued by a bank or *factor* for a buyer, to permit the purchase of goods. The letter is a promise that upon shipment of goods, cash directly from an account will be released to the seller. LOCs are often used for international transactions.

Limited Function Wholesaler: One that offers a partial array of sales support functions for the manufacturer, including some, but not all, of the following: sourcing, warehousing and storage, transportation, research, and financing.

Limited Line Retailer: A *retailer* that sells a variety of products but usually within only a few product categories (e.g., bicycle shop, bakery).

List Broker: A company or individual that makes a commission on renting and selling mailing lists, often serving a managerial role in making and executing list selections and sorting.

Logistics: A term used to refer to "physical distribution" systems.

Mail Order Selling: A method of direct selling in which consumers respond to offers through the mail.

Make-Bulk Warehouse: A storage operation that consolidates smaller into larger loads for reshipping.

Manufacturer's Representative: A wholesaling *agent* that acts as an independent sales force for a manufacturer, usually operating on a contractual basis. The manufacturer's rep typically works within an exclusive territory and specializes either in types of products (e.g., bathroom products) or types of markets (e.g., college market).

Mass Merchandiser: A *retailer* that offers a wide range of products but usually not in the same depth of assortment that a *department store* offers.

Merchandising: The planning and marketing of products to make the products available in the best place, at the best time, at the best price.

Merchandise Mart: Permanent, industry-specific trading location where sellers showcase their wares and buyers come to shop on a regular basis. The toy district in New York City is considered a merchandise mart. Can be considered as a "retail" store for buyers.

Merchant Middleman: A *channel* intermediary who takes title to the products he/she sells.

Multilevel Channel: A *channel of distribution* that includes more than one intermediary between the manufacturer and consumer.

Off-Price Retailer: A *retailer* that sells brand name products at less than the manufacturer's *suggested retail price,* sometimes offering products that are discontinued or damaged at large savings.

Oligopoly: A situation in a market where only a few companies control the supply of a particular product.

One-Level Channel: A *channel of distribution* that includes one intermediary between the manufacturer and consumer, such as a *retail* store.

Outlet Mall: A shopping center that houses *retail* stores that sell excess or unwanted inventory directly to consumers at discounts. The individual stores often bear the names of the manufacturers.

Overstock: Too much inventory.

Pallet: A platform, usually made of wood and measuring 40 to 48 inches, which is commonly used to hold and transport products in bulk quantities of varying heights.

Parent Store: A *retail* store that owns and operates other stores, usually bearing the same name.

Party Selling: A type of *direct marketing* in which representatives take orders from invitees to parties held to sell specific products.

Pay to Stay Allowance: A trade *deal* in which the manufacturer or *wholesaler* pays the *retailer* to keep a product on the shelf when it is threatened with replacement by other products.

Personal Selling: One-to-one, face-to-face transactions with purchasers.

Plan-O-Gram: The printed layout or "blueprint" of how products will be arranged and look on a shelf, based on the number of sections devoted to the manufacturer's products by the *retailer*. Often developed cooperatively by the manufacturer and the accounts.

Private Carrier: Transporters whose services are dedicated to specific companies without government intervention or regulation.

Rack Jobber: See *jobber*.

Referent Power: Channel power transferred from a consensus of influential parties (such as the Grower's Cooperative in the grape juice industry) to parties that they feel operate in the best interest of the industry.

Retailer: The final seller of goods directly to the consumer, whether through a store, catalog, television, etc. Retail establishments include *mass merchandisers, variety stores, home TV shopping channels, catalog houses, supermarkets,* etc.

Returns: The products sent back to a manufacturer because of damages or expirations, or *allowances* provided by the manufacturer for retailer disposal of these goods.

Reverse Channel: When goods and services make their way back upstream from the consumer to the manufacturer or service provider, such as in recycling.

Reward Power: Channel power derived from granting privileges for performing certain actions, such as a manufacturer granting exclusivity to a wholesaler.

Rollout: The methodical escalating distribution of a new product into the marketplace, or existing products into new geographic markets. In a national rollout, a product is released across the country. A market-by-market rollout is a wave of careful releases in which product introduction in new markets is influenced by experience and performance in earlier markets.

Sales Aids: Tools, such as brochures, slides, and *sell sheets,* designed to help the seller present products or marketing programs to the buyer.

Sales Forecast: An estimate of a product's dollar or unit sales for a period of time projected into the future.

Sales Incentive: A reward or bonus for salespeople based on their performance, typically tied to a preset *sales quota* or other goal.

Sales Quota: A dollar or unit sales target assigned to a specific individual or group, from which bonuses and other rewards are determined.

Selling Agent: An agent who operates on an extended contractual basis, sells all of the specified line merchandise or the entire output of his or her principal, and usually has full authority with regard to prices, terms, and other conditions of sale. The selling agent occasionally renders financial aid to his or her principal.

Sell Sheet: A printed *sales aid* used to illustrate or explain a product promotion or other program to the *retailer.*

Shelf Life: The length of time that a product remains in good condition on the shelf, most often used for food products. Federal laws require the practice of *dating,* which indicates to the consumer the last date that the product is safe to purchase for consumption.

Shipper: The outermost container of a product; used to ship goods.

Shopping Goods: Products that are compared by the consumer as to quality, price, and suitability before purchase is made, as opposed to goods that are bought without much consideration (e.g., *impulse goods*).

Shrinkage: Gradual loss of inventory over time due to damage, theft, or mishandling.

Skid: See *pallet*.

Slotting Allowance: See *distribution allowance*.

Sourcing: The process of finding suppliers for raw materials and finished goods and the weeding out of poor from good suppliers to arrive at optimal purchasing positions.

Specialty Goods: Products for which consumers are willing to make a special purchasing effort, such as jewelry, boats, bicycles, etc.

Specialty Retailer: This retailer typically sells a specific type of product, such as a fabric store, deli, hat store, and so on.

Stockout: When a *retailer* unexpectedly runs out of product. Except in rare cases where supply is deliberately limited to build demand and drive up the price (e.g., some toy lines), stockout is to be avoided.

Store Check: A visit to the *retailers* through which products are sold, by marketing and sales people, to look at how products are being displayed, what competitive products are being sold, etc. Store checks enable desk jockeys to get a feel for the real world in which their product competes.

Supermarket: A retail outlet that carries a wide variety of food products as primary lines. Hypermarkets can also be grouped into this category if food is a substantial portion of inventory. *Convenience stores* are considered "mini" supermarkets, carrying limited merchandise, usually those that are purchased frequently, immediately, and with the minimum of thought (e.g., milk, newspapers, cat food, etc.).

Telemarketing: Marketing through the use of the telephone or computer.

Test Market: An actual selling trial of a product or marketing program in a selected market that is representative of ultimate markets. Test markets allow the marketer to evaluate performance on a small scale, from which broader plans can be determined or refined.

Trade Show: A permanent, industry-specific assembly of manufacturers and intermediaries, used as a selling medium.

Traffic: The flow of consumers through a store, or specific part of a store.

Truck Wholesaler: A type of *wholesaler* that sells to, delivers, and collects payment in one operation at the customer's location.

Turnover: An inventory term meaning the number of times during a specific period that a specific volume of goods moves through a channel. Also called a "turn." If a store's normal shipment of greeting cards is ten cases and that store sells out these ten cases four times in one year, four turns have been made.

Variety Store: A *retail* store that sells a wide variety of goods, usually at low price. An example is Woolworth's.

Vending: A direct selling method in which products are sold through automatic dispensing machines, directly to the consumer (e.g., soda machine).

Vertical Channels: Marketing channels in which the manufacturer integrates channel intermediaries into their own operations (e.g., retail stores such as Firestone).

Warehouse Store: Same as a *club store*.

Wholesaler: An intermediary that actually takes ownership of goods, buying and reselling them for a profit, sometimes directly to consumers and other times to retailers, who in turn sell them to consumers.

Zero-Level Channel: Synonymous with *direct marketing*, in which no intermediaries exist between the manufacturer and consumer.

PM TOOLS™
DISTRIBUTION

- Channel Map
- Historical Sales Analysis Worksheet
- ACV Worksheet

CHANNEL MAP

MANUFACTURER/ SERVICE PROVIDER

AGENTS
Commission Merchant
Action House
Broker
Selling Agent
Manufacturer's Representative
Licensing Agent

☐

WHOLESALERS
Full-Service
Partial-Service
(Cash & Carry, Truck, Drop Shipper, Mail Order)

◯

RETAILERS
Department Store
Variety Store
Mass Merchandiser (Discount House, Club Store, Off-Price Retailer, Outlet Mall, Hypermarket, Catalog Showroom)
Supermarket
Convenience Store
Specialty Retailer
Limited-Line Retailer
Chain Store

△

CONSUMER

INSTRUCTIONS: In between the "Manufacturer/ Service Provider" and "Consumer" boxes, draw the appropriate shapes (i.e., square for agents, circle for wholesalers, and triangle for retailers) for all of the intermediaries that are involved with distribution of your product. Write what type(s) of each of those intermediaries are utilized at each step in the shape (e.g., Supermarkets and Department Stores). Draw a line from shape to shape to show the sequence of product movement through the channel.

HISTORICAL SALES ANALYSIS WORKSHEET

BRAND:_____

SALES:

[] Unit vol. [] $ vol.	YEAR 19___	YEAR 19___	YEAR 19___	YEAR 19___
JAN.				
FEB.				
MARCH				
APRIL				
MAY				
JUNE				
JULY				
AUG.				
SEPT.				
OCT.				
NOV.				
DEC.				
Total:				

CHANGE (%):

[] Unit vol. [] $ vol.	YEAR 19___	YEAR 19___	YEAR 19___	YEAR 19___
JAN.	N.A.			
FEB.	N.A.			
MARCH	N.A.			
APRIL	N.A.			
MAY	N.A.			
JUNE	N.A.			
JULY	N.A.			
AUG.	N.A.			
SEPT.	N.A.			
OCT.	N.A.			
NOV.	N.A.			
DEC.	N.A.			
Total:	N.A.			

19__

19__

19__

19__

J F M A M J J A S O N D

ACV WORKSHEET

BRAND: _____

MARKET	ACV ___	ACV ___	% Diff.	Rationale
_____	___	___	___	_____
_____	___	___	___	_____
_____	___	___	___	_____
_____	___	___	___	_____
_____	___	___	___	_____
_____	___	___	___	_____
_____	___	___	___	_____
_____	___	___	___	_____
_____	___	___	___	_____
_____	___	___	___	_____
_____	___	___	___	_____
_____	___	___	___	_____
_____	___	___	___	_____
_____	___	___	___	_____
_____	___	___	___	_____
_____	___	___	___	_____
_____	___	___	___	_____
_____	___	___	___	_____
_____	___	___	___	_____
_____	___	___	___	_____
_____	___	___	___	_____
_____	___	___	___	_____
_____	___	___	___	_____
_____	___	___	___	_____

INSTRUCTIONS: ACV is the percentage of total distribution of a product, based on the percentage of volume moved in those stores (e.g., 75% ACV = product sold through stores that account for 75% of all industry volume). List markets that you wish to analyze. Select a period with which you want to compare the present ACV (e.g., present versus year ago, etc.). Calculate the change and provide a rationale for the change.

SIX

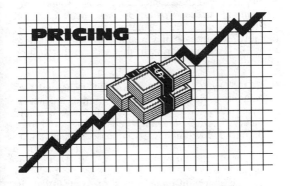

PRICING

TOP-LINE

OVERVIEW

Pricing is the only element of marketing that can be manipulated to produce revenue; all other marketing functions represent costs. When it comes down to the actual contribution of each marketing function to the "bottom line" or profitability of a product or business, pricing is the means by which cash is generated to support and often justify marketing decisions in the other functions. Many elements impact the pricing decision in the organization, including: sales volume, manufacturing costs, allocated overhead, profitability requirements, competitive activity and pricing, marketing programs and their priorities, and others.

If the price of a product is above the consumer's willingness to pay or beyond the perceived value of the product, sales will suffer (no matter how good marketing programs are). On the other hand, if the price of a product is far below the consumer's willingness to pay, the marketer could be forfeiting much needed revenues and profits unnecessarily. The pricing decision is a critical one and should be thought through and arrived at scientifically.

PRICING THEORY

Pricing theory is the explanation of how *economic determinants, consumer behavior and expectations,* and *competitive activities* influence the price and ultimately the purchase of a product. We will also define some basic pricing terms in this section that will be referred to later.

1. **ECONOMIC DETERMINANTS**: Financial analysts often view the pricing function as a quantitative, precise science that is related to microeconomic theory. There is *demand,* the consumer need for a product and willingness to purchase it under various conditions, and *supply,* the quantity of product that is to be offered during a given time period to the consumer.

    There are different levels of competition, in which many (the ideal market), few (*oligopoly*), or only one company or product (*monopoly*) vie for the attention and patronage of the consumer.

    Price elasticity, the response that consumers make to price changes, is measured by many marketers to predict what will happen to the sales of their product if they raise or lower the price by a set amount. Elasticity is determined by many factors, including supply, demand, the number of competitors, the range of prices, whether the product is a commodity or luxury item, the loyalty of consumers to specific brands, the presence of major attribute advantages of one product over another, etc.

    Elasticity is expressed numerically by dividing the percentage of change in volume resulting from a price change by the percentage of change in the price itself. For example, if we increase the price of a racquetball racquet by 10 percent and it results in sales volume loss of only 5 percent, then the elasticity ratio is 0.5. The product's pricing is said to be relatively *inelastic* because the elasticity ratio was under 1.0, meaning the market absorbed part of the price increase and the increase resulted in greater profitability. If the 10 percent increase resulted in a 20 percent volume decline, we can say that the market for this product was *price elastic*.

In general, categories and brands that have strong brand loyalty are relatively inelastic up to the point of profit maximization. We know that consumers who love Nike sneakers are more likely to buy Nike rather than other brands, even if the price were increased over that of competitive brands. But there is a point where consumers will switch if the disparity is too great. This line of demarcation is different for each category and product, and can change in a relatively short time. Marketers seek to come as close to this line as possible, without going over. Finding an ideal *price point* or level that the consumer will accept without adversely affecting the product's profitability is tough, and tracking the history of elasticity of different brands within a category can help to reveal important patterns.

2. **CONSUMER BEHAVIOR AND EXPECTATIONS**: Consumers establish in their own minds the *utility* or degree to which a product fulfills their needs, relative to other products. Some of this perception comes from the availability of products (i.e., from supply and demand), but the rest of consumer perception comes from the individual need and value that is placed on the product itself.

Value is the utility of a product measured against its price. A way of measuring value is the *performance/price ratio*—the perceived value to a consumer that a product possesses (how well a product delivers on its benefits), based on standardized scales set for both performance and price. This means of measurement is often used to help set initial prices, based on perceived value of a new product versus those of existing products.

If a consumer sees a major benefit in one product versus another in the same category, that consumer will pay more to attain that benefit. If a consumer sees a new product idea he/she has never encountered before, the desire to try something new may seduce the consumer into paying a premium for that product. Marketing programs help to communicate a product's benefits to consumers. If these programs do their jobs, the consumer will be willing to pay more.

Consumers are classified in many ways by different companies, based upon their willingness to try new things or existing things with new twists.

Some consumers are considered *innovators,* who will try new products without much concern for price. Others are designated as *laggards,* who will wait until a product is well known before taking the chance—these consumers are typically very price conscious and cautious and will wait for the price to come down. There are other designations in between that follow a bell-shaped curve, with the bulk of consumers somewhere in the middle. These are discussed in greater detail in chapter 3, Product Development.

Behavior also develops from stimuli like familiarity; if a consumer is used to paying a specific price for certain type of product (especially a generic or commodity product such as sugar), pricing will not differ from one product to another in that category or segment, unless a significant change occurs in its supply.

3. **COMPETITIVE ACTIVITIES**: A final determinant in pricing theory is competitive activity in the marketplace. The price of a particular product can be considered fair and reasonable, but if one competitor offers the same or similar products at a huge discount, the fairly priced product will lose out. Competitive activities include more than setting a lower retail selling price for a product, recommended by the manufacturer; they include discounts, incentives, promotional programs, and other elements that all affect pricing and ultimately value to the consumer. To consumers, the *perceived* price point is the final value of the goods after all these things have been taken into account.

Competitive activities are more influential in cases where products are very similar and perceived utility is relatively equal.

Some determinants in pricing do not come from any of these three sources but rather are set by governmental actions, such as the Robinson-Patman Act, which says that a seller's prices must be uniform to all buyers, unless they can be justified by differences in costs. Prices cannot be set in *collusion,* which is an illegal action in which companies band together against the public interest. If they set prices this way, they restrict normal market trade.

THE PRICING PLAN

The pricing plan is strongly linked to the financial business function, just as the product development plan is closely linked with R&D and manufacturing business functions. Because of its direct effect on cash flow, the pricing plan is often the one point of the overall marketing plan that attracts upper management's involvement in decision making. In fact, the marketer often must present pricing analyses and recommendations to higher management, and the responsibility and decision-making power is assumed at that level.

Prior to developing the pricing plan, it is important to get an understanding of pricing dynamics of the category. Tracking competitors' average prices, trade deals, and resulting competitive performance will help to determine the effect of pricing in that particular marketplace. A competitive rack-up of pricing activity both nationally and in specific areas of interest should be conducted. What markets appear to be price sensitive? Where are private label players strong? Where are local low-price products situated? Next, the prior year's pricing plan and results should be reviewed and "lessons learned" and their implications stated. Articulate all of this at the beginning of the pricing plan. Then, these steps are followed:

1. Reiterate pricing *objectives* set in the marketing objectives.
2. Determine pricing *strategies* that support and fulfill pricing objectives.
3. Determine pricing *tactics* that put pricing strategies into action.

PRICING OBJECTIVES

Pricing objectives are already stated in the marketing objectives, although perhaps not elaborately. In fact, pricing objectives are the most directly accountable functional objectives because of their impact on sales and profit requirements in the marketing objectives. Pricing objectives fall into one or more of four major categories: (1) profitability; (2) volume; (3) competition; and (4) image.

1. **PROFITABILITY OBJECTIVES**: These objectives are driven by motives of profit maximization, loss minimization, and rates of return set at much higher levels of the company. As such, pric-

ing becomes very important to the health and budgets of other functions.

Profit maximization itself means that an increase in price of a product would equal the increase in the cost to produce or market the product. In other words, if the price were increased by $0.10, making another $1 MM in revenues, the only way we could sell as much product to make that extra revenue at that price is to increase advertising by $1 MM. We can then say that our profits have been maximized. In another case, if we increased our price by $0.10, but it resulted in $1 MM less in sales, yielding no additional profits, we again can say that profits have been maximized. Marketers try to approximate this profit maximization scenario as closely as possible.

Rates of return are measurements set to give the brands minimum performance or *contribution* to the overall profitability of a business or group of brands. Examples are Return on Investment (ROI), Return on Sales (ROS), and so on. These return rates are expressed in percentages, showing the relationship between one spending variable (e.g., investment, cost of goods, etc.), and profits. For example, if we invest $1.00 and get back $1.15, we have a 15 percent ROI. To take one step further, let's say that 14 percent minimum return on sales rate is required of your brand as a corporate policy, and your brand has a 10 percent ROS. A price increase (or budget cutting in other areas) could be required in order to bring you beyond this minimum.

2. **VOLUME/SHARE OBJECTIVES**: Volume objectives are set in terms of the amount of physical product that is sold in a given period of time. They can be measured in relation to maintaining or increasing actual unit movement, relative unit movement versus competition (i.e., *market share*), or percentage of sales under specific conditions.

Volume objectives are sometimes short-sighted, driving a product to sell as much as possible, regardless of long-term implications. They can, however, be strategic, attempting to preempt or gain leadership over competitors or to gain enough sales of a new product so that a company can afford to produce the product.

Also, if a category is very brand-loyal, then

building volume while sacrificing profits in the short term may pay off in the long term in a healthier business down the road. Volume objectives and the many methods of forecasting are discussed in detail in chapter 5, Distribution.

3. **COMPETITION-BASED OBJECTIVES**: These pricing objectives flow from competitive activity in the marketplace and are often as simple as matching the price of a competitive product in the segment of the category in which a product competes. These objectives usually are set within categories that are very "price sensitive," where consumers react to small changes in price and are not very loyal to brands.

4. **IMAGE-BASED OBJECTIVES**: This type of pricing objective is fueled by a need to establish an image of high quality or exclusivity in the minds of the consumer, as such products as Porsche, Perrier, or Evian have done. Pricing is set extraordinarily high to support these demands, and even though physical utility may not be high, emotional elements such as vanity or *prestige* can very well (and often do) compensate for the higher price.

PRICING STRATEGIES

While many final pricing decisions are determined outside a marketing manager's jurisdiction, the marketer is always in a position to influence pricing decisions. It is part of every marketer's responsibility to seek out, interpret, and present information that can affect those pricing decisions.

Pricing strategies are used to support and fulfill pricing objectives and will differ, depending upon the focus of the marketing objectives (e.g., increase market share versus increase profits), and upon what the other company functions "bring to the party." For example, we may be able to raise prices if the advertising is fantastic. Contrarily, we may have to lower prices because lower-priced private label products are gaining share.

There are five major types of strategies, all of which depend upon all of the factors discussed in the earlier Pricing Theory section. These include: (1) the *cost-oriented strategy;* (2) the *market skimming strategy;* (3) the *market penetration strategy;* (4) the *competitive pricing strategies;* and (4) the *prestige pricing strategy.*

1. **COST-ORIENTED PRICING STRATEGY**:
   The most commonly used pricing strategy today is
   cost oriented, where a company wishes to achieve
   profitability objectives by either setting *target
   profits* to achieve specific rates of return or *markups* and *margins* above their costs. An example of
   a target profit is "20 percent of sales," and prices
   are set to achieve that figure. Markup costing involves figuring the price of a product, based on
   adding a percentage to the cost of the product. For
   example, a 50 percent markup on a product that
   costs $10.00 to produce would render the selling
   price of the item at $15.00.
     Marginal costing involves setting prices based
   on the percentage of profit that is sought. For example, if you wanted to make a 50 percent margin
   or profit on your item that costs $10.00 to pro-
   duce, then you would price the item at $20.00,
   because with a selling price of $20.00, $10.00 is
   50 percent profit. Just make sure that you know
   whether someone is speaking of markups or margins when judging competitive pricing and setting
   your own.
     Cost-oriented pricing strategy is sometimes con-
   sidered to be the "easy way out" but may not be very
   effective, because all of the pricing determinants
   that can impact a product's performance may not be
   considered. Factors such as competitive pricing, perceived product value for the price and product demand should also be factored into the cost-oriented
   pricing decision.
2. **MARKET SKIMMING STRATEGY**: A skimming strategy means charging as much money as the
   market (ultimately the consumer) will bear. A skimming strategy is used to *maximize* profits and is
   based on all of the pricing determinants, such as supply and demand, consumer behavior and expectations, and competitive activities. A skimming strategy is typically short term because it is not sustain-
   able. If high profits are taken in a particular category, a marketer soon finds ten other competitors
   with lower prices have entered the scene because the
   product area was so attractive.
     Products that have major competitive advan-
   tages over other products with which they compete can charge much higher prices if consumers
   feel the benefits are worth it. Skimming strategies
   are most often taken with new product introductions where higher prices can be charged at

introduction if there are no competitive threats in the short run. An example is Rollerblade, which was "the only game in town" for a few years and has only recently been forced to roll back pricing somewhat and to produce lower-priced models because of many lower-priced entrants into the in-line skating market. Skimming strategies can also be taken in competitive markets (usually by all competitors), where demand is much higher than supply (e.g., the bed and breakfast industry in New England), and adjusted regularly as demand goes up and down.

The skimming strategy often can make a company a lot of cash on a new product at inception, and sometimes the product can maintain its price because it has established a prestige positioning, such as Ralph Lauren clothing or Häagen-Dazs ice cream. If this is the case, skimming evolves into a ***prestige pricing*** strategy, to be discussed later in this section.

Finally, if a skimming strategy is taken, the marketer should monitor closely the competitive marketplace and demand for his product.

3. **MARKET PENETRATION STRATEGY**: The market penetration strategy is driven more by volume than profit. In this case, the marketer wishing to get as deeply entrenched in a market as possible charges lower prices and sacrifices some profits. One reason can be that he needs high sales to cover the fixed costs of production. Another can be that there is a high degree of loyalty in the category and he wants to get as many trial users as possible. Another reason can be that he wants to gain a solid foothold in the market before competitors come in to battle his products. The penetration strategy is also used when a new product is introduced in a category so crowded that it is difficult to get the consumer's attention and make the sale.

Procter and Gamble often uses this strategy to maximize market penetration when they introduce a product. This means that they offer a product such as Tide detergent with *bleach alternative* at a price far lower than the competition. By this means, they hope to get a lot of first use of the product in hopes of gaining consumer loyalty and future purchases at the higher price.

Some products or services strive to be the *low-price leader,* selling more of the product than competitors by pricing low. This is often done in "commodity"-based businesses and "staple goods" (e.g., milk, sugar), where there are few differentiating factors between brands.

Sometimes lower prices can yield equal or higher profits in the long run, even though they generate smaller returns, because more product is sold. High volumes afford businesses *economies of scale* and *scope*. Scale economies mean that the more of something you produce, the lower your fixed cost (e.g., salaries, plant, office equipment, etc.) allocated to each unit produced, the lower the cost to produce or market that unit, and the higher your profitability. If you sell a product for $1.00 and your competitor prices a same or similar product at $1.25, it costs you only $0.50 to produce and market in quantities of 10 MM, while it costs him $0.75 to produce and market in quantities of 5 MM. You both make the same profit on each unit, but you made $5 MM gross profit ($0.50 gross profit x 10 MM units) as opposed to his $2.5 MM gross profit ($0.50 x 5 MM units).

4. **COMPETITIVE PRICING STRATEGIES**: These strategies involve setting prices depending upon the activities of others in the market.

A *going rate* pricing strategy relates to the "accepted marketing norm" for a product.

A *guaranteed low price* strategy is one in which a company ensures that its price is lowest, in order to appeal to consumer thrift. This is typically done in retail marketplaces, where the same products are available through many different outlets.

A *defensive parity* pricing strategy is one in which pricing is adjusted with a direct competitor, sometimes even the guaranteed low price in the market. In the latter case, it is used more as a defensive than offensive measure to meet competitive pricing that is lower, so that consumers cannot distinguish and favor competitors based on price alone. An example is the "Nobody Beats the Wiz™" electronics store and the old "Crazy Eddie" stores. The auto industry (i.e., car dealers) also use this strategy, as well as many service providers, such as advertising agencies. In some industries, "standards" are set that determine ultimate pricing (e.g., advertising agency commissions at 17.65 percent).

A *pricing war* is an unfortunate situation in

which competitors all use price as the primary means to attract users. Pricing wars are costly and, as with other kinds of wars, all warriors are hurt.

In industrial and service markets, *competitive bid pricing* often dictates pricing. Competitive bids may be hidden from a supplier's knowledge (*closed bid*), or he may be made aware of competitive quotations (*open bid*). Bid pricing is often a game of chance in this respect, and too often excludes other factors, such as service, talent, and follow-through for the order, which cannot usually be factored into a bid.

5. **PRESTIGE PRICING STRATEGY**: Prestige pricing is a strategy whereby high prices are charged *intentionally* to give the brand a high perceived value, which may or may not be reality based. It is similar to the *skimming* strategy, although skimming is typically short term and prestige pricing is usually long term in scope. Prestige pricing is directly related to the emotional elements of consumer behavior and expectations, and appeals especially to vanity and desire for prestige; the consumer is willing to pay more for a product either to be in vogue or be perceived on a higher social plateau. Other marketing programs must be in place to support this image if the strategy is to work.

PRICING TACTICS

Pricing tactics are simply *setting the prices,* based on the chosen pricing strategies. However, when tactically setting prices and translating those strategies into real numbers, everything that impacts the final price as the product moves from the plant, through the distribution channels, to the ultimate consumer, should be considered. Before we close this section, here are a few key pricing terms and tidbits that will help you in your price setting.

List price is the quoted standard rate of a product to either a business (for industrial goods) or to wholesalers and retailers for resale to consumers at a higher price. *Suggested retail price (SRP)* is a standardized retail price, set by the manufacturer. SRP protects manufacturers by helping to ensure that retailers' pricing methods don't conflict or counter with their own pricing strategies. The SRP is purely directional in nature to the retailer (not mandatory), so some retailers choose to set the price higher in order to increase profits. *Market price* is the final price paid, list price less cash and noncash discounts. *Uniform delivered price* includes transportation costs.

Prices are set for *products,* where the price of a product is constant for the entire product (e.g., most packaged goods); *units,* where price is set for varying measurements of a product quantity with a standard measurement (e.g., ground coffee at $4.99 per pound); and *lines,* where other products in a line affect the cost of individual products (i.e., lines that have "basic," "moderate," and "deluxe" versions or products that need to be differentiated by price to keep them from competing with one another).

Sometimes prices are *differentiated,* meaning that a product costs more to one consumer or business than another, based on geographic location or other legal determinant, because the cost of delivering the product is different from one buyer to another. Another example could be price differentiation by time of year and even in response to how long a buyer takes to pay the invoice. *Net price* refers to a discount based on early payment of invoices. For example, "2% net 10" means that if the buyer pays the full invoice within 10 days, he is entitled to subtract 2% of the total cost of the invoice from his payment.

Discounts are reductions in price offered to the consumer and distribution channels to foster sales. Discounts come in many forms, including payment for shelf space, putting up displays, "price-offs" (temporary price reductions), volume discounts, trade-ins, rebates, advertising allowances. All of these things should be factored into pricing structures when determining tactics. (See chapter 5, Distribution and chapter 8, Promotions for more detailed explanations.)

Retailers often use a deep discounting strategy to offer a *loss leader*—an attractive product at a very low price, often at a loss, in hopes of drawing consumers into stores to buy other products. Car dealers and electronics dealers often offer promotional prices to *trade-up* or get consumers to buy the more expensive product once they have them in the store. *Price lining* is a retail practice of picking one or several price points and grouping all products into these pricing categories (e.g., "all beach toys now $2.99").

Finally, an interesting oddity that you might have noticed more than once is that prices are rarely even or "on the dollar." This is because of a consumer phenomenon called *perceived odd pricing value*. This simply means that consumers look at certain prices or price ranges in emotionally positive or negative ways. For example, consumers perceive a price of $4.99 as significantly lower than $5.00. Consumers are said to perceive anything under $1.00 as much more of an impulse item than anything over $1.00, even by a penny. And, some believe that once you've crossed the $10.00 and $100.00 barriers, you're in new territory and have to reevaluate your marketing plan to adapt to changed consumer perceptions.

PRICING GLOSSARY

Administered Prices: Those set by management and held constant over time.

Base Price: The "sticker price" or "list price," before any discounts are applied or costs added for shipping and handling.

Bottom Line: A buzzword that refers to the profitability portion of a financial statement. All sales contribute to and all expenses take away from the *bottom line*.

Closed Bid: A type in which competitive quotes are not disclosed, thereby limiting ability to price based on the competition.

Competitive Bid Pricing: A type of structure where competitors submit costs of products or services to a buyer and the buyer makes a selection based on those quotations. Can be *open,* where everyone knows what everyone else is quoting, or *closed,* where secrecy is maintained.

Cost Plus Pricing: A common method where price is determined by taking the cost of a product and adding a dollar amount that brings it to the set point of profitability. For example, if you want to make 50 percent on all goods sold, you price a product that costs $1.00 to produce at $2.00.

Dead Net Pricing: Final cost of products after *all* discounts have been applied.

Delivered Pricing: The price of goods to a buyer, which includes freight and other associated costs.

Demand: The consumer need for your product and willingness to purchase it under various conditions.

Demand-Oriented Pricing: Pricing policies that arise from consumer need or *demand* rather than cost. When demand is high but supply is short, prices go up; when demand is low, but supply is high, prices go down.

Derived Demand: Need for a product that is a result of the demand for another product, such as the demand for machinery to produce shampoo because shampoo is demanded by consumers.

Economies of Scale: Savings derived from larger systems, such as production or distribution (e.g., it can cost less per unit to produce 1.5 MM units than 0.2 MM). A certain amount of cost is always present no matter how many units are produced (fixed cost), and a certain amount of cost is variable (incremental cost associated with each unit produced). Larger systems allow the fixed costs to be spread over a greater number of units.

Economies of Scope: Savings derived from sharing knowledge from other areas of your business, such as using optical memory technology developed for the computer division in the VCR division.

Elasticity of Demand: See *price elasticity.*

Free on Board (FOB) Pricing: Sum that is quoted as of a certain inland shipping point, from which the buyer is expected to pay for further shipping.

Full Cost Pricing: Procedure in which all costs (even staff, property, other overhead, and sometimes debt) are considered in setting a price, allowing the firm to recover all of its costs and realize a profit.

Incremental Cost Pricing: Procedure in which only the costs directly attributable to the manufacture and delivery of a product are considered in setting a price.

Inelastic Demand: A situation in which the market (or consumer) is willing to absorb a price increase so that the amount of product sold does not decline when the price is increased. Price increases produce greater profits when demand is inelastic.

Inflation: Increase in price levels that reduces the consumer's purchasing power.

Line Pricing: Procedure in which price is set for individual products within a line, based on relative pricing of the other products in the line. Often the pricing is used to clearly distinguish "close cousins" in products, such as "deluxe" and "super-deluxe" when benefits do not differentiate them sufficiently.

List Price: See *base price.*

Loss Leader: Product offered to consumers at less than cost to attract them to retail stores in hope that they will buy other merchandise at regular prices.

Margin: The profit with respect to sales, expressed as a percentage. If a company manufactures or buys a product for $10 and sells it for $20, that company has established a 50 percent margin.

Markdown: Amount to which the retailer reduces the original selling price (or *suggested retail price*) of a product.

Market Price: The final price paid for a product: the *list price* less cash and noncash discounts.

Market Share: The percentage of sales that a product, line, or company accounts for in a particularly defined market or segment of the market. Is expressed as a percentage and can be measured for different quantities, such as unit volume, dollar volume, etc.

Market Skimming: A *pricing strategy* used to maximize profits where prices are set as high as the market will bear. Often used with new product introductions when no direct competition threatens.

Markup: The amount by which the retailer increases the price of a product he/she sells from his/her own original cost. Markup costing involves figuring the price of a product, based on adding a percentage to the cost of the product. For example, a 50 percent markup on a product that costs $10 to produce would render the selling price of the item at $15.

Monopoly: A marketing situation in which only one company sells a product, having full control over that market.

Nonprice Competition: When a product is priced exactly the same as competitors', so that products will have to compete on a different level.

Odd Pricing: See *perceived odd pricing value*.

Oligopoly: Market structure where relatively few competitors exist and barriers usually inhibit new competitors from entering, such as high start-up costs.

One Price Policy: Selling a product to all like customers for exactly the same price, as opposed to negotiated prices.

Open Bid: A type of *competitive bid* where all quotes are known by or made available to each company involved.

Penetration Pricing: A *strategy* that uses a low introductory price for a new product to speed up the product's acceptance and build volume, before competitors enter the market.

Perceived Odd Pricing Value: Pricing policy based on the psychological phenomenon that consumers look at prices or price ranges in certain emotionally positive or negative ways. For example, consumers perceive a price of $4.99 as significantly lower than $5.00.

Price: The cost of a product to a buyer.

Price Appeal: Practical approach to advertising copy, where the strength of the selling proposition focuses on the price of the product rather than on more emotional components.

Price Channel: The place on a supermarket shelf into which a price slip, often containing the brand name and UPC code, fits.

Price Elasticity: The degree to which supply or demand for a product service will change as a result of the change in price. A price elasticity of 1.0 means that demand will vary exactly and inversely with a change in price. For example, if the price goes up 10 percent, sales go down 10 percent.

Price Lining: A retail practice of picking one or several price points and selling all goods at one of these prices.

Price Point: A standard retail price (e.g., $1.99) used by sellers for two or more items that vary slightly in cost but are perceived as similar in value to consumers.

Price Sensitivity: The tendency for a product's demand to vary based on changes in price. Products that are price sensitive may produce significant increases in sales with small price reductions or may suffer large volume losses from small price increases.

Pricing Differentiation: Offering more than one price for a product in different markets or through different distribution channels. This differentiation must be justified by variations in selling costs, transportation, discounts, and so forth. Differentiation is also used in test markets to test the reaction of consumers to two or more price levels.

Pricing Policy: General guidelines based upon objectives and intended for use on specific pricing decisions.

Pricing Strategy: Element of marketing decision-making that deals with the methods of setting profitable and justifiable exchange values for goods and services.

Primary Demand: *Demand* for a type of product, not any specific brand.

Profit Margin: see *margin*.

Profit Maximization: The point of "optimal" profitability, where the amount of additional money made from further increases in pricing is equivalent either to the loss in revenues from lower sales or the same revenues with higher marketing costs.

Promotional Pricing: Temporary measure in which prices are lowered to generate sales.

Rate of Return: Financial measurements, usually expressed as ratios or percentages, that show the amount of profit that a business produces with respect to a second measurement. For example, Return on Sales (ROS) is a common rate used to show what percentage of sales were profits; Return on Investment (ROI) shows what percentage of profits were derived with respect to investment.

Return on Investment (ROI): See *rate of return*.

Return on Sales (ROS): See *rate of return*.

Selective Demand: *Demand* for a specific product in a specific market.

Skimming Pricing Strategy: See *market skimming*.

Suggested Retail Price (SRP): Also called *list price, sticker price,* or *base price*. A standardized retail selling price, set by the manufacturer. SRP protects manufacturers by helping to ensure that retailers' pricing methods don't conflict with their own pricing strategies.

Supply: The amount of product that is available to the consumer during a given time period.

Trade-Up: A retail tactic to get consumers to buy a more expensive model or version of a product, after they've been shown the less expensive one.

Value: The *utility* of a product, measured against its price.

Variable Pricing: Selling the same products to different buyers and charging different prices, usually through negotiation. This type of pricing is common among street vendors, antique dealers, and similar types of businesses.

Uniform Delivered Price: Price in which transportation costs are included.

Unit Pricing: Price setting measurement in which prices are stated in terms of a measurable unit, such as per pound, per foot, etc.

Utility: The degree to which a product fulfills consumer needs, relative to other products.

PM TOOLS™
PRICING

- Price Elasticity Worksheet
- Competitive Pricing Rack-Up
- Margin and Markup Worksheet
- Price/Performance Matrix

PRICE ELASTICITY WORKSHEET

Product	Price 1	Price 2	Change	Volume 1	Volume 2	Change	Elasticity
___	$___	$___	___%	$___	$___	___%	___
___	$___	$___	___%	$___	$___	___%	___
___	$___	$___	___%	$___	$___	___%	___
___	$___	$___	___%	$___	$___	___%	___
___	$___	$___	___%	$___	$___	___%	___
___	$___	$___	___%	$___	$___	___%	___
___	$___	$___	___%	$___	$___	___%	___

INSTRUCTIONS: Price elasticity is the degree to which supply or demand for a product or service will change as a result of the change in price. List the products you wish to compare. Write in the previous price (Price 1) and the new price after the change (Price 2). Write in the change (Price 2 / Price 1) as +/- a percentage. Write in the sales volume (always $ sales) before (Volume 1) and after (Volume 2) the price change and calculate the change in volume during that period (Volume 2 / Volume 1) as +/- a percentage. Calculate the elasticity by dividing the change in price by the change in volume. If the result is negative: 0 to -1 is good; -1 is neutral; and <-1 is bad. If the result is positive: 0 to 1 is bad; 1 is neutral; and >1 is good.

COMPETITIVE PRICING
RACK-UP

PRODUCT	SHARE	PRICE
_____	_____%	$_____
_____	_____%	$_____
_____	_____%	$_____
_____	_____%	$_____
_____	_____%	$_____
_____	_____%	$_____
_____	_____%	$_____
_____	_____%	$_____
_____	_____%	$_____
_____	_____%	$_____
_____	_____%	$_____
_____	_____%	$_____
_____	_____%	$_____
_____	_____%	$_____
_____	_____%	$_____
_____	_____%	$_____
_____	_____%	$_____
_____	_____%	$_____
_____	_____%	$_____
_____	_____%	$_____
_____	_____%	$_____
_____	_____%	$_____
_____	_____%	$_____
_____	_____%	$_____
_____	_____%	$_____
_____	_____%	$_____
_____	_____%	$_____
_____	_____%	$_____
_____	_____%	$_____

MARGIN AND MARKUP WORKSHEET

COST (A)
$ _____

SELLING PRICE (B)
$ _____

DIFFERENCE (C)
$ _____ (B-A)

MARGIN (The profit with respect to the percentage of price that is profit): _____ (C/B)

MARKUP (The profit with respect to the percentage above cost that price is): _____ (C/A)

PRICE/PERFORMANCE MATRIX

Relative Pricing

Perceived Value	High	Med.	Low
High	**Fair Priced** (prestige priced)	**Underpriced**	**Extremely Underpriced**
Med.	**Overpriced**	**Fair Priced** (neutral)	**Underpriced**
Low	**Extremely Overpriced**	**Overpriced**	**Fair Priced** (Low-end value priced)

KEY:

Brand A _____

Brand B _____

Brand C _____

Brand D _____

Brand E _____

Brand F _____

INSTRUCTIONS: List each brand name in the key. Map the price position of each by writing in the "key letter" (e.g., A, B, C, etc.) of the product in the appropriate place on the matrix.

SEVEN

TOP-LINE

OVERVIEW

It has been estimated that the average American is exposed to between 300 and 1,500 advertisements per day. Some of these messages are more effective than others in reaching the proper audience and communicating the product/service benefit. In the current market environment of budget cutting and cost reducing, it has become increasingly important that the marketer have a thorough understanding of advertising—what it can and cannot do, how and when it should be used, to whom it should be communicated, and how much should be spent doing it.

Advertising is paid communication, mass or targeted, through various media, by business firms, nonprofit organizations, and individuals who hope to inform or persuade members of a particular audience. The objective of advertising is to *sell* a product, idea, or service. Unfortunately, this objective is sometimes masked or forgotten by overabundant creativity that attempts to break through the clutter at the expense of communication of the real product benefit. Creativity is *great,* as long as the benefit message is clear.

Advertising can be classified according to the **medium** chosen to deliver the message. The media include *television* (network, local, or cable), *radio advertising* (network or local), *magazines, newspapers,* and **out-of-home** (billboards, taxi or bus signs, stadium signs, etc.). One of the newest forms is in-store advertising, where LED displays can bring the message to consumers in the aisles or on the shopping carts, or by radio. The chosen media are called "vehicles" because they are the means by which advertising is delivered.

Depending on the scope of the product or service offering, advertising can be done on a national or local basis, to the end consumer or to the trade (retailers, wholesalers, distributors, professionals, or other resellers). It can also be directed at process users, such as manufacturers or farmers. The group that is chosen by the marketer to receive the advertising message is called the **target audience.** A national product may be advertised both nationally and locally, and may target more than one group.

Advertising is done both at a general category level and a particular brand level. For example, the American Dairy Association advertises the benefits of using dairy products, with separate advertising executions for milk, ice cream, cottage cheese, etc. Kraft General Foods Inc., on the other hand, is interested in advertising its particular brand of ice cream, Breyers.

THE ADVERTISING PLAN

Because outside agencies almost always help to develop the advertising plan and always execute it (differing from most of the other functions, which are planned and executed in-house), it is a common practice in marketing to develop advertising plans that can "stand alone." As such, the advertising plan is more extensive than other plans and begins with restating and clarifying the role of advertising, based on the functional direction provided in the situational analysis of the marketing plan.

The advertising plan revolves around identification of and communication of a single or several product benefit(s) to a particular audience. This information plus trends in volume, consumption, the competitive environment, positioning, pertinent related product innovations and opportunities, and the marketer's strengths, weaknesses, opportunities, and threats, are provided by the company to the agency.

Prior to the development of the advertising plan, a rack-up should be prepared of competitors' product advertising. Competitive spending, *dayparts,* types of media used, message, etc., should be included in this analysis. This will help determine optimal advertising and promotion strategies and spending levels. For example, last year you may have spent $1 MM on television, while the average competitor spent $0.5 MM. What was the result of this spending? For example, if competitive spending is expected to go up to an average of $2 MM this year, last year's $1 MM may be inadequate relative to the competition.

Also, a media rack-up should be prepared that compares the effectiveness of various media for your product and identifies new or alternative media available on the market. Finally, the prior year's advertising plan and results, if an existing business, should be reviewed and lessons learned and their implications stated. Articulate all of this at the beginning of the plan. Then these steps are next:

1. Determine the *advertising role* in the overall business strategy, as defined by the marketing plan;
2. Set *advertising objectives* that support marketing objectives;
3. Set *advertising strategies* that indicate how objectives will be fulfilled;
4. Set the *creative strategy* and develop *creative content* and *tactics* that communicate the desired message with the proper emphasis to support advertising strategy;
5. Develop the *media plan,* selecting the appropriate *advertising medium* that is best suited to deliver the creative execution to the desired audience.
6. Evaluate *advertising effectiveness* prior to, during, and after release of advertisements, against the stated advertising objectives.

Of course, as with other functions, set the budget. Rather than trying to meet a set number for a budget, attempt to develop the budget from the bottom up, establish a range of allocation and priorities.

ADVERTISING ROLE

Marketing objectives set goals for the product/business in terms of sales, profit, market share, distribution, household penetration, etc. One marketing strategy may be to utilize advertising to help achieve these objectives if advertising is perceived as a good use of resources in achieving those goals. Thus, the role of advertising as an element of the *marketing mix* will be defined in the marketing strategy section of the marketing plan and depends upon the strength of opportunity it offers in solving the problem or achieving the marketing objectives.

The statement of the advertising role should indicate what the advertising is expected to do to the target audience (i.e., in terms of awareness, behavior, or perceptions), and whether advertising will work alone or in conjunction with other elements in the marketing mix. If it will work with other elements, will it take a primary or secondary role? For example, in a new product introduction, advertising would play a large role in building awareness but might need to work in conjunction with public relations and consumer promotion to build awareness.

Let's say that our marketing objective is to introduce a new apparel line for girls that can be shared with a life-sized doll that our company already sells: "To develop and launch a new line of apparel, targeted to girls six to twelve who are users of our life-size doll line, that delivers key benefits of sharing and interaction with the doll line, contemporary design, and added play value, generates gross sales of at least $10 MM, and delivers net margins of at least 18 percent in the first year of operation." The role of advertising might be stated in this way:

> *The role of advertising is to assist the new introduction in achieving volume and profit objectives, primarily by creating broad-scale awareness of the primary product benefit—fun sharing and interaction; and secondarily by working in conjunction with consumer promotion on the national introduction.*

From this role statement, the marketer can now set more specific measurable objectives.

ADVERTISING OBJECTIVES

The desired end results of the advertising message should be *measurable,* usually in terms of increases in awareness, positive brand perceptions, attitudes, and/or purchase intent.

The advertising objective generally should *not* be measured in terms of sales or volume alone. There are too many intervening variables that may thwart large volume increases. Volume may be *part* of the objectives, but it does not have to be. If advertising has communicated the product benefits *effectively* to the right consumers, they will buy the product, either when they have the need for it or at the next purchase occasion, assuming it is AVAILABLE AT THE RIGHT TIME, IN THE RIGHT PLACE, AND AT THE RIGHT PRICE, and that there is NO CONFLICTING MESSAGE at the point of purchase, through word of mouth or through competitive advertising that will change the prospect's mind. If any of these conditions are not met, the sale may be lost; but advertising has still done its job: it caused the consumer to seek or intend to purchase the product.

Although advertising does not have to be measured against volume, the marketer *should* see an increase in sales during the advertising period. If advertising awareness is strong and the message is getting across positively and volume is not moving, then other elements of the marketing mix must be examined and improved.

Typical advertising objectives have many layers. For a new microwave popcorn product, objectives might be:

> *Generate awareness of Popity Pop in at least 60 percent of the microwave popcorn users. Of those microwave popcorn users who become aware of the product's benefits, establish positive brand perceptions in at least 75 percent of the audience. Of those microwave popcorn users who register a positive brand perception, generate a 50 percent trial purchase intent level.*

These objectives can now be measured after the advertising is running, through marketing research.

ADVERTISING STRATEGIES

The overall advertising strategy is the action plan by which the marketer will achieve his advertising objectives.

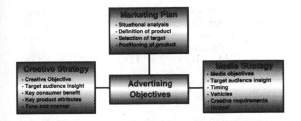

Creative strategy (or copy strategy) and media strategy are subsets of the advertising strategy. Generally, the advertising strategy includes direction on:

- What the message is supposed to communicate about the product.
- To whom the message should speak (target audience).
- Guidelines for effective dissemination of the message (media plan).

CREATIVE STRATEGIES

The creative or *copy* strategy provides direction on the content of the message. The essential input is the positioning statement, which was derived from the situational analysis and the marketing plan. The target audience and the product benefit should have been identified via the positioning statement. The benefit(s) should have been identified as being important to the desired target audience via marketing research. Now, the marketer is ready to elaborate on these points in order to create the most effective message.

The creative strategy will define the target audience in detail and will describe the product benefit that must be communicated, and the product attributes that will support and deliver this benefit to consumers. A good creative strategy communicates how the marketer would like his audience to *feel* about the product and its benefits.

The creative strategy should be written by the marketer himself, or in conjunction with the advertising agency. It should include the following elements:

1. **OBJECTIVE**: This is the *creative* objective, as opposed to the advertising objectives. If you will recall, the advertising objectives indicated measurable

goals in terms of awareness, perceptions, and purchase intent. The creative objective states what you would like to convince consumers to feel or do as a result of the advertising execution.

2. **INFORMATION ON THE TARGET CONSUMER**: This section should provide *insight* into the consumer that you want to reach. It is not good enough to say "current users" or "women aged twenty-five to fifty-four." Talk about your consumer—explain who he/she is, and what he/she wants or needs. Sometimes it helps to picture one person who epitomizes your target and describe him or her—not only in terms of geographics, demographics, and psychographics, but also in terms of how he or she thinks or feels about a situation that is relevant to your product.

3. **KEY CONSUMER BENEFIT**: "Cleans your windows" or "tastes great" are not enough here. The benefit should be worded in a unique way so that it addresses the consumer need or problem to be solved. This benefit could be a tangible result of use of the product, or it could be image related (a psychological benefit that the consumer perceives when he/she uses the product). Make this section interesting and *do* elaborate, but keep it focused on the *key* benefit. Don't confuse the issue by bringing in other minor benefits. Think about what the *one thing* is that you want the consumer to remember or take away from your advertisement, because if you're lucky, he or she will recall one thing.

4. **REASON TO BELIEVE**: Which one or two product attributes will convince the consumer to believe that the product will deliver the benefit? In other words, *why* will Frusen Glädjé deliver the fresh, creamy, *best* taste to ice cream lovers? Because it uses only the finest, freshest ingredients in its product formulation OR because it has "X" years of experience, OR a combination of the two. It is *essential* that you provide the consumer with a reason to believe.

5. **TONE AND MANNER**: This will affect the setting, look, and feel of the advertising executions. It will describe the context in which you would like your message to be delivered. It will help determine the type of actors chosen and the tone of the copy.

Describe the tone and manner in a few sentences or even paragraphs. The more you can describe, the better. Just be sure that the tone and manner described is relevant to the consumer you described above. The tone and manner of the Mazda Miata ads, for example, played an important role in the advertising's success. They took us back to the fifties when life was good, simple, and values were important.

There are a number of key pitfalls to avoid in writing creative strategy:

1. Make sure your *benefit is closely linked to your product* in the communication. If it isn't, another brand may capitalize on your great benefit message.
2. Make sure the product benefit is *valuable to your consumer,* and not just to you! If you market pasta, you may think that purple pasta is a great idea because you are around plain old pasta every day, but the consumer may not agree. Do your research homework.
3. Don't try to say too much. If you are lucky enough to get your target's attention, *keep your message short, uncluttered, and focused.* If you try to convince consumers that your ice cream tastes best, costs less, stays fresh longer, and will help you lose weight, and you do it all in a fifteen-second commercial, chances are they won't remember *any* of it.
4. Don't try to be concise in your written creative strategy. As long as it's focused, explain and describe to your heart's content. *The more you know* and understand about your product and your target audience, *the more you should write.* If you don't know or if you don't write it, your agency won't know either, and will not produce an ad that thrills you.
5. Don't attempt to write a creative strategy until you've u*sed your product yourself* repeatedly and have solicited others to use it and to give you feedback. You may get some great insights from this exercise, and you can ensure that your product does indeed deliver the promised benefit. Ultimately, if the product doesn't deliver, consumers will stop buying it.

In summary, a creative strategy that works will: (1) find and define the consumer segment that seeks your product benefit; and (2) communicate that benefit clearly and link it closely with your product in the consumers' minds.

Just a word about the competitive arena. It's great if you *do* find a unique benefit for your product and can be the first in the marketplace to capture the share that "uniqueness" will bring, and you can preempt competitive entries. After all, consumers who have tried your product and are satisfied are not likely to switch to a new product that offers the same benefit; your competitor will have to spend a lot more than you did to make that happen. But if your product competes in a category where it is difficult or impossible to come up with a unique benefit and cannot claim to deliver the same benefit better than the next guy, advertising can still be effective by communicating *in a more compelling way* than your competitors. If the message is more creative, the benefit may be perceived by the consumer to be greater.

CREATIVE TACTICS

It is the charge of the advertising agency to find a way to translate your well thought out creative strategy into great executions or tactics. The agency must come up with what is often referred to in marketing as "the big idea" and turn it into a themed advertising campaign, translatable through the various media you've selected.

The creative team at the agency will now work on ways to communicate your benefit clearly and with impact through words and pictures. They must make the message memorable, believable, and appealing to your target audience. They must ensure an easy linkage between the product and the benefit. Examples of well-linked product/benefit themes are:

Product	Theme	Benefit
CHARMIN Bathroom Tissue	"Please don't squeeze the Charmin."	squeezably soft
BURGER KING	"Have it your way at Burger King now."	burgers any way you want
CHEER Laundry Detergent	"All-temper-CHEER."	can be used to get all fabric types clean

The combination of a great creative strategy and great creative minds at work at the agency will make for great advertising executions.

Although there are many dynamics at work in the creation of great advertising, there are four basic principles that apply:

1. **TALK TO YOUR TARGET AUDIENCE** in language that they can understand and will appeal to them. Don't talk down to them or above their heads. Recognize that the strength of the message should be tailored to the type of attitude or behavior that you are trying to change or induce. Some messages will require more detailed explanations than others, depending on the result that is sought. Get into the mind of your consumer.

2. **STICK TO THE MAIN MESSAGE** or selling proposition. Don't clutter the ad with support that does not have to be there. Weigh the level of support necessary against the impact of a simple, strong message. You may have to make trade-offs between impact and information.

3. **DON'T LOSE THE SELLING MESSAGE** in state-of-the-art, flowery, cutesy, or symbolic creativity. Your goal is to ensure that your target audience recalls your message and links it to your product. Just ask yourself if the ad makes the sale before you present it to anyone—and if it doesn't, send it back until it does.

4. **HAVE FUN WITH IT**. Let your creative juices flow until something hits you. And the right execution *will* hit you—you'll know it when you get it.

THE MEDIA PLAN

It is the charge of the media planner to determine the best media mix to deliver the marketer's objectives while staying within budget. The media planner is well versed on:

- All of the available media forms.
- Overall cost and cost per thousand reached by each form.
- Segment of audience reached by each form.
- Versatility of each form in terms of geographic and timing considerations.

Some terms used in our detailed explanation of the media planning process should be understood first.

1. **RATINGS**: This is the percentage of households tuned in to a particular television or radio program. If 20 homes out of 100 were tuned to "The Cosby Show" on a particular night, that show had a 20 rating. Ratings are categorized by viewing times, such as Saturday morning, 9:00 A.M. to 10:00 A.M., etc. A rating is calculated by dividing the total number of households viewing that program by the total population of households, either nationally or in a particular area. The rating system is one means by which programmers determine their advertising rates. The media planner uses ratings to calculate the number of people that will be reached by advertising on that program. Both the programmer and the media planner purchase this rating information.

2. **HUT** (Homes Using TV): This is the percentage of households actually viewing *any* television program at a particular time. These television usage levels vary by time of day, geographic area, and by season. *HUT* percentages are used when calculating share.

3. **SHARE**: This is the percentage of HUT tuned in to a particular program. For example, if 50 out of 100 homes are watching TV, and 20 are tuned in to "The Cosby Show," that show has a share of 20 over 50, or a 40 share. While share numbers show a programmer how his offering is doing compared to other offerings in that time slot, they do not give complete information to the advertiser on how many homes are being reached.

4. **GROSS RATING POINTS**: Commonly referred to as *GRPs,* these are the total rating points delivered over the whole or a certain part of the media plan. For example, if a commercial is shown on a show that has a 20 rating, and on another that has a 5, and on another that has a 10, the total GRPs would be 35. If this same schedule ran for four weeks and the ratings stayed the same, the total GRPs from that television flight would be 35 times 4, or 140. GRPs do not account for duplication, so some of the households included in the 140 may have seen the ad more than once. Remember, ratings and GRPs are expressed as a percentage, so delivery of 140 GRP's means that the message has been conveyed to the equivalent of 140 percent of all households.

5. **IMPRESSIONS**: Also known as *gross audience*, impressions are expressed in terms of total number of households viewing programs that contain an ad. In other words, if 10 MM homes watch show A in which you run your ad, and 7 MM watch show B, in which you also run your ad, and your ads run on these shows four times over a four week period, the total number of impressions is 17 MM times 4, or 68 MM impressions. Impressions can also be calculated if you know the total GRPs, by multiplying the GRP percentage by the number of homes with TV sets.

6. **REACH**: This is the percentage of unduplicated households that are exposed to the ad in a given time period. Viewers are counted only once, regardless of the number of times that they see the ad. Media planners will often recommend a mix of advertising vehicles or media in order to reach more unduplicated households.

7. **FREQUENCY**: This is expressed as the average number of times a household is exposed to the same advertising message within a given time period. It is calculated by dividing the total possible audience (*GRPs*) by the number of households exposed at least once to the ad (reach). Thus, if an ad produces 140 GRPs and has a reach of 70, then the average frequency of the exposures is 2.

Researchers have recommended that the minimum effective frequency within a purchase cycle is two, with three exposures being optimal. This principle generally applies to all media forms.[1] Therefore, the media planner should ensure that a large percentage of the target audience is reached at least twice with the ad, rather than averaging the number of consumers exposed to one ad and three ads and arriving at an average frequency of two. Half of that target would not be reached effectively with only one exposure.

Generally, the media planner will have to make trade-offs between high reach and high frequency. The advertising objectives are what will help to make those decisions.

---

[1] Jim Surmanek, *Media Planning*, NTC Publishing Group: Lincolnwood, IL, 1989, pp. 43–44.

With a regional product, and sometimes with a national product that does not have the budget to run advertising everywhere, the media planner will have to choose vehicles that lend themselves to local or regional buys. These buys generally have a higher *CPM* (cost per thousand impressions) than national buys. Choosing the markets that receive the advertising for a national brand with a smaller budget will depend on the objectives. For example, if a brand wants to increase frequency of purchase among current users, it would advertise in the highest *BDI* areas. If a brand wants to increase penetration among competitive category users, it would advertise in high-opportunity markets, or high-*CDI* and low-BDI markets. If the low BDI in a particular market is the result of distribution voids, advertising could help the sales force to fill those voids.

The media plan itself is a written guideline for making the correct media decisions. The structure of the media plan is as follows:

1. **INPUTS:**
   - Advertising Objectives
   - Creative Strategy
   - Consumer Target
   - Product Purchase Cycle
   - Competitive Information
   - Market/Area Priorities
   - Sales Information/Development Indices
   - Budget Guideline
   - Timing of Other Marketing Mix Elements (i.e., Promotion)
   - Any Special Considerations

All of the above inputs will be used by the planner in formulating media objectives and strategies.

2. **OBJECTIVES**: The media objectives are measurable, actionable, desired end results of the implementation of the media plan. They are based upon advertising objectives and are usually expressed in terms of target audience, timing, reach, and frequency. For example, the media objective for a new product introduction might read:

   Achieve high levels of awareness by reaching at least 70 percent of the target audience an average of three times within the first eight weeks of advertising.

3. **STRATEGIES**: The media strategies will outline how the objective will be achieved. Strategies will outline: (1) which media will be used; (2) calendar year timing; (3) quantities of each type of media.

The media selected will be based upon the planner's knowledge of each type and the effectiveness of each in reaching the target audience specified in the stated media objective. The planner will look at demographics and available product usage information about the target audience and try to parallel these as closely as possible with the different media types. Generally, utilization of a media mix rather than one vehicle will provide greater reach. Cost and geographical considerations also come into play in this decision. Major media includes *broadcast* (e.g., television, cable, radio), *print* (e.g., newspaper and magazine), *direct response* (e.g., direct mail), *outdoor* (e.g., billboards), and *point-of-purchase* (e.g., store banners).

Another dynamic involved in media strategy is timing, or *continuity,* of the advertising. A media schedule may be *continuous, flighted,* or *pulsed.* In general, this decision is made based upon the advertising objective, the product's *purchase cycle* and *seasonality,* advertising budget considerations, and the competitive arena.

Continuous advertising may be used in a highly competitive, high visibility product category, such as laundry detergent or soda. These products must consistently fight for their *share of voice* relative to the competition. And since the frequency of purchase is relatively high, continuous advertising keeps awareness and preference levels up.

Flighted advertising is more commonly used for seasonal brands, or brands that don't compete heavily through advertising. A *flight* is a period of time, usually indicated by weeks, that the advertising for a given product will be running. This period is followed by a period of total inactivity, and then there may be another flight. A media planner would not typically schedule a flight during a period of expected slow activity in the purchase cycle, unless the objective is to provide an alternate benefit that might cause consumers to make an incremental purchase at that time.

Another argument for flighting is that awareness levels of the advertising message typically remain up for some period of time after the advertising has stopped. As this awareness level begins to decline, another flight can begin. Marketing research can help determine the "awareness curve" and make recommendations on how to time the flighting for a given product's awareness objectives.

Flighting might also allow the marketer to reach the target audience more effectively (*effective reach*). Reach and frequency within a shorter time period may be more valuable than using consistently lower levels continuously.

Pulsing is continuous advertising, but the difference is that heavy media schedules are interspersed with light ones throughout the year. A product may target a broad consumer base during heavy up periods, and a more narrowly defined audience during lighter periods.

After media objectives and strategies have been outlined, the media planner will choose the scheduling tactics. Tactics will include (but are not limited to) selected areas, length of flight, days to be scheduled, number of announcements daily, selected programming, selected publications or outdoor vehicles, and reach/frequency/GRP calculations by medium. Finally, a budget summary will conclude the plan.

ADVERTISING EFFECTIVENESS AND TESTING

Because such a hefty portion of the advertising budget is spent on media, it is a good idea to *pretest* advertisements before they are placed and run in the media. In pretesting, consumers are chosen to receive the advertisement in a controlled setting. For example, a magazine ad may be tested by stripping the ad into a particular issue of a magazine and sending the "doctored" copy to selected consumers and soliciting their reactions in terms of awareness, message retention, and likeability. For broadcast commercials, selected consumers sit in a room and view commercials, including the one that is being tested, and they are asked to press buttons indicating positive and negative reactions.

Posttesting is done after the ad has run for an acceptable period of time in any given media. The purpose of posttesting is to find out if objectives have been met, and if not, to find out what measures should be taken to correct the situation. Again, let us reiterate that advertising's effectiveness cannot be measured by increased sales alone. Other factors in the mix could be responsible if the increase did not happen. Also, good advertising could have helped to maintain sales that would have otherwise been lost due to other factors or to lessen the impact of a volume loss that would have occurred anyway. Therefore, it is critical that advertising be judged according to the objectives that were set for it to accomplish.

Whether pre- or posttesting, measuring advertising recall can be u*naided,* where consumers are asked to remember all commercials viewed within a given time period; *aided,* where consumers are prompted or clued as to the name of the product, parts of the commercial, etc., and asked to remember the advertisement based on that "help"; and *recognition,* in which consumers are shown advertisements and asked to remember having seen it before. All of this is done to measure awareness and the effectiveness of a message being delivered clearly to its target audience.

In some advertising research *eye cameras* are used to test copy, slogans, jingles, and other creative elements. Eye cameras (there are different types) monitor the movement of the eyes and pupils, which tells researchers how interested a consumer is in what is being exposed to him/her.

Advertisers also need to learn which media work best for their products. Media can be evaluated prior to media placement by several means. First, the marketer should look at advertising for specific products or in the category itself—how they have performed through various media in the past. For a particular category, is television more efficient, or direct mail, or outdoor? Syndicated data is also used to determine where and when a product should be advertised in each medium. For example, if the demographics of a product are boys six to twelve, "David Letterman" would not be a good slot for the advertisement. Syndicated data helps the marketer understand the differences in efficiency between various media.

THE ADVERTISING BUDGET

The advertising budget for a particular product in any given year should be based upon five main concerns:

1. What *volume* must be achieved (level of sales).
2. How much *profit* the product is projected to make (net income).
3. How much advertising the *competition* is doing (or how much you have to fight for your share of attention).
4. What needs to be done in the *marketplace* (i.e., introduce a new product, change a product's positioning, maintain awareness levels).
5. How the *consumer* has responded historically to different types or different levels of advertising done for your product and other similar products (if available).

The planning process in any corporation is likely to be a *negotiation* between those representing corporate or divisional needs, and those who are responsible for marketing a particular product. What the marketing or product manager sees as the realities of the business may not jibe with corporate volume and income goals. On the other hand, it is upper management's responsibility to ensure that product managers are not being too conservative in their projections. Especially in larger corporations, volume and profit goals may go through several rounds of negotiations before final agreement is reached pertaining to one particular business.

The overall advertising budget is normally set as part of the marketing plan and allocated in the advertising plan. The marketer knows the volume and income targets and must allocate spending to each of the marketing functions necessary to ensure that those targets are met. The allocation that advertising receives will depend on its role in the mix, and on the answers to the above five concerns.

ADVERTISING GLOSSARY

Acetate: Clear or translucent and flexible thin plastic sheet or strip that is used for production of *overlays, camera-ready* proofs, and other types of graphics.

A. C. Nielsen Company: Major research and marketing service firm that sells: (1) marketing research data; (2) media research syndication service (Neilsen Ratings); and (3) coupon-redemption services to manufacturers, retailers, and advertising or media agencies.

Advertising: Paid communication through various media, mass or targeted, by business firms, non-profit organizations, and individuals who hope to inform or persuade members of a particular audience. The objective of advertising is to *sell* a product, idea, or service. Advertising is one of the marketing tools that make up the marketing mix.

Advertising Agency: Service organization that contracts with product or service marketers to plan, create, produce, and place their advertising. Agencies vary in the services they provide, from a shop that specializes only in creative (sometimes called a creative boutique) to one that offers a full range (including production, media, and market research) to their clients.

Advertorial: An advertisement that is combined with editorial copy. Usually paid for by the marketer, an advertorial links the product/service to a particular cause, issue, or any items or trends that are of interest to the target audience in order to capture its attention and regard. An advertorial must, by law, be labeled as an advertisement. The main media vehicles for advertorials are newspapers or magazines.

Advocacy Advertising: Advertising that is usually paid for by corporations, consumer groups, or individuals and is designed to influence the target audience's perceptions or attitudes about a controversial issue. For example, The American Cancer Society may pay for antismoking advertising, while a tobacco company may advocate smokers' rights.

Affiliate: An independently owned broadcasting station that contracts with a network to carry its commercials in order to receive network programming. With a string of affiliates (usually one in each viewing area), the network can offer a greater consumer base to the advertiser, and can therefore charge higher rates. The affiliate can also run local commercials during certain allotted times during network programming. A network television station can own and operate only five stations throughout the country, and these five are usually in the largest metropolitan areas. It is to a network's advantage to try to contract with the strongest affiliate in each viewing area. It is to the affiliate's advantage to contract with what it perceives to be the strongest network. Aside from the strength of its actual programming, a network with the strongest affiliate in a given market (sometimes the weaker affiliates have poor reception or poor lead-in programming) will have the advantage.

Agency Commission: Fee that an advertising agency charges a client for sourcing, selecting, and managing work done by other outside companies or vendors (e.g., printing, commercial production, photographers, color separators, etc.). The amount charged the client is usually 17.65 percent of the gross commissionable cost. Services performed inside the agency by in-house or freelance personnel are generally not commissionable.

Also, commission paid to advertising agencies by the media (broadcast or print) for handling the sales and billing of the time or space to their clients. The media generally give the agency a 15 percent discount (slightly higher for outdoor advertising) from the gross advertising billed to the client.

Aided Recall: Research method for testing audience *recall* of advertisements, in which the respondents are prompted by being shown the advertisement or other aids and then asked to remember if they had seen or heard them before. This is one technique that market researchers use to test the effectiveness of advertising.

Air Date: Date on which the program, and the commercial in it, will be broadcast.

Animatic: A series of photographed sketches compiled onto a film strip and synchronized with audiotape. This "unfinished" television commercial will allow the marketer to visualize the finished commercial, before expensive production work is done.

Animation: A sequential series of drawings or illustrations set to film.

Announcement: An advertising message in television or *radio*. Also called a commercial.

Answer Print: First edited print of a filmed commercial, before any color correction or synchronization is done. This is generally presented for client approval.

Arbitron Ratings Company: A major broadcast research service that provides *radio* and television viewing audience measurement data in a variety of formats to broadcasters, marketers, and advertising agencies.

Area of Dominant Influence (ADI): Geographic area made up of all counties influenced by originating stations in a particular television market.

Marketers and advertisers use ADI information to plan the reach of their advertisements.

Art: In advertising, art or artwork can be photography or illustrations that will be reproduced in some form of printed matter or film. While a photograph is generally turned over to the photoengraver as a chrome, an illustration may be either photographed as a chrome or handed over as is as "flat art." Basically, artwork is any printed matter that is not typeset. Typeset matter is called "copy." Normally, the advertising agency will hire commercial artists or photographers to create artwork for their ads.

Art and Mechanical (A&M): A mechanical is essentially a "blueprint" of the ad, laid out with all the art and type elements in exact position and size (or, if necessary, as a percentage of actual size). It is sent with the artwork to the photoengraver to create a "proof" for the printer to follow. Therefore, the term "art and mechanical" is used to describe the matter that is turned over to the engraver for processing.

Audience: Total number of persons viewing or listening to a program or advertising message.

Audience Composition: The makeup of an audience for a particular program, classified by *geographic, demographic,* and/or *psychographic* characteristics. Audience composition helps the media planner decide if the advertising message should be aired on a particular program to reach the desired target.

Audience Duplication: The percentage of the audience for a given advertising message that received that message previously through different media. *Rating* and measurement services estimate the amount of audience duplication.

Audiometer: Electronic device used by *A. C. Nielsen Company* to record audience tuning of television sets. Placed on the television receiver in people's homes, the device records the time the set is turned on, the channel to which it is tuned, and the length of time it is tuned to each channel.

Author's Alteration (AA): Changes made to a final *mechanical* or color proof other than to correct it so that it matches the original artwork. AAs result from the client or agency's desire to change wording or to retouch artwork after some reproductive work has been done, or even after it has been turned over to the printer. Photoengravers and printers charge a premium for the author's alterations.

Availability: The positions in a program or between programs on a given network or station that are available for commercial purchase by an advertiser. Commonly known as "avails."

Barter: The exchange of commercial time from broadcast stations for merchandise or services.

Base Rate: The dollar amount charged for a single advertisement by any advertising medium before any discounts are offered; also called *open rate*.

Billboard: An *outdoor advertising* structure that is normally found in areas of high vehicular or pedestrian traffic. The advertising message is printed on large sheets of poster paper, which are arranged and mounted onto the structure. Billboard size is referred to by the number of poster sheets that it takes to construct it.

Billings: The total of all invoices that an agency has charged to all of its clients. Agency billings include all internal fees, *agency commissions,* and out-of-pocket outside vendor charges. The success of an agency is often measured by billings increases or decreases from year to year.

Bleed: An illustration or copy that extends past the trim mark to the edge of the page so that there is no white border. An advertisement that runs to the edge of the page is called a bleed ad.

Body Text: Copy that is not the headline. Body text normally explains or supports the basic premise or message in the ad.

Brand Awareness: A knowledge that the product or service exists. Brand awareness is often a primary objective of advertising, because it must exist before consumers' perceptions or images of a product can be formed.

Brand Development Index (BDI): Percentage of brand's sales in an area in relation to the population in that area as compared to the sales throughout the entire United States in relation to the total United States population. The BDI shows where the brand's strengths and weaknesses are in terms of product usage. There may be several reasons for a low BDI in a particular market area: there could be distribution holes, a strong regional competitor, or that geographical area may not be likely to use any brand in that category. BDIs are compared against *Category Development Indices* (CDIs) to determine opportunity markets. For example, a brand with a low BDI in an area with a high CDI would theoretically have a good growth opportunity.

Broadcast Media: Media that reach the consumer through the use of electronic transmissions, such as *radio* and television. These media are used frequently by advertisers who want to reach vast numbers of consumers to create and maintain product awareness.

Bullpen: An advertising agency's in-house art studio. The artists who work here produce layouts, comprehensives, and mechanicals. More recently, agency bullpens are equipped with computers that can produce advanced graphic designs and can even set type. Mechanicals of this type can be delivered to a color separator on computer disk.

Cable Television (CATV): Community antenna television system through which signals are disseminated to subscribers' homes by cable and paid for by subscription. Signals transmitted by cable provide clearer reception and offer many more stations and programs than regular television can.

Camera-Ready: Term describing a *layout*, including *artwork* and *copy*, that is ready to be photographed or otherwise reproduced.

Campaign: Series of advertising messages or promotional pieces that are related by a central idea or theme that is or can be translatable to various media forms.

Category Development Indices (CDI): Percentage of total category sales in an area in relation to the population in that area as compared to the sales throughout the entire United States in relation to the total United States population. The brand will look by area at the strength of the category in which it competes to determine where opportunities lie.

Circular: A single sheet of paper that contains one or more advertisements, usually distributed locally by hand. Circulars can also be used as package inserts and in direct mail envelopes. They are often used by local retailers in a given community to announce a sale or to create awareness of a new business.

Circulation: The number of copies of a publication that is distributed via subscription and via newsstands. The circulation is one method of setting advertising rates. In broadcast, circulation denotes the number of homes owning a set within the station's coverage area.

Classified Advertising: Advertising appearing in newspapers or magazines that is arranged according to specific categories or classifications. Examples are automobiles for sale, real estate, and the personal ads.

Closing Date: The final date or "deadline" that is set by a publisher or broadcaster for a receipt of reproducible advertising material for a given issue or program. The advertising agency generally creates a timetable for production by working backward from the closing date.

Color Separation: Process of separating full color chromes or flat *art* into red, yellow, blue, and black by a photographic method, for the purpose of reproducing the original. Most artwork is made up of a combination of these four colors. The separations are made onto four distinct pieces of film, which are turned over to the printer, along with a color proof. The printer then knows exactly what color combinations must be attained to duplicate the artwork.

Comprehensive (Comp): Tight *layout* of an advertisement, with all the type and *artwork* elements in place, created by the agency to give the client an idea of how the final ad will look.

Consumer Franchise: The current loyal users of a particular brand.

Controlled Circulation: Selective distribution of publications, usually free, to individuals or businesses.

Cooperative Advertising: A single *campaign* that is sponsored or paid for by two or more manufacturers, retailers, or a combination of both.

Copy: All written material in an advertisement including *headlines, subheadings,* and the body *copy.* Advertising agencies usually employ copywriters, who work in conjunction with art directors in creating advertisements.

Copyright: Exclusive rights to their original work (including advertisements) granted by United States law to authors, artists, and musicians. A copyright protects the original work from being copied, reprinted, sold, or used by someone else without express consent.

Copy Testing: Measuring the effectiveness of the message in advertisements and commercials; often used when introducing a new product or repositioning a product, in order to assess one kind of appeal over another, one product benefit over another, or perhaps one price over another.

Cost per Thousand (CPM): The cost of reaching one thousand individuals (or homes) by a given medium. CPM is the generally accepted measurement that media buyers use to compare the cost effectiveness of various media choices. The CPM is determined by multiplying the total cost of the ad by 1,000, and then dividing that by the total audience reached.

Coverage: The percentage of homes or individuals that can potentially be exposed to a medium (or the percentage of homes within the reach of that medium).

Creative Boutique: Advertising agency that offers only creative services.

Dayparts: Division of the day into time segments to reflect changes in *broadcast* programming patterns and audience composition. Commercial time may be purchased by the daypart (rather than by the program), and its cost is based upon the average size of the audience for a specific daypart. Morning drive time is an example of a *radio* daypart where there is a large audience of career-minded individuals, driving to work. Dayparts typically follow a standard pattern, although they are set individually by stations. Typical television dayparts may be as follows:

7:00 A.M.–9:00 A.M.	M–F	Morning
9:00 A.M.–4:30 P.M.	M–F	Daytime
4:30 P.M.–7:30 P.M.	M–F	Early Fringe

7:30 P.M.– 8:00 P.M.	Sun–Sat	Access
8:00 P.M.– 11:00 P.M.	M–Sat	Prime Time
7:00 P.M.– 11:00 P.M.	Sun.	Prime Time
11:00 P.M.– 11:30 P.M.	M–F	Late news
11:30 P.M.– 1:00 A.M.	M–F	Late fringe
1:00 A.M.–	Sun-Sat	Late night

Direct Response Advertising: Advertising to which the consumer must respond by mail or phone to receive the product or service offered. This may be considered to be a form of sales.

Drive Time: The morning or afternoon hours *daypart* of the *radio* broadcasting during which people are generally driving to or from work. Morning drive time is 6 A.M. to 10 A.M.; afternoon drive time is 3 P.M. to 7 P.M.

Effective Reach: The number of individuals (or homes) reached by a media schedule at a given level of frequency.

Efficiency: The relationship of media cost to audience delivery.

Engrave: Cut, etch, or incise *artwork* and type on a metal surface for reproduction by a printing process.

Exposure: A person's receipt of an advertising message, through any medium. The number of exposures achieved by a media schedule is an important quantitative measure of the effectiveness of an advertisement. Qualitatively, this should be correlated with the number of exposures received by the *target* audience. For example, a tennis racket advertisement that is seen by 5,000 tennis players may be more effective than one that is seen by 100,000 members of the general public (without regard to whether or not they play tennis).

Eye Camera: Used to test *copy,* slogans, jingles, and other creative efforts. Eye cameras (there are different types) monitor the movement of the eyes and pupils, which tells researchers how interested a consumer is with what he/she is being exposed to. Types of eye cameras include one that photographs reflected light from the eye and another that videotapes the responses of the eye, recording dilations of the pupils in response to interesting stimuli.

Film: Strip of plastic or celluloid with a silver emulsion light-sensitive coating, available in a wide variety of forms and used for the production of photographs, motion pictures, or television video.

Fixed Position: In *broadcast,* a commercial unit purchased with nonpreemption guarantees. In *print,* a position guaranteed to the advertiser in specified issues of the periodical.

Flighting: Concentrated periods of heavy advertising, followed by periods of complete inactivity. In flighting, advertising typically is on view for a specified number of weeks, goes off for a specified number of weeks, and then resumes, and so on. Each activity period is known as a flight. Awareness is typically retained during some period of advertising inactivity and begins to diminish at a given point. Marketing research helps to determine the most effective flighting schedule for a given product and advertising campaign.

Frequency: This is expressed as the average number of times a household is exposed to the same advertising message within a given time period. It is calculated by dividing the total possible audience (*GRPs*) by the number of households exposed at least once to the ad (*reach*). Thus, if an ad produces 140 GRPs and has a reach of 70, then the average frequency of the exposures is 2.

Fringe Time: The *daypart* hours that directly precede and follow prime time, usually 4:30 P.M. to 7:30 P.M. and 11 P.M. to 1 A.M. EST.

Gatefold: A printed page that folds out, increasing the dimensions of the ad.

Geographics: The characteristics of a population or homogeneous groups or segments, based on physical location (Northeast, West Coast, etc.).

Gross Audience: Total number of individuals (or households) in a print or broadcast media audience, without regard to the duplication.

Gross Rating Points (GRPs): Commonly referred to as GRPs, these are the total rating points delivered over the whole or a certain part of the media plan. For example, if a commercial is shown on a show that has a 20 *rating,* and on another that has a 5, and on another that has a 10, the total GRPs would be 35. If this same schedule ran for four weeks and the ratings stayed the same, the total GRPs from that television flight would be 35 times 4 or 140. GRPs do not account for duplication, so some of the households included in the 140 may have seen the ad more than once. Remember, ratings and GRPs are expressed as a percentage, so delivery of 140 GRPs means that you have delivered your message to the equivalent of 140 percent of all households. Media planners use gross rating points as a method for designing a media schedule in attempting to deliver a maximum number of GRPs at a minimum cost.

Headline: The boldest or most prominent word or group of words in a *print* advertisement. The headline must attract attention and compel the reader to go on to view or read the other elements in the ad. Some popular techniques used to arouse interest in headline copy are: posing a question, promising a product benefit, or the use of key attention-getting words such as "new," "incredible," "introducing," and "free." Research has proven that the headline is a major factor in print advertising effectiveness.

Heavy-up: Heavy concentration of advertising for a short period of time and/or in selected market areas. A heavy-up strategy can be used to defend a product against erosion in brand share, to capitalize on a seasonal trend or pattern, to close distribution voids, or to defend against competitive incursions.

Homes Using Television (HUT): The percentage of homes that have their television sets turned on as compared to the total number of television households in that area.

Impressions: The sum of all exposures to an advertising message.

In-House Agency: A department within the marketer's own company that creates advertising for it.

Independent Station: A *broadcast* station not affiliated with any network.

Insert: Separately printed page or pages to be added to or bound into a publication.

Insertion Order: An order by an advertising agency that specifies to a publisher the ad size, position, *circulation,* agreed-upon price, and date that the ad is scheduled to appear.

Institutional Advertising: Image-building advertising done by a corporation to enhance its company image rather than any of its specific products or businesses.

Key Line: Same as *mechanical* (see *art* and *mechanical*).

Layout: An artist's rendering of the proposed advertisement, submitted by the agency to the client for review and comment. There are three types of layouts, depending upon the extent to which they accurately and completely represent the finished product: a rough layout, a revised layout, and a final or comprehensive layout.

Lead Time: The amount of time necessary to deliver the job by the deadline.

Listener Diary: A continuing written record kept by members of a viewing or listening audience. This data is used by research companies to determine *ratings*.

Local Media: Metropolitan or community *newspapers, magazines,* or *broadcast* or cable stations that concentrate primarily on serving the needs of the locality in which they operate.

Magazine: Periodical publication that contains editorials and advertisements. Although they are usually sold via subscription or newsstands, the bulk of the revenue comes from the sale of advertising space. They are attractive to media planners because they usually target specific consumer groups. Reproduction quality of magazine ads is usually excellent.

Makegood: A gratis repeat of an advertisement in *print* or in *broadcasting,* to compensate for an error on the part of the seller of the space or time. The error may be due to a cancellation of the spot for some reason, or a poor reproduction of the ad.

Makeready: Performing all the functions involved in getting a printing press ready to print a run, such as filling the inks, preparing the paper feeder, setting the side guides, and so on.

Market Segmentation: Division of the total market or *audience* into subsections in order to target certain segments based upon *geographic, demographic,* and/or *psychographic* criteria. This process allows for more effective use of advertising dollars.

Mass Media: Media that effectively reaches broad audiences, without regard to market segmentation. *Television* and *radio* networks and broad-reach magazines and newspapers are considered to be mass media.

Mechanical: See *art and mechanical*.

Media Buy: Purchase of time or space in an advertising medium, such as *radio, television,* or *print* space. The media-buy decision is based upon the amount of money available, the number of exposures desired, the target market the advertiser wants to reach, the frequency of the exposure desired, the number of people each medium will reach, and the impact each medium will have on the message.

Media Plan: A plan that includes objectives, strategies, timing, and budget for advertising media for a specific product or products, and then outlines the specific media, *GRPs, reach,* and *frequency* offered by each, along with cost.

Media Schedule: Schedule of media selections, dates, and times for the advertisements in the *media plan*.

Media Weight: The total volume of *audience* to be reached by an advertising *campaign* in terms of the number of commercials and *print* advertisements.

Medium: Vehicle through which an advertising message is delivered to the *audience*.

Merchandising Credits: Promotional activities provided by a medium free or at a nominal charge when space or time is purchased for advertising. A certain program in a few local markets may be chosen to do this.

Network: A group of affiliated *television* or *radio* stations interconnected for the simultaneous broadcast of programs and advertisements.

Open Rate: See *base rate*.

Outdoor Advertising: Advertisements that are posted on vehicles located outside of the home (in public places), such as *billboards,* subway signs, bus posters, stadium signs, taxi tops, etc. It is the most cost-effective medium, and is best used when there is a simple message or visual to be communicated.

Pass-Along Readers: Readers who did not purchase the publication but have read it (and the advertisements in it) because someone passed it on to them, or because they picked it up in a waiting room situation.

Point: Standard vertical type measurement unit, 1/12 of a pica or 1/22 of an inch.

Point-of-Purchase Advertising: Advertising at retail that capitalizes on the impulse nature of some purchases. This may include end-aisle displays, header cards, shelf strips or "talkers," aisle signs, freezer cards, etc. See the glossary for chapter eight for more detailed explanations.

Preproduction (Prepro): A meeting prior to photography or filming where the objective is to choose beforehand any props, backgrounds, models, etc., that will be used on the day of shooting.

Prime Time: The *daypart* hours when viewing or listening is at its peak on television or on *radio*. With television, prime time is during evening hours, usually 8 P.M. to 11 P.M. (Monday-Saturday) and 7:30 P.M. to 11 P.M. (Sunday) EST. In *radio,* generally 6 A.M. to 10 A.M. and 3 P.M. to 7 P.M. EST, during morning and afternoon *drive time*. Advertising space is costed out at a premium during these hours.

Print Media: Media other than that which uses electronic signals for message transmission. The *print* media include all magazines and newspapers.

Production: The final creation of the actual *print* or a *broadcast* advertisement.

Puffery: Descriptive copy in an advertisement that does not make any refutable claims about a product. Also called "romance copy."

Pulsing: Continuous advertising that alternates between periods of heavy and light activity.

Radio: A type of *broadcast* media, in which electronic transmissions are sent through the airwaves to deliver an auditory message to listeners.

Rate Base: The published circulation of a *print* vehicle upon which advertising rates are based.

Rating: The percentage of households or individuals that are tuned in to a particular TV or *radio* program, with the size of the total potential viewing audience as a base. The potential audience is all households within a geographic area that have the ability to receive the broadcast. Each rating point represents one percent of the households making up the potential audience. Thus if a program has a rating of 20 (20 rating points), it would mean that 20 percent of the households in a particular geographic area had sets tuned in to that program.

Reach: Total size of the *audience* exposed to an advertisement at least one time through a particular medium or a particular time period, or in a total media schedule. It may be expressed for part or all of a *media schedule*.

Rebate: Credits or refund given to an advertiser when the frequency of insertions or commercials becomes high enough to earn a discounted rate. The discount is normally applied retroactively to the advertisements previously run at the higher rate.

Recall Research: Marketing research technique used to evaluate the effectiveness of an advertisement by testing the respondent's ability to remember the advertisement or any of its specifics. Recall may be *aided* or prompted, or *unaided*.

Recognition Test: Similar to *recall research,* except that consumers are shown stimuli and asked if they remember having seen it before.

Rep: The representative of a particular advertising medium who calls on the marketer or media planner to sell space or time.

Retouching: Method of color correcting or enhancing artwork after it has been photographed. This is usually done electronically today, as it is a very expensive process. The *artwork* must be scanned into a computer, and the retoucher charges for hourly time spent on the corrections or enhancements.

Rollout: A term used to describe a product, a marketing program, and/or an advertising schedule that is introduced into more and more areas as time goes by.

Run-of-Paper (ROP): Also called "run-of-press." It is an arrangement that allows the newspaper to place the company's ads in any position within the paper that is available.

Share of Audience: Also called "share." Percentage of households or individuals that is tuned to a particular station, *network,* or program, as compared to a base of all *televisions* or *radios* in use at the particular time. Share differs from rating in the following way: If there are a hundred total possible recipient households for a broadcast, and twenty are tuned in to a program, the program has a rating of twenty. However, if sixty TV sets are turned on, and twenty are tuned in to a particular program, the program has a 33 share.

Shoot: Photography or filming or videotaping of a *print* ad or *broadcast* commercial.

Simmons Market Research Bureau (SMRB): A syndicated service that provides product usage data and other media *audience* information.

Split Run: A testing technique in which two different ads are run in a *circulation* of a publication, so that each individual receives one ad or the other. This is used to compare awareness and response.

Sponsorship: The purchase of multiple *announcements* within a program, which allows advertisers to receive a bonus.

Spot Ad: *Broadcast* advertising time purchased on a market-by-market basis.

Spread: Article or advertisement that appears across two facing pages in a publication.

Storyboard: A sequential series of *art* illustrations and *copy,* depicting the planned action for a *television* commercial. Allows the client to visualize and revise the commercial prior to *production.*

Subhead: Line of copy that is secondary to the *headline,* that usually adds to or explains the thought provoked by the headline.

Supplement: A newspaper section that is arranged and editorialized in a magazine *format.* Usually found in Sunday papers.

Syndication: The sale of a particular program on a market-by-market basis to local stations.

Tag: Short announcement, usually a promotion of some sort, that is placed at the end of a *television* or *radio* commercial. In print, a tag line may be used to reinforce a thought or to unify a campaign.

Target Audience: The group of people whom the marketer wants to reach with his message—those for whom the product offering is intended. The target *audience* is defined in terms of demographic, geographic, or psychographic characteristics, such as age, education, income, purchase behavior, etc. Also referred to as "target market."

Tear Sheet: A clipped page of an actual *printed* ad, usually submitted to the advertiser as proof of insertion. A tear sheet is normally attached to the invoice.

Telemarketing: Two-way use of the telephone as the medium to perform certain marketing functions—e.g., receiving orders or inquiries from customers. Marketers may make use of an 800 number (free of charge to callers), or a 900 number, where the consumer is charged a fee for the call. Telemarketing allows the marketer to predetermine informational needs from the customers.

Tent Card: A folded card, in the shape of a tent, that carries a *printed* advertising message. Tent cards are frequently used in restaurants and bars, found on the tables or counters, and are a form of *point-of-purchase* advertising.

Testimonial: Statement by a "real person" in an advertisement to show user endorsement of a product or service. Sometimes the person is representative of the target audience, and other times the person is a celebrity or an "expert."

Theme: The main idea that brings together an advertising *campaign* or look. It is normally the most memorable portion of the ad and usually contains the intended message in a creative fashion.

Thumbnails: Miniature sketches or rough *layouts* used to develop print advertising concepts. Thumbnails are normally kept internally at the agency, and an art director will choose the strongest concepts to work up in a tighter form for client presentation.

Trade Advertising: Advertising directed to the middlemen (e.g., wholesalers and retailers) who sell the manufacturer's product to the ultimate consumer. The objectives of trade advertising are to promote distribution or to gain special displays or other incremental promotions of the advertised product.

Trademark: Registered brand name, *logo,* symbol,

or *copy* used to identify a product or service. Regulated by the U.S. Patent Office. A manufacturer may not use any words or symbols for which another manufacturer holds the trademark.

Transit Advertising: Advertising message carried on or around the stations where people use public transportation, or on the transportation vehicle itself.

TV Market: An unduplicated *television* area to which a county is assigned on the basis of highest share of viewing.

Unaided Recall: In *recall research,* a method of measuring advertising effectiveness by determining, without prompting, whether people remember seeing or hearing a particular advertising message.

Values and Life-styles (VALS): Identification of consumer segments based upon psychological and sociological characteristics.

Vehicle: Any method through which any advertising message is disseminated to the *audience. Television, radio,* and *magazines* are examples of vehicles.

Voice-Over: Recorded voice or sound, the source of which is not seen during the advertisement.

Word-of-Mouth Advertising: A message about the product that is communicated from one customer of a product or service to a family member, friend, or acquaintance who may be a prospective customer for the same product or service. May be positive or negative.

PM TOOLS™
ADVERTISING

- Target Audience Profile—Demographics
- Target Audience Profile—Geographics
- Target Audience Profile—Psychographics and Buyer Behavior
- Creative Advertising Strategy
- Media Calculations Worksheet
- Master Media Flight Schedule

TARGET AUDIENCE PROFILE

DEMOGRAPHICS

AGE	SEX	CHILDREN IN HOUSEHOLD	HOUSEHOLD INCOME	EDUCATION	PROFESSIONAL STATUS	COMMUNITY TYPE
☐ < 6	☐ Male	☐ 0	☐ < 30K	☐ < High	☐ Blue Collar	☐ Urban
☐ 6 - 12	☐ Female	☐ 1	☐ 30 - 40K	☐ High	☐ White Collar	☐ Suburban
☐ 13 - 18		☐ 2	☐ 41 - 50K	☐ College	☐ Homemaker	☐ Rural
☐ 19 - 24	**MARITAL STAUS**	☐ 3	☐ 51 - 60K	☐ Graduate		☐ Other_____
☐ 25 - 34	☐ Single	☐ 4	☐ 61 - 70K	☐ > Graduate		
☐ 35 - 44	☐ Married	☐ 5	☐ 71 - 80K			
☐ 45 - 54	☐ Divorced/ Separated	☐ ≥5	☐ > 80K			
☐ > 54						

NOTE: Other categories can be added, such as religion, race, nationality, social class, specific occupation, and family life cycle.

TARGET AUDIENCE PROFILE
GEOGRAPHICS

KEY:

☐ PRIMARY
☐ SECONDARY
☐ TERTIARY

N

PRIMARY DENSITY

☐ Urban
☐ Suburban
☐ Rural

INSTRUCTIONS: Pick a color or pattern (e.g., diagonal lines, vertical lines) for each of the audiences in the Key (i.e., Primary—most important target; Secondary—moderately important; and Tertiary—least important but still in the plan) and fill in the boxes. Fill in the markets on the map with the appropriate colors or patterns. You can also check off whether the population density of your Primary target is Urban, Suburban, or Rural.

TARGET AUDIENCE PROFILE

PSYCHOGRAPHICS AND BUYER BEHAVIOR

PSYCHOGRAPHIC PARAMETERS:

Personality

_____

_____

Life-style

_____

_____

_____

BUYER BEHAVIOR:

Purchase Frequency _____ (wks / mos / years)

Purchase Occasion	☐ Normal	☐ Special	
User Type	☐ Non-user	☐ Ex-user	☐ New user ☐ Regular user
Usage rate	☐ Light	☐ Medium	☐ Heavy
Brand Loyalty	☐ Low	☐ Medium	☐ High

Benefits Sought:

_____

_____

_____

CREATIVE STRATEGY ADVERTISING

BRAND POSITIONING:

For _____(target audience),
_____ (brand) is the_____
(qualifier, e.g., "only," "first," "leading," etc.)
_____(category) that_____
_____(benefits).

OBJECTIVES:

_____
_____
_____
_____

**INFORMATION ON TARGET
CONSUMER:**

_____
_____
_____
_____

KEY CONSUMER BENEFITS:

1._____
2._____
3._____
4._____
5._____

REASON TO BELIEVE:

_____
_____
_____
_____

TONE AND MANNER:

_____
_____
_____
_____

MEDIA CALCULATIONS WORKSHEET

GROSS RATING POINTS
(A cumulative measurement used to calculate the percentage of audience that receives a message in an advertising schedule.)

UNDUPLICATED REACH X FREQUENCY MESSAGE EXPOSED = GRP

_____ % of audience X _____ times message exposed = _____

COST PER THOUSAND
(The cost of reaching one thousand individuals or homes by a given medium.)

COST OF AD / TOTAL CIRCULATION / 1000 = CPM

$ _____ / _____ / 1000 = $ _____

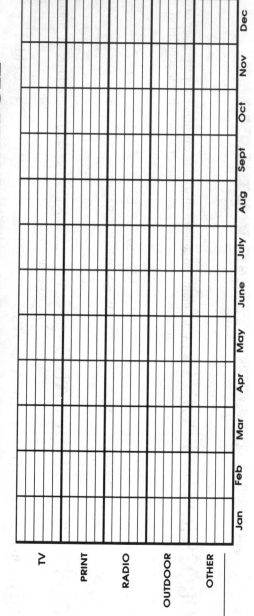

EIGHT

TOP-LINE

OVERVIEW

While advertising generates awareness and can stimulate purchase intent by virtue of communication of product benefits, promotion provides an extra tangible *incentive* in an attempt to "close" the sale. This is not to say that promotion cannot also be used to generate awareness—it can and it is, but that is usually not its *primary* role.

The charge of promotion is to *provide incentives to sell, buy, or use* a product. These incentives are usually tangible, in the form of some reward for product purchase. Sometimes the reward has monetary value, as in *coupons* or *premiums*. Sometimes the reward is the communication of a new way to use the product, such as a recipe leaflet in the package. In an organization, promotion is usually called "sales promotion." Sales promotion can be further divided into two subgroups—*consumer promotion* and *trade promotion*. They differ in that different incentives or *reasons* to purchase and/or use the products or services are directed at one of two groups: (1) consumers, and (2) trade.

Consumer promotions are used to influence the consumer or consumer groups to purchase or use products. The consumer target is normally defined in the marketing plan, and the promotion plan is written with this identified target in mind.

Trade promotions are targeted toward everyone in the "distribution channels" between manufacturers and users of products, including: (1) *sales force,* including the internal sales force, brokers, distributors, wholesalers, and jobbers; and (2) *retailers,* including supermarkets, mass-merchandisers, department stores, specialty stores, catalogs, and home-shopping networks. The objective is to provide incentives to one or more of these groups to either buy or support the products that the marketer sells.

THE PROMOTION PLAN

The promotion plan involves identification of the best way for promotion to help achieve marketing objectives within its defined role in the marketing plan. Much thought and analysis goes into the decision to run that $.50 coupon in the Sunday paper the week before Halloween, or to give away that free sample at the county fair. What type of behavior among the target audience is desired? What types of offers are likely to get a response from this target audience? Which promotional vehicles will best reach this audience? What is the best timing? The planner must answer each of those questions.

Before the promotion manager begins to write the plan, he or she should do three things: conduct a competitive analysis, prepare a "lessons learned" summary of the previous year's results, and take the time to research the latest promotional vehicles available.

Competitive information is available as raw data from a few tracking agencies. In competitive categories, the promotion manager should subscribe to such agencies for this data and manipulate and analyze it to the extent necessary. Some of the information that might be of interest concerns comparative spending levels, coupon values, timing, and vehicle use.

A lessons learned summary should include analysis of the redemption or response rates of previous promotions, along with corresponding share and/or volume data as appropriate. Any testing that took place in the previous year would be evaluated (i.e., varying coupon values to ascertain maximum efficiency level). Recommendations would then be made for repetition, deletion, or improvements to previous events.

Perhaps one of the most overlooked aspects of promotional planning is allowing for time to meet with suppliers of different promotional vehicles. All through the year, suppliers and creative agencies send brochures and call to attempt to set up meetings to present their wares. Often a busy schedule places this at the bottom of the promotion manager's "to do" list. The planning process suffers when the manager is unfamiliar with all of the options available.

Once the "preplanning" process is complete, and the promotion manager has been given the necessary elements of the marketing plan, he or she is ready to sit down to write the promotion plan. There are five key steps in development of the promotion plan:

1. Determine the *promotion role* in the overall business strategy, as determined by the marketing plan.
2. Set measurable *promotion objectives* that support marketing and overall business objectives and plans.
3. Set *promotion strategies* that are best suited to fulfill objectives.
4. Set *principles and guidelines* for most effective deployment of funds.
5. Select the appropriate promotional *tactics* and executional elements that are most in line with strategies.

THE PROMOTION ROLE

The role of the various marketing functions, one of which is promotion, is determined in the marketing strategy section of the marketing plan. The marketer has several marketing tools in his arsenal, and it is his job to determine the most effective mix of these tools that he can use to fulfill marketing objectives. The functional role statement will define the contribution that the function is expected to make and what the function is expected to accomplish.

Although there are exceptions to every rule, generally, promotion can be expected to play a major role in the product's marketing mix when the:

1. Product is a new introduction;
2. Product is a reintroduced/relaunched product;
3. Category in which the product competes is very competitive;
4. Product and/or category is very price/value sensitive;
5. Product must defend itself against a competitive new product introduction; and
6. Composition or elements that make up the product itself have some special news or advantage that needs to be demonstrated or experienced in order to be realized.

Conversely, promotions can be expected to play a lesser role in the product's marketing mix when:

1. Product dominates the category in which it competes;
2. There is little or no competition or competitive promotional spending;
3. Product is very price inelastic.

PROMOTION OBJECTIVES

After the marketing strategies and the role of promotions in supporting those strategies are determined, it's now time to set promotional objectives. These are derived directly from marketing objectives and strategies and will state the desired results of the promotion efforts for the year.

We use the "W's" system to remove most confusion in writing objectives. Promotional objectives build on marketing strategies by adding these four elements:

1. Desired consumer response or *what* you want to accomplish with promotion (e.g., stimulate trial, increase purchase frequency, encourage larger size purchase);
2. Consumer target or *who* (e.g., non-users, heavy users, light users, health-conscious women, weight-conscious men);
3. Promotional timing or *when* (e.g., during peak holiday seasons, during contraseason or off-season, during back-to-school time periods, during peak diet periods);
4. Areas or *where* (e.g., national sales area, key high-volume areas, opportunity markets).

Thus, an outline for stating a promotion objective is as follows:

	among
(what)	
	during
(whom)	
	, in
(when)	
	.
(where)	

You can insert any of the above examples into the blank spaces and arrive at your objective statement. The key is to take marketing objectives and strategies and translate them into promotion objectives.

If a marketing objective is to introduce a new flavor of ice cream, and a strategy is to utilize advertising and promotion to gain broad-scale awareness and trial, the promotion objective might be stated as follows:

Generate trial among at least 10 percent of heavy users of ice-cream during introductory peak ice cream consumption period in the national sales area.

Notice that there is a performance percentage stated in this objective, upon which the success of the promotion can be assessed later. It is essential to set up the methodology for evaluation at the time that the objectives are being written—and this is where promotion connects with marketing research. Evaluation in this case can be a combination of analysis of redemption or response rates to trial-oriented consumer promotions, a look at market share and source of volume of the new flavor, and/or a postpromotion survey of a sample of the target audience.

Although we gave only a consumer promotion example here, promotion objectives target both the consumer and the trade. Some generic promotion (what) objectives to consider in planning include:

1. Generate trial (consumer).
2. Increase frequency of purchase (consumer).
3. Counter competitive activity (consumer or trade).
4. Increase usage ideas and occasions (consumer).
5. Induce "trade-ups" to larger size or bulk products (consumer).
6. Get feature pricing, display, or other trade support (trade).

7. Reduce or increase trade inventories (trade).
8. Expand or improve distribution (trade).
9. Buffer a planned price increase (consumer and trade).

Before we go on to strategy development, we should take a look at each of the "W's" in our objective and define them in as much detail as we can. For example, if part of our objective is to reach nonusers, just who are they? Urban, middle-class consumers, women, men, kids, health-conscious people? The more precise the answer to this question the more effective the vehicles will be that are chosen later to deliver the promotional offers.

PROMOTION STRATEGIES

Promotion strategies outline how we will go about achieving promotion objectives. Strategies provide the *direction* necessary to develop specific promotional programs that accomplish our objectives. We've been through the who, what, when, and where in developing our promotion objectives; the promotion strategy is the "how." It's okay if strategy statements repeat some of the information in the objective statement, or some of the "W's."

Simply stated, our strategy is complete if we take the example of the promotional objective above and add the word "by" plus two elements:

1. **TYPE OF PROMOTIONAL OFFER:** Provides direction on the *type* of offer, in terms of both value and nature (e.g., trial value percentage of purchase price, multiple purchase economic incentives, incentives that encourage purchase *continuity*).
2. **SCOPE OF PROMOTIONAL VEHICLE**: Provides direction on the choice of the delivery vehicle for the offer (e.g., broad-reach vehicle, targeted vehicle, package delivered).

Thus, our strategy statement might read:

> *During June, the peak ice cream introductory month, generate trial among heavy users of ice cream by delivering broad-reach trial-value economic incentives that are at least 40 percent of the purchase price, and by direct product sampling in high ice cream CDIs.*

Now, let's take a look at the many different types of consumer and trade promotion tactics, or the various offers and vehicles that can be used to achieve objectives.

PROMOTION TACTICS

Promotional tactics are all those tools that the marketer has at his or her disposal to achieve objectives. A tactic itself is a combination of the choice of an offer (or an incentive) and a vehicle, the method by which the incentive will be delivered. It is essential that the marketer know what each of the offers and vehicles can do strategically, and that the tactics are carefully chosen for their ability to get at the objective. It is very tempting when an exciting tactic is presented to choose it without considering the strategically appropriate purpose. This is the trap that one must carefully avoid. Let us review some of the more common offers and vehicles in the promotion repertoire.

PROMOTION OFFERS: Promotion offers are the promotion "devices" we have at our disposal to achieve our objectives. They present incentives that can produce desired purchase behaviors from various consumer or trade targets.

If you have developed your objectives and strategies well, selecting the offer should be relatively easy, as you've narrowed down your choices by ruling out those that don't support or further your strategies. There are nine "core" types of consumer offers, each with different strengths and probable effects:

1. **COUPONS:** These reduce the price of a product at retail. They are primarily used to drive both trial and repeat purchases and to create a competitive point of difference. Coupons are used as cash at the register to buy the product(s) covered, but they are worth almost nothing (e.g., 1/100 cent) if redeemed without purchasing the product. Coupons always have *coupon terms*, which include the instructions for handling by the consumer and retailer and a date of expiration.

   There are several types of coupons: the cents-off coupons (discount savings are deducted at the register when one or more of a product is purchased), *BOGO*s or *B2G1*s ("buy-one-get-one free, buy-two-get-one-free, etc." where the purchaser gets two for the price of one or three for the price of two, and so on), and *joint purchase or companion* coupons (another product, often related, is free or discounted when two or more other products are purchased at the same time).

Couponing is viewed extremely positively by the consumer. High-value coupons and free-with-a-companion purchase coupons can motivate trial. Multiple purchase requirement coupons can be extremely effective in generating incremental purchases during a peak season and in achieving a pantry-loading objective. Coupon values/offers can be manipulated to fit many objectives, making this tool one of the most flexible that the marketer has at his disposal.

Disadvantages of couponing are that at "normal" values it mostly subsidizes current users, has a high incidence of **misredemption** (coupons are accepted for other products by accident or oversight, or after the expiration date) and **malredemption** (coupons are illegally stolen, sold, and redeemed), and produces clutter. Cents-off couponing generally does not add value to a brand; rather, persistent couponing may actually **demote** the product. Nonetheless, couponing has come to be expected in certain product categories and must be done to keep up with competitors where brand loyalty is low.

2. **PRICE OFFS:** The most common form of promotion, in which the cost of a product is simply discounted at retail. ("This week, World Famous Ice Cream just $1.99/gallon!") Often the result of trade **allowances,** which are monetary incentives to the trade to run these offers periodically. The retailer publicizes these *"feature prices"* in the store circular and with *shelf talkers* or special *displays*.

Price offs are successful in encouraging pantry loading by current users and some level of brand switching.

3. **PREMIUMS:** Rewards, other than cash, offered to the consumer for purchasing a product or series of products. Provide competitive edge and excellent reason for purchase if executed well. Types of premiums include: *free at point-of-sale premiums* (those offered with the purchase of a product, either packaged with the product or somewhere in the store, providing immediate gratification); *free in mail premiums* (those offered free through some

consumer action—usually mailing in for it with proof or proofs of purchase); *self-liquidating premiums* (those offered either at point-of-sale or through mail-in where the consumer pays the manufacturer's cost of the premium, including what it costs to process and get the premium to the consumer). In any case, for greatest appeal the premium should have a logical connection with the product.

While point-of-sale premiums may be successful in attracting brand switchers, it is unlikely that the premium will attract a non-category user. Mail-in premiums encourage continuity among current users but are generally not effective in attracting new users. Another disadvantage is that the delayed reward and effort necessary on the part of consumers makes for low response rates. Generally, premiums are not often used in new product introductions, because this may take consumer attention away from the product.

4. **SAMPLING:** Provides consumers with a chance to try the product before actually purchasing it. Very effective tool to drive trial purchases. Often used to introduce new products and product improvements or in new or undeveloped markets. Can be delivered as a portion or as a serving at store level or at another targeted location, in a trial-sized package that is either free or specially priced at the store, or through direct mail. Retailers like in-store sampling because it creates strong merchandising support and usually moves a lot of product while it is taking place. Disadvantages to the manufacturer are the high expense and difficult logistics involved.

5. **EVENTS:** Live sponsorship of a happening, such as "comedy night," sports event, and so on. Works well for brands that are considered "image" or "lifestyle" driven. Often an *overlay* (additional layer) to other types of offers and often done in conjunction with on-site sampling.

6. **GAMES, CONTESTS, SWEEPSTAKES:** Usually low-cost promotions that involve chance (sweepstakes and games) or competition (contests) to win prizes. A purchase may be required for entry to a contest (where skill is required), but by law a purchase cannot be required for sweepstakes or games involving chance only. Often used as an overlay and varies widely in its effectiveness. Can be used to create excitement, to build store traffic, and to encourage display activity. May be used to en-

courage purchase continuity if "collect and win"-type structure is used. Generally, should be supported by advertising to achieve maximum effectiveness.

7. **REFUNDS:** Monetary rewards offered to consumers in exchange for proofs of purchase, usually through the mail. Refunds are often a much higher value than coupons because of the lower percentage that are redeemed. They are used in connection with a purchase continuity strategy or to encourage multiple or incremental purchases among current users, although high value refund offers may induce trial.

8. **CLUBS**: Membership offer with tangible benefits, such as monthly newsletter, discounts, etc. Good for establishing ongoing communication between a brand and its consumers, and building and maintaining brand loyalty and continuity in competitive categories. Generally, clubs are most effective when brand purchase frequency is high, and where maintaining an ongoing relationship with loyal consumers helps to keep them in the franchise.

9. Bonus **PACK:** Package promotion that offers the consumer an additional amount of the product free. This can take the form of larger containers or multiunit packs. This tactic encourages current users to load and is a tiebreaker in low brand-loyalty categories. The disadvantage is that special packages must be developed, and often additional distribution allowances must be paid to the trade.

In trade promotion the following techniques are used:

1. **TRADE DEALS**: Offers that are used in the short term to either gain distribution for a product or increase trade support of that product. The most frequently used trade deal is the *allowance.* Allowances are discounts in the form of monies given to the trade in exchange for performance. The payment is made either by a deduction from an invoice or a check from the manufacturer.

    Types of allowances include *buying/slotting allowances* (discounts/payments to offset the expense of putting products on the shelf), *promotion allowance* (payments for moving products out of the warehouse and into the store during a specified period), **buy-back allowances** (a deal to the wholesaler or retailer to repurchase more of the product after a deal period has ended), **advertising allowances** (discounts/payments for retailer advertising of your products), **display allowances** (discounts/payments for giving your products special display space in the store or using merchandising materials that you provide).

Other types of trade deals are free merchandise (premiums, **dealer loading,** etc.), and fees (e.g., shelf restocking fees).

Some manufacturers regularly make products available to the retailer at discounted prices during particular time periods. This is done in an attempt to gain more sales during critical times, and to ensure feature prices at retail. This is especially true with products in highly competitive categories and with highly seasonal products.

2. **POINT-OF-SALE MATERIALS**: Any promotional material located at retail, at the "point of sale/purchase" that houses products and/or carries promotional offers. These are often given to the trade as added incentive to display the product.

3. **SALES KITS AND COLLATERAL**: Sales tools, such as manuals, brochures, product sheets used by the sales force, distributors, brokers, and so on, to give the trade a reason to carry or support a product.

4. **CONTESTS, GAMES, AND SWEEPSTAKES**: Same as its consumer counterpart, but targeted to the trade and their families, often tying into consumer programs running at that time. Usually used to get the trade excited about a consumer promotion and supportive of it. Frequently, trade contests use display-building as the criterion.

5. **RETAILER COUPONS:** Coupons may also be delivered by the retailer. Retailer-delivered coupons are commonly known as "recus" in the promotion business. These coupons are delivered to consumers via retailer circulars but are offered to the retailer and paid for by the manufacturer.

PROMOTION VEHICLES: There are many vehicles by which promotional offers can be delivered to the consumer. Choice of the vehicle depends on who the target consumer is, the scope of the offer (broad or targeted, national or regional), and the type of offer that is to be delivered. Here are some of the more widely used consumer promotion vehicles:

1. **FREE-STANDING INSERT (FSI):** This is the four-color coupon insert that is found in most Sunday newspapers. It is not produced by the newspapers themselves—it is supplied by independent suppliers. The "big three" FSI suppliers are Product Movers, Quad Marketing, and Valassis Inserts.

   FSIs continue to be the most widely used couponing vehicle, because of the relatively low *cost per thousand* (somewhere between $7.00 and $7.50/M for a full page), the broad reach (offers 52 MM-plus national circulation), and the strong advertising value (you can get a full four-color page to deliver a message and coupons). Also, consumers who use coupons know to look there every week.

   The only way that one can narrow down a target utilizing FSIs is geographically. One can buy part of the circulation offered, with little or no cost penalty (there is a small minimum charge, but most marketers are likely to exceed that anyway). They tend to cover the largest papers in A and B counties only (cities and suburbs surrounding cities). FSI suppliers will supply marketers with a newspaper list that is grouped by area, and the marketer can pick and choose the areas to be covered on a newspaper level.

   One major disadvantage of FSIs is the long lead time required to execute. Film is due at the supplier approximately eight to ten weeks prior to the *drop date*. Therefore, FSI executions must be planned well in advance, and thus, this method is not a fast way to respond to a critical marketing situation. Still, marketers regard FSIs as the most efficient way to reach a large number of consumers, and the trade often bases promotional or distribution decisions on whether the product will be promoted in an FSI.

2. **NEWSPAPER ROP:** Manufacturers may run ads containing promotional offers right on a newspaper page, called a *run of press*. Offers are best run on the

day of the week that the newspaper features ads pertaining to that category. For example, "best food day" (BFD) is normally Wednesday, when the papers run the food ads from manufacturers and food chains. The food marketer would place his ad or coupon in the co-op food section in the paper.

Newspaper ROPs usually produce a lower rate of redemption than do FSIs, all other things being equal. However, ROPs require very short lead times (often less than a week), while FSIs require about ten weeks. ROPs are often used to "fill in" in conjunction with FSIs, which do not cover all of the local papers. This is called "ROP fill." ROPs are also powerful when used in conjunction with a special sales effort, or as leverage in getting feature prices or circular ads with the trade. For example, if a salesman tells his accounts that an ROP will be running with a BOGO offer, the account will be sure to stock up on the product for the anticipated need.

3. **SUNDAY SUPPLEMENTS:** Special supplements included in the Sunday newspaper (e.g., *Parade* magazine) or wholly purchased and dedicated to a company (e.g., Caldor's sale circular). Usually full color.

4. **MAGAZINE:** Magazines are sometimes used for promotional advertising and sampling. Examples include a print ad adapted to contain a coupon or mail-in offer, or a glued envelope that the consumer takes to a card store to get the card to go with it. There is a special promotional vehicle called Thematics that is supplied to "women's service" magazines during certain key months. Thematics is a heavier, cardboardlike paper stock insert that is bound into the magazine and contains coupons, recipes, mail-in offers, and some advertising space. Thematics is especially effective for recipe-oriented products.

5. **DIRECT MAIL:** There are several companies that run cooperative direct mail programs throughout the year. An example is Donnelley's Carol Wright. Recently, direct mail suppliers have offered the manufacturer the ability to target the mailings to specific audience segments, along with the option of doing a broad-reach general mailing. Examples of the types of segments a marketer is able to reach via direct mail are Hispanics, young families, seniors, African Americans, health-conscious adults, and children.

While direct mail vehicles generally have a higher CPM than FSIs, the redemption rates tend to be higher due to their more targeted nature. Direct mail can be used to deliver just about any type of offer, including samples.

6. **PACKAGE-DELIVERED**: Premiums, coupons, and other promotion offers are packed or printed on or inside a product package. It may be the manufacturer's own package, or another product's package. An offer on or in another product's package is called a *cross-ruff*. Marketers may use their own package to deliver an offer when they want to encourage continuity or as a tiebreaker in a competitive category. Offers directed at a product's current users may or may not be "flagged," or advertised on the front of the package or on point-of-sale materials, while offers designed to induce brand switching must be flagged or otherwise communicated to be effective. Another product's package may be used to generate trial from a user base that is perceived to be similar in nature to the users of the original product. Cross-ruffs work best when the products are highly related (e.g., peanut butter and jelly, cereal and milk, syrup and waffles, etc.).

7. **IN-STORE OR POINT-OF-SALE:** Any promotional offer made at the store level, such as in-store sampling, near-pack premiums (free or at a discount with purchase of the product), special displays, and point-of-sale collateral materials, such as stack cards, shelf-talkers, static-clings (for the freezer case), tear pads.

A relatively new category of in-store vehicles is that of automatic coupon dispensing machines. The most popular example is a machine that electronically delivers a coupon at the checkout when a "trigger" product is purchased. The most popular service using this method is Catalina Marketing's COUPON SOLUTION. Act Media has a device that is placed right on the shelf near the product, is locked, and dispenses one coupon at a time when a consumer presses a button.

Other electronic couponing devices have been tried and have failed, including "frequent shopper programs" like Citicorp's Reward America which would give the consumer automatic price-offs when the participating items were scanned at the checkout. Retailers now control many electronic frequent-shopper programs that are store specific, including the issuance of store cards, sometimes tied to check-cashing cards.

8. **EVENTS**: Although events are listed in the offer section, they are included here because the event itself can be the vehicle by which promotional offers are delivered. Marketers sponsor the type of event that attracts large numbers of the target audience.

9. **EDUCATIONAL MARKETING AND CO-OPERATIVES:** A recent new trend is marketing products through the educational system. This vehicle effectively delivers targeted coupons to households and multiple long-term brand impressions to children and families, supported by high-content educational programs and scholarship and grants programs in the schools. Because budgets are so constrained in the educational system, high-content sponsored programs such as these are welcomed and sought after by schools, principals, teachers, students, and parents.

Promotion is a science in which innovation is constant, and more tools than we mention here are being introduced as creative marketing people meet new challenges.

PROMOTION GUIDELINES

The tactical elements of the promotion plan should not be written until certain guidelines are established. Guidelines give general direction on several elements:

- Vehicle mix;
- Offer mix and value;
- Frequency of events;
- Timing of events;
- Any other considerations specific to that organization.

Several factors will need to be considered when establishing guidelines, such as promotion objectives and strategies, competitive activity, lessons learned from previous years' events, seasonality, and budgetary limitations. Here is an example of guidelines for the vehicle mix:

We will utilize a broadreach FSI for the product's introduction, to ensure maximum distribution and consumer awareness and trial. We will also utilize strong point-of-purchase incentives during the entire peak season, due to the impulse nature of the purchase. This will afford us with a point of difference on our major competitor, who dropped two FSIs last season, and had no point of purchase activity.

A similar, short guideline statement should be written for each of the bulleted points listed earlier.

TACTICAL DETAILS

After objectives, strategies, and promotional guidelines have been written AND sanctioned by anyone who needs to approve them (such as the product manager), the tactics must be chosen and the details outlined in the plan. Gaining approval of the first part of the plan before the tactical details are worked out will save much time and effort.

The tactical or event details include: (1) the event description; (2) the vehicle; (3) the offer type and value; (4) scope or circulation; (5) cost details; and (6) rationale statements. These details are normally listed by product line, and then chronologically. It is recommended that a consistent "user-friendly" format be used when writing out the details.

It is at this stage in the planning process where creativity comes in. How will the events be structured and work together to achieve and optimize objectives and budget? Is there a "big campaign idea" or new twist that might serve to create excitement about the product? Is it strategically appropriate for any of the events to "tie-in" with another brand or product?

While the creative direction for the event(s) does not need to be decided at this point, one should think about the creative possibilities when constructing the flow of events.

At the event-costing stage **redemption** rates must be estimated for each offer. The estimate comes from analysis of past redemptions on the product when the same delivery vehicle was used (from the lessons learned summary). If no past history exists for a particular vehicle, estimates can be made based upon other products' performances that have been published by the vehicle supplier, or by discussions with the coupon

clearing house or redemption center account person who handles the product. Experience is the best teacher when it comes to estimating redemption rates. For those just beginning in the business, your boss can be a great resource.

A combination of circulation, offer value, and estimated redemption rate will make up the variable or redemption portion of the event cost. Here's the formula for costing out the redemption on an FSI with a circulation of 50 MM, a coupon value of $0.30, coupon handling charges of $0.10, and an estimated redemption rate of 3 percent:

$$50 \text{ MM} \times (\$0.30 + \$0.10) \times .03 = \$600 \text{ M}$$

The redemption portion of this program will cost $600,000. If the offer requires any other handling costs (fulfilling anything, compiling names, judging, etc.), the fulfillment house can estimate the postage and handling cost per respondent based upon the offer requirements, size and weight of the item if a mail-back is necessary, and estimated volume of respondents.

The fixed cost portion of an event is comprised of the distribution (or space) cost and the artwork and production cost of all program elements. Distribution includes postage costs for direct mail, execution of a sampling program, space costs for an FSI, etc. It is usually measured by a **CPM** for printed matter, and a per store or per day cost for sampling. Artwork cost includes the fees for the creative agency, photography or illustration, mechanical development, typography, etc. Production cost includes color separations and film, and printing or producing the items.

Staying with the FSI example used, assume that the CPM for a full-page FSI is $7.25. The artwork generally costs about $20 M, and the film separations will cost about $5 M. Thus, the space cost for a circulation of 50 MM is calculated as 50 M × $7.25, or $362 M. The total fixed costs are then $387.5 M. When redemption is added, the total program cost is $987.5 M.

When comparing tactics, the promotion manager should determine how many packages of the product will be sold based upon the various estimated redemption rates of each tactic. For example, the above FSI will move 50 MM × 3% = 1.5 MM packages of product. In contrast, a targeted direct-mail piece may have higher fixed costs, but the expected redemption rate will also be higher. A promotion manager must weigh the cost/benefits of each program considered.

CREATIVE GUIDELINES

Once we have decided which tactics to use, we can establish creative guidelines for each event. Like the creative strategy document in advertising, promotional creative guidelines direct the agencies that will be working on the creative executions. The structure of these guidelines may vary, depending on the promotion strategy for the year. For example, if one cohesive promotional campaign will be utilized, the creative guidelines may look very much like an advertising creative strategy. On the other hand, if the promotional events planned are tactically different, then a different set of guidelines may be developed for each instance. Creative guidelines include the following items:

1. **PROMOTION OBJECTIVES AND STRATEGIES**: The objective that the particular tactic addresses should be reiterated here. The strategy that directed the tactic should also be written.
2. **PROGRAM SPECIFICATIONS**: These include a brief description of the program or vehicle (e.g., "full-page FSI"), the drop date or time frame of the program, a description of the offer, and the scope or circulation of the offer.
3. **COMMUNICATION PRIORITIES**: This is a list of the points that you want the creative to cover. It is essential that these items be listed in order of priority. The first priority should be what you wish to be the main focus of the execution. The agency will take these priorities and create an ad that orders them properly according to the direction. Examples of communication priorities are: (1) appetite appeal; (2) package registration; (3) offer communication; (4) recipe delivery.
4. **TONE AND MANNER**: As in advertising, the tone and manner describe the desired "feel" or character of the execution. It may be "holiday festive and fun," or "soft and subtle." It may be "light and airy" or "bold and bright." The tone and manner established generally coincides with the brand image and positioning.
5. **COPY ESSENTIALS**: List any legal requirements, bullet points, etc.

6. **TIMETABLE**: This starts with the date that guidelines will be released to the agency and ends with the date that the film must be turned over, or the product shipped, etc. The necessary steps in between will vary according to the type of event and the organizational requirements.
7. **APPROVAL SIGNATURES**: All those who will have to approve the creative execution should also approve the guidelines, which should be routed for signature and comment. The originator of the guidelines may revise them after all comments are received, and before they go out to the agency.

PROMOTION EFFECTIVENESS AND TESTING

Tracking the success or failure of promotional executions is essential, yet it is often overlooked. This evaluation becomes part of the "lessons learned" summary that is utilized for the following year's planning process.

It is a promotion manager's responsibility to set up tests within the promotion plan. Tests can be done to determine optimal coupon or refund offer values by varying the values within a particular market area. The *A/B Split* method, for example, can vary coupon values within one particular newspaper that is receiving an FSI. An analysis can then be done to evaluate the cost of running a higher-value coupon against the benefit, or additional redemption rate achieved. While consumers claim to prefer higher-value coupons in general, the use of lower-value coupons in lower-priced products or in categories where there is little competition may be effective enough.

Tests can also be done to determine redemption tendencies by geographical area, by running the same value coupon in different areas, and changing the scanner code so that redemption can be read separately. It may be determined that couponing is simply not cost effective in certain areas. The information can also be used to help pick and choose areas when budget does not allow for a full coupon drop.

Other testing options include: two or more different

vehicles used to deliver the same offer, to test vehicle effectiveness versus cost; and deletion of an offer from control markets to determine if the lack of a promotion event in some areas (versus others that receive the event) had a negative effect on volume or share.

If at all possible, the promotion manager should work with market research to set up testing options. As the offers mature, the evaluation should be done and applied to the following year's planning process.

Some of the things that a promotion manager should look at are: redemption rates (by vehicle, geography, and coupon value), share bumps around the promotional period, and incremental features/displays gains as a result of the promotion. All this should be weighed against the cost of the event. Of course, awareness may be aided by promotional activity as well as advertising. This can be measured in the same fashion as described in chapter 7, Advertising.

PROMOTION GLOSSARY

A/B Split: Testing method whereby different offers are run within the same distribution vehicle or newspaper, in order to determine the optimal effectiveness. For example, in an *FSI* run the circulation of one or more newspapers may be split equally between two different *coupon* values, to test *redemption* differences as compared to cost of using higher values. This testing should be done in as targeted a section as possible and as randomly as possible, because coupon sensitivity dynamics vary with geographical areas.

Ad Slick: Glossy paper containing reproducible line art of product package, logo, etc., supplied to a retailer for use in the creation of promotional ads. Also supplied to creative agencies and newspapers for creation of other promotional materials.

Advertising Allowance: Payment made to a retailer or wholesaler for advertising the manufacturer's product. Proof of performance is required before payment is rendered. Proof is normally a *tear sheet* of the retailer's printed ad or an affidavit certification for broadcast ads.

Allowance: Discount offered to a retailer or wholesaler by a marketer, usually payable either by manufacturer's check or off the invoice.

Ballot Test: Research method used to survey selected households to determine likelihood of response to a *promotional offer*.

Barter: The practice of trading products or services for media placement or other promotional elements.

BFD (Best Food Day): The busiest food shopping day; the day of the week when manufacturers run their *ROPs* and food chains run their *feature ads*. It is usually Wednesday.

BOGO (Buy-One-Get-One Free): A type of *coupon* or on-pack *premium* offer that gives away a free product with a purchase of the same product. The objective of this type of promotion is to get the consumers to "load" their pantries with a product. Other reasons for this type of offer may be to liquidate supplies of an old product, either because it is getting close to the *expiration date* or to make room on the shelf for a new product entry. Also referred to as B1G1F, extendable to B2G1F, etc.

Bonus-Pack: A type of package promotion that gives an additional amount of product for the same price as the usual amount, normally done by increasing package size for a limited time. The package is usually "flagged" with the extra bonus amount indicated clearly. Sometimes a complementary product is attached to the product package free of charge, such as when hair conditioner is offered free with the purchase of shampoo, or a toothbrush is offered free with the purchase of toothpaste. The objective of this type of promotion is to gain trial of a complementary product, or to encourage *brand switching* by offering *value added* to the purchase when compared to the competitive offerings.

Bottle Neck Hanger: A type of package promotion that hangs a promotional offer on the neck of the bottle.

Bounceback: A *coupon, refund,* or *premium* that is sent to the consumer after he or she responds to another offer—i.e., if a consumer sends away for a free *sample*, the sample is sent with an additional coupon for the next purchase. Bouncebacks are used to encourage repeat purchase and/or continuity.

Brand Switching: Consumer practice of switching or alternating purchase among different brands in a particular category. Many promotions are designed to encourage brand switching (to YOUR brand) or to discourage switching (away from YOUR brand) by users of the category. Brands that have a high degree of loyalty are less sensitive to brand switching. Commodity items such as coffee or sugar are subject to a high degree of brand switching.

Business Reply Card (BRC): A preaddressed postcard supplied to consumers to reply or respond to a *promotional offer*. It may be postage-paid by the marketer, or may require a stamp. An envelope supplied for the same purpose is called a BRE. This tactic is used to facilitate and thus increase response.

Buy-Back Allowance: A special offer made directly after a deal period to the wholesaler or retailer to repurchase more of the product after the supply of the purchase made on deal has been exhausted.

Buying/Slotting Allowance: A specific amount of money or discount given by the manufacturer to the buyer in exchange for purchase of a specific quantity of product during a specified time period. This type of trade *deal* is normally done when a new product is introduced, or when the salesman needs to push a greater than usual amount of product through the distribution channels. Instead of cash, a specific amount of free goods may be offered with purchase of a required amount.

Cause-Related Promotion: Technique that includes donations to a cause or charity as part of the consumer hook.

Clearing House: A service that receives, groups, and counts *coupons* from retailers, and submits them to the manufacturer for payment.

Club: A *continuity*-focused promotion in which the consumer is granted membership and is entitled to special communications, offers, and other benefits. Offers usually center around collection and submission of proofs of purchase. This technique is used to build and maintain brand loyalty by establishing ongoing communications between the manufacturer and the product's customer base.

Consumer Promotion: The practice of providing incentives to the consumer or consumer groups to purchase or use products. Techniques or tactics include *couponing, sampling, bonus packs,* and *premiums*.

Contests: Promotions that require an entry by the consumer that calls for skill rather than chance. These entries must be judged by an independent source. It is allowable to require proof(s) of purchase for contest entry (see contrast to *sweepstakes*).

Continuity Programs: Promotions that reward the consumer for collection and submission of proof(s)-of-purchase, or that encourage the purchase of more than one of the product for a match and win game, etc. To maintain continuity, the rewards are sometimes sent with additional *bounceback* purchase incentives, such as coupons. Continuity programs are good for building purchase frequency and brand or trademark loyalty. Sometimes continuity offers will be structured to reward consumers for purchasing flavors or varieties different from the base brand. Marketers should be careful that the number of proofs required is a reasonable stretch for the consumer within a certain time period—otherwise interest will be lost and the program will be ineffective. Continuity programs are attractive to heavier users.

Co-op Promotions: Promotions in which several manufacturers share in the cost of distribution—i.e., co-op *FSIs* or *direct mailings.* This results in a lower *cost per thousand* than if a manufacturer were to run solo with the promotion.

Cooperative Advertising: A type of *allowance* whereby the retailer and the manufacturer share the message and the cost of the ad.

Cost per Thousand (CPM): Cost to reach 1,000 people with a message through one of many media (same as advertising usage of term). This is often used as a measure to compare the efficiency of various promotional vehicles, along with response rates expected through use of each vehicle. See *Cost per Thousand* (Advertising glossary) for more detail.

Count and Recount: An offer of a specific amount of money to be given to a wholesaler or retailer for each case moved out of the warehouse during a specified time period. The name comes from the fact that the salesperson must count the beginning inventory and then return to recount the inventory at the end of the period.

Coupon: A printed piece, usually "dollar bill" size (5-1/2 × 2-3/16) or IBM size (3-1/2 × 2-3/16), that offers the consumer a stated value or discount. This can be a cash discount when the product is purchased, free product, or another product at a lower price or free with purchase of the first product, etc. The discount is applied to the merchandise by the cashier at the time of the sale. A coupon normally contains *coupon terms,* the brand logo or photograph of the product, *retailer copy* or instructions on *redemption,* legal restrictions, and a bar code for scanning. Many retailers are offering to double manufacturer coupons in order to attract customers, some on a specified day of the week, and others on a continuous basis. The retailer pays the difference between the stated coupon value and the increased value offered to the customer.

Coupon Elasticity: Term used to describe the level of sensitivity of a brand or a product category to coupons. Relatively higher redemption rates indicate a high degree of coupon elasticity. Coffee and cereal are two categories with high coupon elasticity.

Coupon Terms: Instructions on a coupon telling the consumer and retailer how that coupon actually works. Terms include the amount of savings, purchase requirements, restrictions, *expiration date,* etc.

Creative Guidelines: Also called "communication guidelines." The direction a client (or marketer) gives to the creative agency that is creating the ad or designing the event. This document should list objectives, strategies, copy, and visual essentials in order of priority (communication priorities) and specifications.

Cross-Couponing: *Coupons* offered in or on other products' packages or through other products' promotions. This is a targeted tactic and is appropriate to use if the user of the other product is very similar to your targeted consumer. Products sought for this type of promotion are usually complementary (used together), and/or have a consumer base that is desirable to the couponing marketer. Can be used to attract new users and/or expand brand usage.

Cross-Ruff: A type of *cross couponing* that is delivered on or in packages.

Deal: Any type of promotional pricing offered to the trade.

Dealer Loader: A *premium* offered to the wholesaler or retailer for buying a specified amount of product. An attractive *display* case that can be reused by the retailer after the product in the display is sold is one type of dealer loader.

Demotion: Word used to describe a promotional strategy that relies heavily on discounting, *BOGO*s, etc., thus negatively affecting the quality image of the brand.

Direct Mail: A *promotional vehicle* that presents the offer directly to the consumer's household or place of business through the mail. Direct-mail businesses offer either a broad-reach (non-targeted) vehicle, or mailings to more targeted audience segments. While the *CPM* of direct mail vehicles tends to be higher than *FSI*s, the coupon *redemption* rate is usually higher as well, sometimes resulting in a better "cost per coupon redeemed."

Display: A special structural unit designed to hold and exhibit product in a retail environment. It may be built by the retailer or created and shipped by the manufacturer. Sometimes the cases or pallets in which the product is shipped can make up the display. Signage, such as a *header card,* for additional advertisement usually accompanies the display. An end-aisle display is located at the end of the shopping aisle and is considered to be a most desirable location.

Display Allowance: A retailer incentive offered by the marketer in exchange for the placement of a secondary *display*. Due to the large number of manufacturer requests for displays, retailers can often choose to honor those that involve higher volume/ higher profit items.

Display Contest: A promotional technique targeted to the trade or the retailers that offers a competitive reward for creation of product *displays*. This tactic is used by manufacturers when creative display of their products can make a major difference in sales, usually during a peak seasonal period.

Drop Date: The date that the *promotional event* or *offer* is to be received by the consumer.

Duplication: Describes the percentage of the audience that receives the promotional offer more than once. To maximize effectiveness, marketers want their mailing lists "dupe-eliminated" to ensure the greatest number of unduplicated deliveries.

800 Number: Toll-free telephone number that marketers set up to receive consumer responses to a *promotional offer.*

Electronic Couponing: A method of *couponing* in which the consumer receives a coupon printed out right at the store. In the most popular type, the coupon printout is linked to the checkout scanner, and it is printed out according to which products were purchased and scanned. The manufacturer can choose which products will "trigger" the release of his coupon. This technology is in its earliest stage and is likely to become a prominent force in the promotion repertoire very soon.

Escalating Coupon or Refund: A method of rewarding the consumer in progressively higher amounts with more value as the amount of purchase requirements increases. A manufacturer may bounce back coupons or cash refunds in exchange for a variable number of proofs of purchase. For example, a consumer may get $1.00 back for three *proofs-of-purchase,* $3.00 back for six proofs-of-purchase, or $5.00 back for eight proofs-of-purchase.

Event: Often referred to in the context of "event marketing," where the product or the corporation is involved in the sponsorship or creation of a live activity, to attract attention for the product. This type of promotion has a partial objective of linking the product with the life-style associated with the event, because a large proportion of the target market is likely to be present at or interested in the event. Product *sampling* and *premium* giveaways are often done at the events.

Expiration Date: The last date that the manufacturer will honor the *promotional offer.* This date must be clearly printed on the offer to limit the manufacturer's liability.

Feature: A *promotional offer* provided by the retailer, usually in the form of an ad in a circular offering a special price. This is most effective when combined with a *display.* Manufacturers ultimately pay for these features by offering *allowances.* The key is for the manufacturer to secure the optimal timing for the feature, relative to competitors.

Free Offer: Perhaps the most attention grabbing type of offer in the promotion manager's repertoire, whereby the consumer is offered something free, either with no purchase requirement (purely for a trial objective) or (most frequently) with a purchase requirement stipulation. The most frequently used free offers are: free product with purchase of one or more of the same product; free product with the purchase of a complementary product; or free complementary product with purchase of the manufacturer's product. In the last two examples, two or more tie-in partners may split the redemption cost of the offer. There are legal requirements that the qualifier for the free offer be clearly stated in the promotional copy, close in proximity to the word FREE and in type at least 1/3 the weight and height.

Frequent User Promotions: *Continuity*-based promotions that offer incentives related to *proofs of purchase*. Promotions are designed to maintain and increase frequency of purchase among the current user base.

FSI (Free-Standing Insert): An advertising insert, printed separately from the newspapers and supplied to them for insertion. FSIs are most often found in the Sunday newspapers and are filled with full-, half-, or third-page manufacturers ads, most frequently containing *coupons, mail-in certificates,* and other *promotional offers.* A *cooperative* FSI is an extremely cost-efficient coupon delivery vehicle, particularly when a manufacturer wants to reach the broadest range of consumers. Although they can be geographically targeted, FSIs are considered to be the most popular broad-reach vehicle.

Fulfillment: The process of "fulfilling" the terms of a *promotional offer* to the respondents. This includes collecting and opening all mail, sorting the requests, processing the *refunds,* packing the *premiums,* etc., and mailing the materials back to the respondent. The fulfillment costs to the manufacturer normally include labor and postage. Companies normally use a "fulfillment house" to do this.

Gang Cut: Refers to batches of *coupons* that never reached the consumer being illegally cut and submitted for payment to the manufacturer or the *clearing house.* This is called *malredemption. Clearing houses* have been trained to detect gang-cut coupons by looking for uniformity in batches.

Group Promotion: Promotional event in which several brands participate (either from the same manufacturer or different manufacturers). It usually has a theme within which each participating product fits strategically.

Header Card: Also known as a "riser card." This is a printed cardboard extension attached behind a display that usually contains promotional artwork and an announcement of a *feature* price or other bonus.

Impulse Purchase: A decision to buy that takes place while the consumer is at the store or was not preplanned. Products that are believed to be high impulse purchase items should make use of displays or in-store promotions, rather than out-of-store, media-delivered vehicles.

In-Ad Coupon: A manufacturer's coupon that is placed in a retailer's circular. The manufacturer is normally responsible for the *redemption* costs.

In-Pack Offer: Promotional items that are found inside the package, such as *coupons* or *premiums*. The outside of the package is usually *flagged* to announce the offer.

Incentive: In promotion, any offer that motivates consumers or retailers to purchase the product. The type and value of the incentives and the vehicle by which they are delivered will depend on the promotion objective.

IRC (Instant Redeemable Coupon): Peel-off or tear-off *coupon* placed on the product, meant to be used with that purchase. They are normally attached by a manufacturer's sales force to deal with an urgent situation. This technique is designed to move product off the shelves quickly—either to make room for a new or improved similar product that the manufacturer wants to sell in, or to preempt a competitive event. This is a type of *demotion* and should not be used by the marketer as a tactic on a regular basis. The tactic may be viewed by consumers and retailers as a "fire sale," and the perceived quality of the product may suffer. IRCs typically have very high *redemption* rates. Many of those that are not presented for redemption are probably "extras" that never make it onto the packages, or that have fallen off.

Licensing: A technique whereby the manufacturer pays for the right to use a popular character or trademark in promotional materials, packaging, or even as a product name.

Loss Leader: A product that is offered and featured in ads by the retailer at a price that may be below cost, in order to attract customers to the store. Usually, the product chosen is one that is extremely popular during that time period—such as turkey, stuffing, or pumpkin pie at Thanksgiving. The retailer (of course) hopes that the extra customers brought in by the loss leader will do the rest of their shopping at the store and proceed to purchase the profitable items.

Lottery: An illegal promotion that requires purchase to win a prize, based upon chance and not on skill. With any promotions based on chance, there cannot legally be a purchase requirement—the manufacturer must offer the consumer an alternate means of participation.

Mail-In Certificate: A small tear-off sheet (at retail) or printed box to be cut out (on an *FSI* or other printed media) that a consumer must complete and mail to the manufacturer in order to receive a *promotional offer*. It requires the consumer to use his own envelope and stamp, and usually requires proofs of purchase. *Re-*

demption on mail-in certificates is usually very low, because most consumers find them to be cumbersome.

Malredemption: Illegal collection and submission for payment of manufacturer's *coupons* by unethical persons. The coupons were not used by consumers to purchase product, yet the manufacturer must bear the cost of paying them. Ultimately the consumers suffer because the manufacturer's profitability suffers, thereby resulting in possible price increases or future cost-reducing effects on product quality.

Media Merchandising: A *promotional offer* by a medium, usually offered free of charge to an advertiser as an extra incentive for purchasing space. Common types include a magazine offering a reader contest involving use of the product and free distribution of promotional materials to readers.

Merchandising: The activities directed to making a product available and displayed at retail. Also, promotion of a product by displaying it in a more attractive, desirable, and easier-to-buy situation. This term is commonly used when a product is displayed in a retail outlet in a place or position other than its normal spot, usually next to a complementary product or on a prominent end-aisle or near checkout *display*.

Merge/Purge: The combination of multiple *data base* lists, and elimination of *duplicate* or other undesirable names.

Misredemption: The *redemption* of any *coupon* without a correct corresponding product sale. The consumer may, knowingly or unknowingly, turn in the coupon for a product that is not the one intended in the offer and have this coupon accepted by the checkout clerk. Coupons that have confusing terms are subject to higher levels of misredemption. Differs from *malredemption* because it is less blatantly and purposefully carried out.

Near-Pack Offer: Usually refers to a *premium* available near the product, offered free or at a discount with the purchase of that product. This is a very difficult vehicle to "sell in" to retailers, because of space and handling considerations. On the other hand, if the retailer is convinced that it will greatly increase product sales (and thus, his profitability) he is more likely to accept it.

900 Number: A telephone line set up to receive consumer responses to *promotional offers,* whereby the consumer pays for the call.

On-Pack Offer: An incentive that is found on the product package. This may be a *coupon* or *premium.* The most effective on-pack premiums (for adults) are those that directly relate to the product use. For children, it is more likely that the premium that's the most fun will have the most influence.

Overlay: An added-value aspect to a promotional event, usually a delayed reward offer used in addition to an immediate incentive.

Pantry Loading: A promotion objective in which the consumer is encouraged to buy more of the product than would be purchased under normal circumstances, thus "loading" product into the pantry. To achieve this objective, a high value incentive is offered for a multiple purchase.

Piggyback Strategy: A promotional strategy whereby the trial of the promoted product is linked to the purchase of another product that enjoys high household penetration and good purchase frequency. The promoted or "weaker" product "piggybacks" onto the strength of the carrier product.

Point-of-Sale (POS) Material: Promotional materials located at the place where the consumer makes the product purchase. Items included in this category include: *shelf talkers, displays, tear pads* or *take-ones,* and *header cards.*

Premium: An incentive other than cash that is offered in connection with purchase(s) of the product. It may be offered *in-pack, on-pack, near-pack,* or as a *bounceback.* This type of promotion is viewed as adding value to the product, rather than demoting it. Premiums at the store level are used to encourage brand switching by category users rather than trial by nonusers, since the premium itself is rarely of enough value to encourage a new purchase behavior. Premiums offered as a bounceback are used to encourage more frequency of purchase.

Promotion: Marketing activity designed to encourage the purchase or additional use of a product or service by providing an extra incentive to the target audience. That incentive may be any *promotional offer,* or an attractive display at retail that catches the consumer's attention.

Promotion Allowance: Discount or rebate offered by a manufacturer to a retailer or wholesaler in exchange for product displays, ads, or features.

Promotion Offer: The actual device or incentive that is used to achieve promotion objectives. Types of offers include *couponing, product samples, premiums,* and *refunds.*

Promotion Vehicle: The method by which the promotional offer is delivered to the target audience. Types of vehicles include *FSI*s, direct mail, packaging, *sampling,* etc.

Proof of Purchase: An identifying symbol or receipt that proves that the consumer has purchased the product, usually specified by the manufacturer in the terms of a *promotional offer* as being acceptable. Common proofs include UPC symbols from the package and box tops. For the consumer to receive a promotional offer, proofs of purchase are normally required to be sent along with a mail-in certificate.

ROP (Run of Press): Refers to an ad printed in a newspaper, the placement of which is determined by the newspaper rather than the manufacturer. *Promotional offers* run in newspapers usually have very low *redemption* rates, but they are popular with the trade and are executable with very short lead time.

Rebate: Term used to describe a *refund* given for the purchase of high-ticket items, such as household appliances or automobiles.

Redemption: To turn in *coupons* or to mail in the materials required for *refunds* to receive the benefit of the *promotional offer*.

Redemption Rate: The percentage of total consumers exposed to a *promotional offer* who respond to it or "redeem" it. *Redemption rate* is one tool for measuring the success of a promotional offer. The higher the redemption rate, the more product is moved, and the fixed costs of the promotion (creative and distribution costs) are amortized over a greater number of product sales.

Refund: A monetary reward sent back to consumers who mail in for it, along with the required *proofs of purchase*. Because they do not offer an immediate reward, refunds are generally of a higher value than *coupons*, and are subject to much lower *redemption rates*.

Sales Incentive: A reward offered to the sales force for performance that achieves a goal or exceeds expectations. To create more excitement, a sales contest may be run related to distribution or sales objectives.

Sampling: A trial-oriented consumer *promotional vehicle* that allows the consumer to try the product (offer) for free, either through a demonstration (usually at the point of purchase) or by delivery of an actual packaged sample for use at a later date. Distribution methods for the latter include in stores, at a special event, or via direct mail. This is one of the most expensive promotional techniques and also one of the most effective if targeted properly. A salable sample may be distributed to retailers in a special trial size that can be sold for a small amount of money.

Seeding: With respect to a *sweepstakes*, the act of planting the winning number or symbol in or on certain packages, cards (for mail-in nonpurchasers), or other *promotional vehicles*. Strict security measures should be taken during this process, to ensure that the winning pieces are not diverted.

Self-Destruct Coupon: Two *coupons* designed so that they overlap, whereby cutting out one will render the other one useless. The coupons usually present different values or offers, and consumers can choose the one that most appeals to them.

Self-Liquidating Offer (SLO): A *premium* that is offered to the consumer for a price that covers all manufacturer costs, including purchase of the premium and *fulfillment*. The consumer still gets the item at a discount, while the manufacturer does not have to absorb any costs. *Proofs of purchase* are normally required along with the cash payment from consumers.

Self-Mailer: A *direct mail* piece that is designed so that it can be mailed without an outer envelope.

Sell Sheet: A printed piece distributed to the sales force that provides details of upcoming marketing support, including advertising and promotion. This assists the sales force in making presentations to buyers.

Shelf Talker: A type of *point of sale material,* usually displayed on the shelf near the product it advertises. It is commonly used to communicate a *feature* price or to draw attention to a new product.

Sorry Copy: Written words that instruct the consumer on how to receive the *promotional offer* when supply of the offer device has been exhausted. This is frequently printed on the riser card that contains a *tear pad* or *take-one,* and is visible only after all sheets have been removed.

Stack Card: A posterlike card that is hung near a product *display* that may contain promotional *copy* and product photographs.

Static Cling: A printed piece of point-of-sale material that is made out of plastic and can stick to smooth surfaces without any other adhesives. This is normally used for freezer cases.

Sweepstakes: A *promotion offer* that enables a person to win a prize by chance. Differs from a *contest,* where skill would be involved in the entry. If a marketer runs a sweepstakes offer, there cannot legally be a purchase requirement attached to the consumer's ability to enter. While it is generally easier for the consumer who purchases the product to enter (i.e., mail-in certificate and instructions are found on or in the package), the marketer must provide an alternate means for the consumer to receive instructions and to enter the sweepstakes. The winners of the sweepstakes are determined by a random drawing. Games are considered to be a type of sweepstakes, because they normally do not require a high level of skill. Examples of games are: instant win, collect and win, rub-off, match and win. Sweepstakes generally have good advertising value, as they can create excitement. The promotional success of a sweepstakes really depends on the level of advertising support it receives.

Tear Pad: Pads made up of tear-off sheets most commonly containing either a promotional offer or a recipe. Most *promotional offers* found on tear pads are not immediately redeemable at the checkout and require a mail-in with proofs of purchase to get the item offered. Sometimes called *take-ones.*

Tie-In Promotions: A promotional event in which two or more products or manufacturers provide a joint offering. For a successful tie-in, the products should relate well to each other in the consumer's mind. Tie-ins are a means of stretching promotional dollars, while providing added value for a brand. They are especially effective if one manufacturer believes that he can get a great benefit from reaching another product's consumer base.

Trade Promotions: Promotions used to motivate the trade either to buy or support the marketer's products. The "trade" represents all factions that influence product availability to the ultimate consumers (e.g., retailers, wholesalers, broker reps, the sales force).

Traffic Builder: A promotional event that attracts incremental customers to a retail store.

Turnkey Program: A packaged promotional event that requires little executional effort by the marketer.

PM TOOLS™
PROMOTION

- Creative Guidelines Promotion
- Promotion Planner, Part 1 and Part 2
- Master Promotion Planning Schedule
- Tie-In Worksheet
- Coupon Redemption Tracking Worksheet

CREATIVE
GUIDELINES
PROMOTION

BRAND POSITIONING:

For _____(target audience),
_____ (brand) is the _____
(qualifier, e.g., "only," "first," "leading," etc.)
_____ (category) that_____
_____(benefits).

OBJECTIVES:

_____
_____
_____
_____

STRATEGY:

_____
_____
_____
_____

COMMUNICATION PRIORITIES:

(e.g., taste, usage, value, brand registration, etc.)

1._____
2._____
3._____
4._____
5._____

TONE AND MANNER:

_____
_____
_____
_____

OTHER:

_____
_____
_____
_____

PROMOTION PLANNER PART I

PROJECT DESCRIPTION

OBJECTIVES

BUSINESS
SALES
USAGE
WRITTEN

0 Increase Awareness	0 Increase Consumption	0 Other
0 Increase Trial Purchase	0 Increase Repeat Purchase	0 Other
0 Increase Usage Freq.	0 Increase Usage Applications	0 Other

MEDIA & VEHICLES

ADVERTISING TIE-IN
PROMOTION TIE-IN
PROMOTION VEHICLE(S)

0 TV	0 Print	0 Radio	0 Outdoor	0 Direct Mail	0 Other
0 Coupon	0 Premium	0 Sampling	0 Event	0 Sweepstakes	0 Other
0 FSI	0 In-pack	0 On-pack	0 Near-pack	0 Bonus-pack	0 Mail-in Offers

0 Display   0 Other Point-of-Sale _____   0 Other

SPECIFIC BOOKS,
DAYPARTS, LOCATIONS,
OR OTHER EXECUTIONAL
DETAILS

PROMOTION PLANNER PART 2

TIMING

	0 < 2 mos	0 2 - 4 mos	0 4 - 6 mos	0 6 - 8 mos	0 8 - 10 mos	0 10 - 12 mos	0 > 12 mos
DEVELOPMENT							
EXECUTION	0 QI	0 QII	0 QIII	0 QIV	(year)		
SPECIFIC MONTH(S)							

COVERAGE

SCOPE   0 National   0 Regional   0 Local

IF REGIONAL (check regions)   0 Northeast   0 Mid-Atl   0 Southeast   0 Midwest   0 Mountain   0 Pacific   0 Other ____

BUDGET (fill in all that apply)

TV	$ _____	IN/ON-PACK	$ _____
PRINT	$ _____	SAMPLING/EVENT	$ _____
FSI	$ _____	DISPLAY/POINT-OF-SALE	$ _____
OTHER ____	$ _____	OTHER ____	$ _____

TOTAL BUDGET: $ _____   0 estimated   0 actual

MASTER PROMOTION PLANNING SCHEDULE

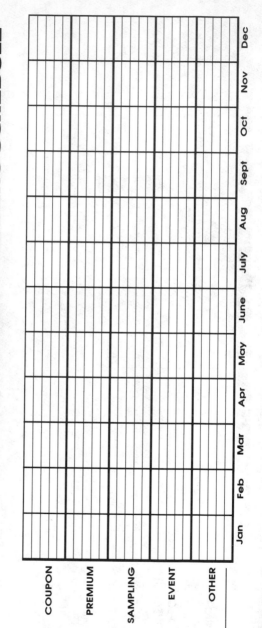

	Jan	Feb	Mar	Apr	May	June	July	Aug	Sept	Oct	Nov	Dec
COUPON												
PREMIUM												
SAMPLING												
EVENT												
OTHER												

TIE-IN WORKSHEET

CATEGORY AND POSITIONING

CATEGORY(S) _____

1st Preference _____
2nd Preference _____

SIC _____
SIC _____

IMAGE   0 Downscale   0 Mainstream   0 Upscale   0 Superpremium

PRICING   0 Economy   0 Mainstream   0 Premium

OTHER POSITIONING INFO _____

CONSUMER TARGET (check appropriate box or box ranges):

CHILDREN

- Sex	0 Male	0 Female			
- Age	0 < 6	0 6 - 9	0 10 - 12		

ADULTS

- Sex	0 Male		0 Female	0 Male	0 Female
- Age	0 19 - 24	0 25 - 34	0 35 - 44	0 45 - 54	0 >54
- Marital Status	0 Single		0 Married		0 Separated/Divorced
- Children in Household	0 0	0 1	0 2	0 3	0 4 0 5 0 > 5
- Household Income	0 < 30 K	0 30 - 40 K	0 41 - 50 K	0 51 - 60 K	0 61 - 70 K 0 71 - 80 K 0 > 80 K
- Education (highest)	0 < High School		0 High School		0 College 0 ≥Graduate 0 Other
- Professional Status	0 Blue Collar		0 White Collar		0 Homemaker 0 Other
- Environment	0 Urban		0 Suburban		0 Rural

TEENS

0 Male	0 Female	0 Female	
0 13 - 14	0 15 - 16	0 17 - 18	

Other Target Info. _____

DISTRIBUTION

COVERAGE   0 National   0 Regional (specify) _____   0 Local (specify) _____

PARTNER ACV LEVELS _____

COUPON REDEMPTION TRACKING WORKSHEET

	Value	Timing	Vehicle	Markets	Creative	Redemption
MARKETS:						
National	$ ____	____	_____	N A B C	P M G E	____ %
Market A ____	$ ____	____	_____	N A B C	P M G E	____ %
Market B ____	$ ____	____	_____	N A B C	P M G E	____ %
Market C ____	$ ____	____	_____	N A B C	P M G E	____ %
	$ ____	____	_____	N A B C	P M G E	____ %
	$ ____	____	_____	N A B C	P M G E	____ %
CREATIVE:	$ ____	____	_____	N A B C	P M G E	____ %
Poor - P	$ ____	____	_____	N A B C	P M G E	____ %
Mediocre - M	$ ____	____	_____	N A B C	P M G E	____ %
Good - G	$ ____	____	_____	N A B C	P M G E	____ %
Excellent - E	$ ____	____	_____	N A B C	P M G E	____ %
	$ ____	____	_____	N A B C	P M G E	____ %
	$ ____	____	_____	N A B C	P M G E	____ %

NINE

TOP-LINE

OVERVIEW

Public relations is the organizational function that seeks to create and maintain a positive image and an ongoing two-way relationship between the organization and those who are in any way affected by the organization's practices. Depending upon the issue, the public relations (PR) function will determine which public segment to target with positive communication, with the objectives of gaining attention, winning goodwill and approval, and receiving positive *endorsements*. One of the advantages PR has over advertising and promotion is the use of free media publicity.

When it comes to marketing, public relations is among the most invisible functions within a company. By its nature, PR must not appear to be self-serving, and thus must stay away from "the hard sell." Consequently, the function often does not get the "glory" that other marketing functions enjoy when their programs work well. In fact, many marketing managers do not know what public relations can do for their products; they budget little for it and do not take the time to learn about it and use it properly. PR is viewed as being one of the least "measurable" functions in the marketing mix—but this does not have to be so, as you will see later in this chapter.

While most marketing programs target the ultimate consumer, public relations programs can effectively target those "experts" who can have a tremendous influence on the ultimate consumers (food connoisseurs, physicians, cause related organizations, community leaders, and the like). And, of course, public relations tries to find ways to utilize the news media in order to obtain favorable references to the product or the corporation.

As an element of marketing, public relations is really a combination of *publicity* and *promotion.* It is concerned with communication, creativity, and ethics. It must be a strategic process in line with marketing objectives. The communication is normally highly targeted, so the message must be carefully designed. In marketing a specific product or service, the news or the message that is communicated by the PR function can pertain to the product directly or create goodwill around the product so that consumer awareness and attitudes will be positively affected.

Publicity is an informational aspect of public relations. In a new product introduction, it seeks to give information about the product's unique benefits—and that may be newsworthy in and of itself; or it may seek to relate the introduction to another concern or an event that will attract attention. With a mature product, PR may work with promotion to create news or excitement.

The PR function may be called upon to write and send *press releases,* design informational *brochures* and disseminate them to the target audience, choose and hire a credible *spokesperson,* or research other causes and/or organizations that may form positive relationships with the product or service offering.

Public relations as a function tends to receive high levels of recognition during periods of crisis management, such as the Tylenol tampering incident and the Exxon oil spill. No doubt crisis management is an essential part of PR; however, it is important to note that public relations should be a *continuous* process within an organization and should not merely exist to react when problems arise. If a company has always presented itself in a positive light, with honesty and integrity, and has always had an open relationship with the media, the ability to rise above a crisis situation is greatly enhanced.

A final important note: While the steps in the planning process described here apply to the function of public relations in general, the examples cited concentrate on only one subset of public relations—that which is concerned with marketing a product or service. Public relations is a much greater force and has a much greater role in organizations than just to assist in achievement of marketing objectives. There are many excellent books on the subject for those who wish to learn about the "big picture," such as those that are in the reference list at the end of this book.

THE PUBLIC RELATIONS PLAN

As with advertising and promotion, the public relations planning process begins with a competitive rackup and a "lessons learned" summary. Competitive information is available from old newspapers, trade articles, television broadcasts, etc. Many companies utilize clipping services—services that exist to collect all published information on any subject and sell it to interested parties. A summary of lessons learned should include analysis of how effective past efforts were. Recommendations can then be made for repetition, deletion, or improvements to previous events. When the PR plan deals with a product introduction or revitalization, the plan arises from a marketing objective, and public relations is assigned a strategic role. After all of this is articulated, the public relations plan follows these steps:

1. Define the problem at hand and set *objectives*.
2. Conduct *research* to obtain insights into the public segment(s) that the organization wishes to influence.
3. Develop public relations *strategies* or an action plan to achieve the objective.
4. Develop public relations *tactics* to bring strategies to life, and execute.
5. Evaluate the *effectiveness* of the programs and make further recommendations if applicable.

PUBLIC RELATIONS
OBJECTIVES

As in any other type of planning, the public relations objectives should be as specific as possible, and measurable. The planning process starts with an understanding of current public perceptions of the organization or of a specific business within the organization. It feeds off of the marketing plan and uses marketing objectives as the guideline for setting public relations objectives.

Definition of the problem at hand is the first step. "Problem" as described here is not necessarily a problematic situation; it is simply the marketing situation that public relations will play a role in addressing. Examples of marketing problems are a new product introduction or stemming a decline in a mature product. An analysis of how public relations can play a part in the successful achievement of marketing goals is dependent on the knowledge of the product, its target audience, and its benefits. There may or may not be existing negative perceptions that must be overcome. If there are, the job of public relations will be more difficult and involved, so it will be expected to play an even greater role.

The public relations objectives should include: (1) the *target audience;* (2) the *time period* of the desired action; and (3) the *desired outcome* of your actions. An example of a public relations objective for the successful introduction of a new isotonic sports beverage called PowerSips could be:

> *During the key introductory period of April through June, generate awareness and positive perceptions of PowerSips among 25 percent of the sports beverage consumers.*

This may be done by targeting influencers, such as major outdoor sports personalities, to gain positive endorsements. These endorsements could then be published in media that are pertinent to the target end-users. PowerSips could sponsor sporting events in exchange for signage and other exposure. All of this will be part of the strategic action plan, described later. The point is, the objective is the basis from which the research will be done, and the strategies written.

A critical factor in setting objectives is the budget. The public relations practitioner must act as an advisor to marketing management as to what the budget allotted to a PR program can be expected to achieve. Realistic objectives should be set accordingly.

Timing is also an important factor. Generally, if public relations is expected to change existing negative perceptions, a longer campaign will be necessary. Negative attitudes develop very quickly and, once they are present, are changed very slowly. On the other hand, a new product introduction may narrow the time frame of the campaign to a short period directly preceding and during the introduction.

PUBLIC RELATIONS RESEARCH

Public relations research involves defining and obtaining key insights into the target audience, and an analysis of pertinent environmental or other external trends or situations that may affect the nature of the communication. Well-conducted research will result in optimal use of dollars.

In public relations, identification of the target audience is twofold: one is the target audience that the marketing plan has identified as the consumer, and the other is the target audience that is in a position to influence those consumers' opinions. As in advertising, the audience chosen as the target of the public relations effort will determine the methods and the media used to reach it effectively.

One goal of conducting research is to determine the true opinions and attitudes of the target group(s), in order to identify potential "trouble spots," and to tailor and deliver the message in the best possible way to reach these groups. A second goal is to determine and examine other underlying forces that will affect perceptions about the product. Research will reveal the facts and will thus lend credibility to a public relations plan.

The types of research that may be applied to the study of both the environmental trends and the target group(s) include: reference books, news stories, existing consumer response data (letters and phone calls that a company has received from consumers regarding similar products), existing surveys done by other professional or trade organizations, and informal personal contacts. More formal research methods involve the use of scientific sampling methods, in which the sampling is set up specifically for the problem at hand. In this method, a representative sample is selected and questioned by mail, by telephone, or through personal interviews.

PUBLIC RELATIONS STRATEGIES

At this stage, the objectives have been written and research has been done. Now the strategies for execution of the objectives will be chosen and the tactical elements defined. What the message will be, and how, when, and to whom the message will be communicated will be outlined in the action plan. A set of communication guidelines should be written for each project, including objective, strategy, key communication priorities, and tone and manner of the communication.

Now that the target group or groups have been defined, the message must be tailored in a way that will appeal to their motivations—or to their self-interest. It must be delivered in the right vehicles and at the right time. For example, if an organization is launching a delicious new nonfat dessert next month (to coincide with the onset of the summer season), one public relations strategy might be:

> *Utilize press party for food editors of women's service magazines to preview the product directly prior to the launch and the big summer dieting issue.*

A gala luncheon was planned for food editors of women's service magazines, and the dessert served. The editors were told (in a creative way) after the dessert was eaten that there was no fat in it. Of course, previous research has shown that a representative sample of food connoisseurs had liked the dessert.

In the above fictional example, the targeted group was food editors. The message was that this great new dessert delivers all the taste and none of the fat. It was done using a gala luncheon, where no expense was spared. It was done one month before the product launch, so that the timing would be right for the following month's magazine insertions. The media selected were women's service magazines, which attract large numbers of the ultimate target audience, which is women aged thirty-five and over. The PR practitioner knew that all of the magazines would be focusing on ways to slim and trim down in a future issue. The practitioner also knew, through research, that negative attitudes and suspicion exist among consumers regarding nonfat desserts, because there have been several recent entries into the market that fell short in delivering good taste. Therefore, it was elected to wait until the lunch was over to reveal that this was a nonfat dessert. The message tied in with the advertising theme: "If we didn't tell you, you wouldn't know the difference."

Other strategies for the launch of the dessert might be to send literature to or to have parties at health clubs and diet centers, and to send press releases and samples to health and diet-oriented publications. The cartoon character *Cathy* could be licensed as a "spokesperson" for the new nonfat dessert, and the press releases might include special comic strips created for the launch.

PUBLIC RELATIONS TACTICS

PR tactics are the actual *communications* of the PR strategies. Communication involves the formation of the message with the intent to inform or persuade members of a particular target group and the dissemination of that message through the proper media. Primary to effective communications, then, is a thorough understanding of the target group and what motivates it.

We use the term "communication" interchangeably with *execution,* because execution of the PR program always involves some form of communication. Execution of the public relations plan involves the following steps:

- Developing, writing, and gaining approval of communication guidelines.
- Creating a schedule.
- Deciding on the tactical vehicle for communicating the message.
- Briefing chosen spokesperson on company position, manner of delivery, and any other pertinent facts.
- Planning any events, parties, or news conferences, sending out invitations well in advance.
- Preparing and sending out any written communication, such as press releases.

A written set of communication guidelines will provide everyone involved in the process and execution with clear focus and priorities. Included in the guidelines should be objective, strategy, tactical description, key communication priorities, tone and manner of the communication, and a timetable. See chapter 8, Promotion, for more detailed information.

Depending on the program desired, the basic steps may be added to or altered. The vehicles chosen to deliver the message to the target audience will depend on the strategy, the budget, and the target audience. Many tactical vehicles are available to the marketer, including, but not limited to, the following:

1. **PRESS RELEASE**: Ready-to-use communication disseminated by an organization to the news media. It is important to write communication guidelines *before* communication is written and disseminated, because press releases are often "shortened" by the *gatekeepers* not always by content importance, but by the position in the release. Points at the end of the release will have a disadvantage. Therefore, priority copy points should always come first in the order of the communication.

   Getting press releases published is not an easy task. Available "white space" is limited, and you are in competition for this space with every other press release issued for every publication. You can help unlock some of the doors by: (1) keeping the release short and to the point, as a journalist would, because no one wants to sift through paragraph after paragraph to edit and rewrite; (2) making it "newsy" and interesting at the same time; and (3) timing it correctly so that there is time enough before deadline to permit it to be read.

2. **FEATURE ARTICLE**: A story that contains background and other points of interest that enlarge upon the main topic or subject matter.

3. **BROCHURE**: A printed piece made up of six or more pages, authored by an organization to describe a product or event in detail to the target groups.

4. **FACT SHEET**: An informational communication containing essential facts about an event or product or service, usually disseminated to the media.

5. **NEWSLETTER**: An internally produced periodical communication designed to inform key members of a target audience, usually containing

news and feature stories that improve perceptions of the product or business.

6. **PRESS CONFERENCES**: A gathering of the press, called by an individual or a spokesperson for an organization, to provide information and to allow for questions about a particular event or subject.

7. **PARTIES**: A gathering utilized to assemble important members of the target audience (usually credible influencers) in an attempt to gain positive press or word-of-mouth communication with the ultimate target audience.

8. **PUBLICITY STUNT**: An unusual event or other dramatic communication designed specifically to gain the attention of the news media.

9. **EVENT SPONSORSHIPS**: Participation in and funding by a compa.ny or product of specific events that are important to the target audience. The objective is to gain goodwill and positive press.

10. **INTERVIEW**: Personal communication by a key member of the organization (usually an experienced company spokesperson) with the press.

11. **SLIDES AND PHOTOGRAPHS**: Usually included with press releases, e.g., product shots, logos.

12. **WORD OF MOUTH**: Form of advertising or publicity whereby information is disseminated from one person to another, without the media. This type of publicity can be most effective or most detrimental, because of higher levels of source credibility.

The credibility of the source of the information is key to the target group's acceptance of the message as the truth. The news media are viewed as being extremely credible because they presumably report on the facts and are not paid for any endorsements. The use of authoritative spokespeople to communicate the message is also a means for gaining credibility.

Another key factor for effective communication is the past history of the organization that is disseminating the message. This is why it is important that organizations maintain a continuous stream of positive public relations. Major corporations (with some exceptions) are generally viewed as being highly credible because they have devoted much time and many resources to effective public relations.

In formulating the communication, the message should be clear, understandable, and devoid of technical or other complicated jargon that is familiar to no one but those in the particular organization or field. Finally, PR practitioners should recognize that diversity exists among potential target groups and should research the appropriate ways to tailor the messages.

When the public relations activity pertains to marketing, the PR practitioner must take care that the communication is in line with the messages that other marketing functions are disseminating. Public relations practitioners should make use of brand identity to the greatest extent possible, including brand name, logo, or other equities and trademarks. All communication guidelines, programs, and printed materials should be reviewed by the marketing manager to obtain optimal synergies.

CRISIS MANAGEMENT

The public relations function of an organization is perhaps at its highest level of visibility during *crisis management*. A disaster involving deaths, accidents, or an environmental crisis will put an organization at the top of the news, whether or not it is directly responsible for the disaster. The way that the organization involved in a crisis chooses to respond publicly, and the extent to which it is prepared to respond, can make all the difference in the world in terms of loss of sales and loss of public trust.

A case in point is the impeccable way that Johnson & Johnson handled the Tylenol cyanide deaths. Experts warned that the incident would mean the end of the Tylenol brand name. But Johnson & Johnson acted without hesitation to pull all of the product off the shelves until the investigation was complete. It maintained a policy of openness and cooperation with the press and with government investigators. The result was that although Tylenol lost a significant amount of brand share during the crisis, the brand rebounded and recaptured 32 percent of the original 37 percent share that it had held before the incident.[1]

---

[1] Wilcox, Dennis L., Ault, Phillip H., and Agee, Warren K., *Public Relations: Strategies and Tactics*, Harper & Row, New York, 2nd ed, 1989, p. 350.

PR EFFECTIVENESS AND TRACKING

Tracking the success or failure of PR executions is critical to building long-term communications with your target audience, as well as understanding the messages' viability and delivery. This evaluation becomes part of the "lessons learned" summary that is utilized for the following year's planning process. Evaluation of the public relations programs relates directly to the stated objective(s). It is not an easy task with respect to marketing because the PR objectives are usually similar to the advertising objectives, albeit on a smaller scale. How can we know how much more one contributed to the achievement of the objective than the other, especially if both forms of communication are occurring simultaneously? Yet, it is important to management to know whether the cost of any program has been justified.

A standard set of evaluator questions can be developed, to which customized questions can be added according to program specifics. The standard set would include:

1. Was the quantity of media exposures acceptable?
2. Did the message effectively reach your target consumers?
3. Was the message communicated clearly and understood by your target consumers?
4. Did your message have the desired impact on your target audience?

Quantity can be measured by counting press mentions and feature articles. A clipping service might be used to do this. However, this is not always indicative of the productivity of the public relations practitioner because the media act as gatekeepers, deciding what is newsworthy. Another method for measuring productivity considers the total quantity of information disseminated by the PR practitioner, regardless of whether the information was published in the media.

Quantity should be used as only one of several evaluatory measures. One well-written and well-placed news release is more valuable than twenty that do not get published.

Alongside quantity is the measurement of exposures to the target audience achieved. The cost of the program needs to be justified according to the cost per targeted individual reached. With this formula, utilization of targeted media becomes more efficient than utilization of broad reach vehicles. One feature article placed in a highly targeted magazine might be worth more than ten mentions in general newspapers because it reaches relatively higher numbers of the target audience.

Whether the message was communicated clearly and fulfilled the communication objectives of the PR practitioner can be measured by analysis of the published materials for inclusion of key communication points previously stated in the communication guidelines section of the action plan. Existing computer analysis methods can measure in percentages the appearance of each of the key copy points.

Audience awareness and understanding of the message can be ascertained through surveys. The audience can be asked via telephone or mail survey or focus groups whether they associate a particular message with a particular product, much as is done in recall testing in advertising. Measurement of audience awareness and understanding will help to evaluate whether or not the message was written and disseminated effectively.

The last measurement technique is to evaluate how the audience that received and understood the message was affected by it. The key here is that the marketer wants to see positive attitude *changes* as a result of the communication.

The main technique used to measure attitudinal change is called the **benchmark study,** which surveys target group(s) before and after a public relations campaign. The percentage of attitude change is then recorded.

Effective evaluation depends on setting reasonable objectives in terms of the role public relations will be expected to play with the budget allocated. Also, the achievement of these objectives should be able to tie back to the PR campaign specifically and be isolated from other elements in the marketing mix. Marketing research co-workers might be able to make this task a little easier.

FINAL WORDS

As we mentioned earlier, public relations is probably the most underutilized tool in the marketing mix. This is partly a result of the limited understanding among marketers about what public relations can contribute to the marketing of a product or service, and partly a result of the perception that it does not make a *measurable* difference in the fulfillment of marketing objectives.

Publicity is public relations's informational arm. It can help to sell products or services by informing the pertinent target group(s) about innovations or recent news about a mature product. It can do this with a high degree of credibility through selected media and programming, which the audience deems to have no bias. It can target groups that have a great deal of influence on the ultimate consumers. If it is done correctly, it can be as effective as advertising, and cost less.

New product innovations can create big news. PR seeks to build this excitement to its maximum potential. We will see this in action later, when we outline the role of public relations in the introduction of SunSplash. PR can also help to reposition or revitalize a mature product by hyping an anniversary, communicating a newer, contemporary usage, or creating events that capitalize on nostalgia. It can work in conjunction with advertising and promotion by creating media excitement or "news" about an upcoming event or campaign, and by supporting the message that is disseminated by the other functions. It can be an extremely powerful tool in helping to sell a product.

PUBLIC RELATIONS GLOSSARY

Advance: Printed information or story distributed before the event.

Agenda-Setter: A term usually used to describe those who choose, write, and report the news, because they determine what the content and tone of the pieces they report on will be.

Annual Report: A corporate information document distributed to employees and stockholders to inform them on the "state of the company." This document must be filed each year with the Securities and Exchange Commission.

Benchmark Study: A research technique that evaluates the target group's attitudes about the subject of the public relations campaign, both before and after the campaign.

Bio: Abbreviation for the detailed biography a PR practitioner prepares for a client, usually for release to the media.

Blurb: A short published or reported mention of the subject of the PR communication.

Booker: A person who places clients into forums that give them public exposure, such as talk shows.

Boomerang Effect: Term describing a phenomenon that occurs when an individual or group reacts to the message in a way that is opposite from the communicator's intention.

Brochure: A printed piece made up of six or more pages. Authored by an organization to describe a product or event in detail to the target groups.

Cheesecake: Photos that capture attention through the display of feminine "sex appeal" visuals.

Circular: A single printed sheet distributed by hand or mail; usually used to announce an event or to champion a cause.

Clipping Service: A service that clips and sends to companies published materials (articles, advertisements, etc.) that mention or pertain to a specific subject. Utilized by organizations to keep tabs on what is published about themselves or their competitors, and as a method of evaluating the effectiveness of a public relations campaign.

Clipsheet: A preprinted sheet of stories and pictures sent to publishers so that they can clip the ones that they wish to use. Has the advantage of allowing publishers to see the printed length and format of the stories, and increases the chance that the information will be published "as is" from the source.

Communication Audit: A study with the objective of determining which public relations communications are reaching the target audience, and also to reveal what else the group desires to know about the subject.

Conservation: The practice of supporting a public's current opinion and working to reinforce it so that it doesn't change.

Conversion: Communication aimed at swaying a public's opinion from one side of an issue to another.

Corporate Advertising: Paid communication that is done to enhance the image of a corporation. It is usually not specific to a particular product or service that the corporation offers—the message is more institutional in content.

Courtesy Bias: Tendency of survey respondents to give the answer that they believe the interviewer wants to hear, or the "correct" answer, rather than saying what they truly feel.

Crisis Management: Term that refers to the way an organization will respond to the public in an emergency situation. The way such a situation is handled will make a great deal of difference in the ability of the organization to recover from the crisis.

Dateline: The first line of a story which states the date and place of origin.

Endorsement: The publicly communicated positive opinion of a respected or well-liked figure, usually solicited by a public relations practitioner. The person chosen to deliver the endorsement is usually an opinion leader on the subject.

External Publication: A communication an organization releases to an audience outside of the organization itself.

Fact Sheet: An informational communication containing essential facts about an event or product or service, usually disseminated to the media.

Feature Story: A story that contains background and other points of interest that enlarge upon the main topic or subject matter.

Filler: A story (usually short) that is added to a publication or broadcast more to "fill up" space rather than based on its merits.

Flack: A derogatory term describing a press agent in the entertainment business.

Free-Loading: The acceptance of gifts or entertainment by those in a position to communicate to the target group, presumably in exchange for a favorable report.

Gatekeeper: A person who weeds through organizational communication to determine what will be reported and how it will be reported. This is usually a news editor, writer, or a reporter.

Hotline: A toll free telephone line set up by an organization to respond quickly to a situation. This is often arranged in times of crisis management so that the news media can have quick access to the organization spokespeople.

Internal Publication: Communication directed to employees or other members of the organization.

Issues Management: Term that describes the control exercised by an organization through identifying and responding to issues that are of concern to the public(s) that the organization serves.

Junket: A trip arranged for members of the press by the organization seeking publicity, usually to bring the press to the site of the newsmaking event.

Literary Agent: Person who represents an author in dealings with a publisher.

Lobbyist: Representative who presents an organization's point of view to members of Congress or other government agencies.

Message Entropy: The breakdown or dissipation of the original message as it goes through the communication channels.

Muckrakers: Term originating in the early 1900s, referring to writers who publicly exposed misconduct by industry and government. This group contributed greatly to consumer and employee awareness of wrongdoing and started many movements for change.

News Release: Also called *press release*. Ready-to-use communication disseminated by an organization to the news media.

Off-the-Record: Information given to a news reporter that is not intended for publication. Journalistic code of ethics prevents the printing of material when it is made clear by the source that it is "off-the-record." The purpose of disseminating this information may be to provide a lead or a direction for the reporter to follow without getting the source involved.

Opinion Leader: Person in a respected or authoritative position whose stated opinions will influence members of particular target group(s).

Pilot Test: Pretesting of a public relations message on a small segment of the target audience before general release, to gauge reactions.

Press Agent: Person whose job is to publicize certain individuals.

Press Conference: A gathering of the press, called by an individual or a spokesperson for an organization, to provide information and to allow for questions about a particular event or subject.

Press Kit: A file distributed to members of the media that usually contains news releases, photographs, and background information on a particular subject.

Press Release: A printed statement or other material that is distributed to the press for publication, constructed in the language that the author wishes to convey. Also called a *news release*.

Promotion: In public relations, a special event or activity that is designed to create interest around a product or an organization.

Public(s): Audience segments that an organization seeks to inform or influence with its communication.

Publicity: Information about a particular event or interest of an organization, disseminated by way of a carefully selected "newsy" message or information to the media, without payment to the media. The media decides the "news worthiness" of the message and frequently eliminates it or edits it to suit its needs.

Publicity Stunt: An event or other dramatic communication designed specifically to gain the attention of the news media.

Public Relations: The organizational function that seeks to create and maintain a positive image and relationship between the organization and those who are in any way affected by the organization's practices.

Puffery: Unsubstantiated copy or information designed to "romanticize" a product or to put a product into a favorable light.

Sidebar: A secondary story placed near the main story to discuss a side issue, sometimes appearing inside a box within the larger story.

Slick: Coated paper containing reproducible line art or copy—usually used for brand logos.

Social Contract: Term used to describe an organization's obligation to the public.

Source Credibility: The level of acceptance of a representative by the target public based upon sincerity and perceived expertise.

Split Message: Communication of two or three different messages to separate audiences to determine which is most effective.

Spokesperson: A chosen or self-elected person who speaks for the cause or organization.

Talk Show: TV or radio program where the guest has an opportunity to champion his cause or showcase talent.

Trade Journal: Magazine targeted to a particular industrial or professional group.

Word-of-Mouth: Form of advertising or *publicity* whereby information is disseminated from one person to another, without using the media. This type of publicity can be most effective or most detrimental because of unusually high levels of source credibility.

PM TOOLS™
PUBLIC
RELATIONS

- Creative Guidelines Public Relations
- Public Relations Checklist

CREATIVE
GUIDELINES
PUBLIC RELATIONS

BRAND POSITIONING:
For _____(target audience),
_____ (brand) is the_____
(qualifier, e.g., "only," "first," "leading," etc.)
_____ (category) that_____
_____(benefits).

OBJECTIVES:
_____
_____
_____
_____

STRATEGY:
_____
_____
_____
_____

COMMUNICATION PRIORITIES:
(e.g., taste, usage, value, brand registration, etc.)
1._____
2._____
3._____
4._____
5._____

TONE AND MANNER:
_____
_____
_____
_____

OTHER:
_____
_____
_____
_____

PUBLIC RELATIONS CHECKLIST

☐ **PRESS RELEASE** _____

☐ **FEATURE ARTICLE** _____

☐ **BROCHURE** _____

☐ **FACT SHEET** _____

☐ **NEWSLETTER** _____

☐ **PRESS CONFERENCE** _____

☐ **PARTY** _____

☐ **PUBLICITY STUNT** _____

☐ **EVENT SPONSORSHIP** _____

☐ **INTERVIEW** _____

☐ **SLIDES / PHOTOGRAPHY** _____

☐ **WORD-OF-MOUTH** _____

TEN

MARKETING PLAN FOR

SolarTech

SunSplash!

This fictional marketing plan was written to illustrate the principles and practices presented in each of the chapters of THE POCKET MARKETER. *It is intended to give you a sample of what actually can go into a formalized marketing plan and should be used for directional purposes only.*

Because of the enormity and variety of information that can be included in a real marketing plan, we have purposely left out areas that were beyond the scope of meeting the stated goal, such as budgeting analyses and details, protracted discussions in the functional plans, and supporting research data appendices. The format that we present here is abridged; and because we have taken certain creative liberties, you may find minor inconsis-tencies or exaggerations in content.

This case is a work of fiction, although it is based on a real industry and the parallel reality of the manner and shape in which the industry functions. However, any of the people, places, situations, and companies referred to or depicted in this plan are entirely the product of the authors' imaginations. Any resemblance to actual events, locales, or persons, living or dead, is entirely coincidental.

SolarTech

THE CASE

INTRODUCTION

Courses in business schools often make use of case studies—actual or mock histories of problems in marketing. As an experiential learning exercise through role play, students are asked to examine cases and come up with what they believe to be the best solutions. We fully support utilization of the case method and now present the basic case of a single fictional company and product. We have constructed an actual marketing plan to enable you to see the principles outlined in THE POCKET MARKETER come to life.

The name of our fictitious company is SolarTech, a market leader in the suncare products industry. SolarTech's challenge is to launch a new product called SunSplash, the extension of a business plan conceived and written by one of the authors at the Wharton School of Business. But before we get into the scenario, let's learn a little bit about the SolarTech company itself.

SolarTech
SUNCARE PRODUCTS

The SolarTech Suncare Products company is a leading manufacturer of one of the most popular brand names in suncare in the United States today, employing over an 18 percent share of the fragmented $520 MM suncare market. It is a ten-year-old privately held company that produces a full line of suncare products (including suntan lotions, oils, balms, and sprays) in two domestic manufacturing plants, and licenses its name to various sunglasses, apparel, and linen manufacturers.

SolarTech is distributed by food store and drug store brokers to thousands of accounts across the United States, Caribbean, and some parts of Western Europe, and is supported by national and local advertising and promotion campaigns, and public relations.

SolarTech products are generally positioned as upscale, premium-priced, and technologically advanced. However, SolarTech products are purchased by consumers across a wide demographic range and have appeal aspirationally to lower-income brackets as well, despite their high price tags. Consumers view the image positioning of SolarTech as "high end" or "upscale" on a scale from 1 ("downscale") to 5 ("upscale").

These ratings were based on the composite rating of a group of attributes that consumers claimed made up "image," including packaging, price, name and logo, spokespersons, advertising, and others.

SolarTech had its humble beginnings in the back room of the New Wave surf shop in Malibu. The shop was owned and run by Ron Sperry, a local surfing hero on the West Coast and Hawaiian circuit, presently the director of promotions for SolarTech. The year was 1981, and Ron spent much time with two of his surfing buddies, Hershal Crain and John Terrance Langley, who were graduate students in chemistry at the local university.

Crain and Langley were experimenting with sunblocking formulations in order to come up with a greaseless suntan lotion especially for surfers that could be used both on their bodies and their surfboards to protect the colors from fading in the sun.

The three threw in together, and John Langley financed the start-up venture with his trust fund to produce a line of suntan lotions called Body n' Board for surfers and their equipment. What began as a crazy notion and interesting diversion for the young scientists turned out to have an uncanny appeal among the dudes and dudettes of the LA coastline, and a small fad began in June of 1982.

Not until 1986, however, did SolarTech begin its climb to success and go national with the introduction of a technologically superior sunscreen called Ultra-Screen, developed by Crain and Langley at their new research lab in Long Beach.

During this period of increased public awareness of sun poisoning, skin damage, and skin cancer, most of the suncare products were offering SPFs (sun protection factors) at 6 and higher. An SPF of 2 meant that the sunscreen let you stay in the sun twice as long as nothing at all; 6, six times as long, etc. In fact, by 1989, over 50 percent of the lotions on the shelf were SPF 6 or above. However, although high-SPF sunscreens were desired by consumers because of their protective properties, they had a major consumer drawback—that is, one had to stay in the sun many times longer to get the same tan they used to get with lotions that contained no sunscreen or sunscreens with low SPFs.

UltraScreen was a breakthrough—a unique new formulation which protected the skin against harmful UVB rays and long-term damage from the sun but allowed sun worshippers to tan much more quickly. A lotion with UltraScreen with a SPF of 6 (six times the protection of skin alone) would allow people to tan three times faster, or as if they were wearing a lotion with an SPF of only 2.

SolarTech was in the unique position to offer suntanning products at higher SPFs with its UltraScreen formula, which protected consumers against burning, as did the higher SPF products on the market, but allowed consumers to tan as fast as the lower SPFs. SolarTech's advertising slogan—"Tanner. Quicker. Safer."—registered very high recall scores. Since 1986, SolarTech has grown while other small players lost share or folded altogether in the crowded suncare market.

Over the years, however, competitors had managed to circumvent SolarTech's technology patent, and other products making similar claims to SolarTech's "Tanner. Quicker. Safer." slogan had become available. When everyone incorporated the technology into their products, the original benefit no longer distinguished UltraScreen from its competitors, and it was almost a tie ballgame again. SolarTech still had the edge that being first out with an innovation brings. Nonetheless, SolarTech has been looking for new ways to innovate its lines and reestablish its reputation in the industry as the technological leader that people count on for innovations in the suncare category.

THE
Sun Splash!
OPPORTUNITY

Traci Harlow, product manager for bottled lotions at SolarTech, was reviewing the volume tracking reports of SolarTech's three-ounce portable lotion pack one June morning when she noticed something very interesting. The newly repackaged three-ounce lotion now exhibited a major bump in sales volume (plus 70.4 percent as compared with the same quarter a year ago). The new package was a medallion-shaped plastic container hung on a neon string to be worn around the neck. "Hmmm," Traci thought, "perhaps there is more to the idea of 'portable' lotion or sunscreen than meets the eye."

That afternoon, Traci visited the office of President John Langley to discuss her findings. Traci felt that when an already successful brand grows that fast and that much in a crowded market, the effect might be just the tip of the iceberg. It appeared that the portable sunscreen sourced most of its volume by category expansion, not by cannibalization of other SolarTech products. John Langley gave his blessing for Traci to investigate the overall concept of "portable" sunscreen—its market potential as a core concept and how SolarTech could best take advantage of such potential if it existed. So, having scarcely researched or tested the three-ounce medallion idea, she set out to learn everything she could about the phenomenon to see if she could understand it, quantify it, and translate it into a new product if the opportunity existed.

BUSINESS OBJECTIVES

- To grow sales by at least 60 percent and ROS from 8 percent to 17 percent incrementally over the next three years.
- To reestablish the company's position as technology leader and innovator both with consumers and within the industry.

BUSINESS MARKETING STRATEGY

- To introduce innovative, new high-margin products that will expand the suncare category and command positive attention in the industry.

PROJECT MARKETING OBJECTIVE

- To develop and launch a new breakthrough line of suncare products to recreational (primary) and protection-only (secondary) suncare products users, that
  1. Delivers key benefits of portability, disposability, and easy, clean application;
  2. Expands the suncare category by at least 2 percent; and
  3. Achieves a 2.7 percent market dollar share, and generates gross sales of at least $14.5 MM and net margins of at least 12 percent, in the first year.

I. PREMISE

The concept of "portable sunscreen" has a high utility with consumers and is a need that has not been fully met and should be capitalized upon. We have found that this concept is a strong enough platform upon which to build a new line of suncare products.

The basis for this premise was the recent performance of our three-ounce Waterproof Lotion. Sales of the three-ounce have been flat for the past three years; however, the release of the new "neck hanger" package with string in April yielded volume increases far beyond expectations and normal precedent. June quarter reports showed a plus 70 percent bump in volume, as compared with the same quarter a year ago.

This success was found to have been derived almost exclusively from the repackaging of the product, built around the concept of "portability." We will take this opportunity in the marketplace much further with the introduction of a line of portable sunscreen products—*SunSplash*.

II. SITUATIONAL ANALYSIS

BUSINESS OBJECTIVES AND STRATEGIES

SolarTech business objectives, from the three year operating plan, are as follows:

1. **MISSION STATEMENT**: To become the world's leading technological and product innovation company in the suncare category, and to achieve and maintain at least a number three ranking in the United States and number five worldwide.

2. **LONG- and SHORT-TERM OBJECTIVES**:

   (A) To grow sales by at least 60 percent (from $115 MM to $185 MM) incrementally over the next three years;

   (B) To grow net profitability from 8 percent of sales to 17 percent of sales incrementally over the next three years. Growth objectives by year (YA refers to "Year Ago"):

   - <u>YEAR 1:</u>
     $140 MM sales (+21.7% vs. YA)
     12% ROS (+50% vs. YA)
   - <u>YEAR 2:</u>
     $165 MM sales (+17.9% vs. YA)
     15% ROS (+25% vs. YA)
   - <u>YEAR 3:</u>
     $185 MM sales (+12.0% vs. YA)
     17% ROS (+13% vs. YA)

   (C) To reestablish the company's position as technology leader and innovator both with consumers and within the industry.

Based on business objectives, overall strategies in each functional business domain for year one include:

1. **R&D**: To optimize research and development capabilities and resources.
2. **FINANCE**: To optimize financial systems and capital resource management.

3. **MANUFACTURING**: To reduce cost at the plant, and to gain efficiencies in sourcing and purchasing materials.
4. **OPERATIONS**: To reduce physical overhead expense.
5. **MARKETING**:
   - To introduce innovative, high-margin products that will expand the suncare category and command positive attention in the industry.
   - To support core products and make spending more efficient and tied to the bottom line.
   - To strengthen distribution of current core products domestically and expand distribution in foreign markets.
   - To develop programs that strongly communicate these advancements to the industry and consumers.

MARKET ANALYSIS

WORLD LEVEL: Consumers have become acutely aware of the dangers of skin damage from the sun as reports continue to show a dangerous depletion of the ozone layer and an uptrend in skin cancer. Although the FDA's 1978 report found that factors beyond a sun protection factor (SPF) 15 did not provide incremental protection, recent discussion of the causes of skin damage and cancer, the depletion of the ozone layer, and similar topics have fueled consumer demand for higher-factored products nonetheless. Higher protection-factored products usually command a premium price ticket. The advantage of using SPFs higher than 15 is that a lighter application produces the desired effect.

Products above SPF 40 do exist, such as SolarTech's Maximum Care 42. These products are all doing reasonably well and are growing steadily. Today nearly 50 percent of all sunscreens are above SPF 6, compared to just 30 percent three years ago.

These trends are likely to continue and gain momentum, increasing the demand for sunscreen products with higher SPFs and perhaps "sunscreen on demand" products that meet the need for protection "on the go" in a variety of settings.

INDUSTRY LEVEL: Outdoor sports and the sale of recreational equipment are on a major upswing, with 22 percent annualized growth over the past three years, and this is expected to continue. The number of people involved in outdoor activities is up nearly 14 percent over the past three years, and the frequency with which they engage in such activities is up nearly 36 percent in that same time period. This has positive implications for suncare products that target the active individual. This increase in outdoor recreational activity may create the need for new sun protection products and peripherals that are readily accessible and easy to use. The notion of "portable sunscreen" capitalizes on this untapped opportunity.

BUSINESS/CATEGORY LEVEL: The suncare category is alive and thriving, with retail sales totaling $487 MM last year. The market is currently divided into four main segments, based on usage behavior: (1) *tanning* oriented (no or low sunscreen) products; (2) *recreational* activity products; (3) *protection only* products; and (4) *cosmetic* products with sunscreen. Presently, the market breaks down as follows:

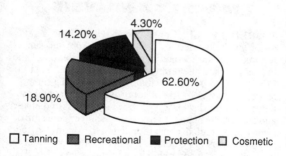

□ Tanning   ▨ Recreational   ■ Protection   □ Cosmetic

Segment growth is illustrated below, showing sharp declines in the tanning segment and steady growth in the other three segments:

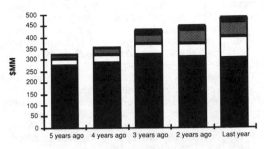

Strong overall category growth is projected to continue through the next three years, to reach $642 MM (plus 32 percent). Recent category growth has been primarily attributed to new product entries that are targeted specifically to the various usage segments.

No upcoming legislation is expected in the category, except for a possible FDA mandate to list allergenic warnings for certain sunscreen agents, such as PABA. This does not impact SolarTech or *SunSplash,* as all of our products are PABA-free.

SolarTech maintains a third place position in all usage segments based on share of unit volume, except cosmetic, where it does not compete. SolarTech's overall market share of volume last year was 18.7 percent. SolarTech's volume segment shares this past year were: 19 percent tanning, 25 percent recreational, and 14 percent protection, and 11 percent misc. (e.g., sunless tanning lotions, accelerators). SolarTech's overall share of dollar volume was higher at 23 percent, reflecting a prestige pricing posture greater than the industry average.

Broken down by distribution segment, mass market growth rate is 16 percent annualized over the past five years. Recent channel breakdown analysis showed that the largest channel is drugstores, with 37 percent segment share and 21 percent annualized growth over the past two years. Supermarkets and department stores are experiencing growth of 19 percent as well. Specialty store distribution (e.g., beach shops, resort hotels, etc.) accounts for 21 percent segment share, with declining growth because of recession and declining beach and "tanning only" applications.

Analysts believe that the expected growth trends represent a considerable opportunity for line expansions and new product introductions over the next three years. Internationally, we see a corresponding growth pattern of European sales of suncare products rising 12 percent last year, to reach U.S. dollar equivalents of $411 MM.

Technology likely will be the differentiating force for companies of the nineties, and into the next century. We are well positioned as the technology leader, and consumers and the trade expect the innovation to come from us. The *SunSplash* initiative supports these factors and will reinforce this image.

The move to higher sunscreen SPFs has afforded the larger players the opportunity for line expansion, and may open the door for successful new product entries by smaller entrepreneurs. Although the FDA's 1978 report recommended a ceiling of 15 on the effectiveness of SPF factors, world level issues previously outlined have fueled consumer demand for higher factored products. This is evidenced by an increase in the percentage of higher SPF products from 30 percent to 64 percent of the category over the last five years.

Another formulation trend is toward waterproof (must sustain four twenty-minute swims) and water resistant (must sustain two twenty-minute swims) lines, to increase efficiency of the sunscreen. Perspiration alone dilutes the effectiveness of a nonwaterproof sunscreen by more than 50 percent, and waterproof products have been receiving positive press in general interest media. The media also report that sports enthusiasts suffer the most, because they are either caught without sunscreen, or the sunscreen they are using wears off before they can get back to the tube or bottle. This is a perfect audience for *SunSplash* to include in its targeting.

The final formulation trend is away from PABA (para-amino benzoic acid) as a sunscreen, because of its potentially harmful effects on the skin. The evolution has been steady, with many products moving to PABA derivatives or replacements that do not cause allergic reactions or skin irritations. Manufacturers are also increasingly including skin softeners and conditioners in their formulas. SolarTech uses no PABA in any of its products and is migrating toward more purely hypoallergenic ingredients.

Another trend of late is the slow merging of cosmetics and sunscreens. Many of the cosmetics producers are formulating makeup lines with sunscreen, or introducing self-tanning products. We do not compete in this segment but may be able to copack portable versions with our technology under noncompetitive trade names.

Marketing strategies are the key differentiators among products. A recent study compared product attributes across the brands and found little differentiation between the products other than positioning and packaging. While some use PABA and some do not, some have fragrance and some do not, and some are in cream form while others are oils, most products were found to be equally effective. Consumers have not absorbed this principle at all; the market is not price sensitive, and the lower-end products have minimal share. Suncare is a luxury purchase to consumers, like cosmetics, and the consumer buys against claims, packaging, and tangible secondary benefits such as texture, application method, etc. Effectiveness is not a competitive issue.

This knowledge has spurred many of the manufacturers in this industry to apply heavy marketing savvy to their efforts to expand margins. And every marketer in those companies is looking for the differential advantage. Recent marketing programs have focused on these "secondary" tangible consumer benefits with much success, and many companies are opting for pure positioning elements as their claim to fame. For example, some companies have positioned lines of different lotions based on age group and gender (e.g., Bronzebaby Little Ones, Caribbean Savvy Toddler Tint, Anugu for Men). Still others have positioned lines based on emotional issues. All perform relatively on a par for the primary benefit of shielding the harmful rays of the sun but are appealing to that secondary set of differentiating positioning and image-based characteristics.

The most interesting trend of late, and the one that has the most impact on our premise, is the movement to alternate delivery systems to increase portability and convenience. Entrepreneurial start-ups have woven successful little niches for themselves, with spray mousses and gels. Amphobe gel is a trendy new product introduction that has caught the major players by surprise, commanding a price of $4.35 per ounce for a one-ounce tube. But the most interesting new product introduction is a suntan oil dispensing machine, manufactured and distributed by Sun-

Slaves, Inc. The machine covers consumers with a ten-second spray for $.50 and can be found on beach boardwalks and swimming pools. The one major flaw is the amount of maintenance involved. But the popularity of the device suggests two things: first, that convenience is a tangible benefit that has yet to be fully explored with the demanding consumer; and second, that the vending machine is a viable, untapped lucrative channel.

In conclusion, major recent industry trends include the move to higher SPF levels, the increased use of hypoallergenic and skin conditioning formulas, and the exploration of alternative delivery systems focusing on convenience.

With the rise in the recreational user segment, portability and even "single-serve" sunscreens will become increasingly valuable benefits over the next decade. Upscale products from cosmetic manufacturers will now directly impact our business.

PRODUCT LEVEL: Consumers reported in personal interviews that the new three-ounce waterproof packaging allowed them to bring the sunscreen with them when they left their blankets on the beach, took a ride on their bicycles, etc.

However, consumers reported that while it solved the problem of portability, it did not go far enough (i.e., it was still inconvenient to wear around the neck). Also, it still resulted in messy lotion residue on their hands after application. It was found that initial trial purchases drove the 70+ percent increase in second-quarter sales. However, only 30 percent of interviewed consumers said that they would definitely buy the product again— a relatively low repeat level.

While the benefit of portability was an extremely attractive concept, the product did not follow through on translating this benefit. Thus, our incremental volume is likely to ebb over the next season, due to falloff of trial users and minimal repeat purchase.

Given this information, there appears to be a major opportunity to capitalize on the unfulfilled need for portability by development of a product line that meets that need in practice as well as in theory and addresses what we have identified to be the consumer concerns.

Exploratory research was conducted. Eight focus groups were held with four different age groups, including male and female young affluent professionals (aged twenty-five to forty); male and female young adults (aged twenty to twenty-five); male and female teens (aged sixteen to nineteen); and male and female active, mature adults (aged fifty and over). Individuals selected for the groups were screened for usage of suncare products (purchased products on at least two occasions within the last year) and were considered to be "somewhat active" to "active," participating in outdoor activities at least once per week. The teen groups were also screened for trial of the three-ounce waterproof SKU, since they had been the primary target.

Initial open discussions focused on current suncare product offerings and usage. Later inquiries focused on concepts of "portability" and convenience (with respect to various user applications and behavior), and possible forms, delivery systems, and extensions of the core concepts. Following are the key results and implications:

- *Low loyalty to any given brand,* although 50 percent of purchases made were based on a known brand name. In the teen groups, 32 percent of purchases were made based on what a respected member of a peer group used. Typically, more than one brand was owned at any given time, and different sun protection factors were used during a given tanning session or for sun protection. For recreational users, only one product was used at a time. Mature adults reported slightly more brand loyalty than the other groups, using more familiar brand names. All respondents admitted that they would try a new brand if it were to have a distinguishing feature (e.g., Bronzebaby Sprayilizer). Thus, a portable sunscreen product may initially draw reasonably high trial numbers. This supports the data collected on our three-ounce SKU.
- For *tanning applications* (a declining seg-ment), more than one SPF lotion or oil was applied during a tanning session. Most common was SPF 2 for arms and legs, SPF 6 for shoulders and back, and SPF 8 for face, neck, and chest. Convenience was not rated as important to beachgoers, as beach trips are almost always premeditated, and carrying several different suncare products was not a problem. Portability/convenience scored a 3.6 across all groups for the sun worshippers in the groups, on a scale of 1 (not important at all) to 10 (extremely important or desired), slightly higher for the teen groups and lower for the ma-

ture adult groups. Therefore, the tanning segment is not a good target for a product that focuses on portability.

- *For recreational applications* (a growing segment), portability/convenience was rated an average of 8.2 across all groups. Sunscreen "on demand" had a strong *protection* utility to all groups, while the teen group also mentioned safer *tanning* while doing outdoor activities. Disposability was also discussed, and rated an average of 8.7 across groups. One participant called it "sunscreen on the go," which we thought to be interesting. "No mess afterward" rated an average of 8.9 among the recreational set. This segment seems to be an excellent target for a sunscreen product that focuses on portability, disposability, and, if possible, results in little or no mess after application.

- *For protection-only oriented individuals* (for use in those situations that require sun protection regardless of activity), portability/convenience was rated a high 9.2 with the mature adult group, and 6.9 among all other groups. Young professional parents with children below six years old reported the second highest rating, at 8.6. They indicated that they would use a portable, disposable sunscreen product extensively with their children. It appears that the protection-oriented user segment is a good secondary target for the new product.

- *For cosmetic application*, low ratings were given, as women typically applied moisturizers with sunscreen in the home before going outdoors. This is not a good target segment.

- *Few focus group participants were primarily concerned with price,* and consumers said that they would be willing to pay a premium for highly portable, disposable suncare products. However, this may be because they are used to purchasing one or two suncare products each season. The issue may get bigger when consumers begin to use the disposable product beyond the initial novelty.

- *Ideas for portability* covered mini-lotion samples, wrist tubes, neck-hanging tubes (like the three-ounce waterproof), belt dispensers, and towelettes. Towelettes were favored over the other options 3:1, based upon ease of application, cleanliness, and disposability. Disposable lotion packets (like hotel shampoo foil packs) held some interest in the groups but were viewed as being "messy" in application and therefore undesirable. Consumers were really excited about building on the idea of towelettes. Other ideas that surfaced were: a "sports quencher" towelette of carbonated water that could be stored in a cooler, baby lotion towelettes, and insect repellent towelettes. Overall, towelettes appear to be the most popular form for our new product, if the labs can develop and we can produce at a reasonable cost. Once pricing is determined, we will test the concept again.

- *High SPF factors were favored* by 83 percent of the participants over factors below SPF 6. Applications for the younger groups included safe tanning while engaging in sports and recreational activities (e.g., bicycling and roller-blading), while older groups saw protection while running, walking, or golfing as the main concern. Thus, our product should appeal to this range of needs, i.e., our line should concentrate on SPF 6 and above.

- *Packaging was considered to be a strong element* in the decision making process, and many new products were tried each season, based upon package appeal. Among younger consumers, especially teens, more than 60 percent of "tanning" purchases are impulse, or at the point of need (the beach). Among other groups, only 25 percent were impulse purchases. Over half the consumers admit to being strongly influenced by packaging or presentation at the point of sale (i.e., displays).

Based upon the above findings, we believe that: (1) we should target recreational and protection-oriented individuals in a wide range of ages; (2) we should concentrate on higher SPF formulations; and (3) high margins could be taken on a portable product because of the perceived high utility to consumers and the general price inelasticity of the category. We will test this further once pricing is established. Final conclusion from the first round groups was to begin development of prototypes, brand name, and packaging in several forms, focusing on towelettes as the delivery vehicle. We also decided to investigate a number of good ideas for line extensions and spin-offs that were brought up in the groups.

SWOT ANALYSIS

The *SunSplash* venture meshes well with our strengths and the opportunities that exist.

STRENGTHS	WEAKNESSES
1. PRODUCTION: Excellent production capabilities: we have existing wet-fill equipment at the plant (from last June's sampling programs) and the know-how to execute a quick start-up. **2. R&D:** Our technical research group has already indicated that they can formulate a towelette that performs properly, and has already experimented with sunscreen agents on a towelette from studies done for the outdoor furniture industry three years ago. Tech Research is already conducting bench top experiments for this project with early indications of success. **3. DISTRIBUTION:** We have strong distribution in ski resort areas, which may allow us to develop transferrable product from one market to another, thus cutting our postsummer take-back costs down significantly and raising our margins—something no other competitor can presently do.	**1. CAPITAL INVESTMENT:** In additional equipment (estimated at $625 K, with associated risk exposure). To be noted is that this type of equipment could be sold easily at depreciated value or could be leased with option to buy for one year. **2. RESOURCES:** We have limited manpower resources at present, and this project will put a strain on existing staff capabilities.

Barriers to entry will have to be erected wherever possible and as soon as possible to prevent immediate erosion of the share that we hope to establish. We must not only enter the market but also capture and secure the entire niche before other competitors have time to turn around their own products. This development effort must be kept as quiet as possible, precluding any type of market testing, which will not give us the sound read we usually like to take before we roll national with our products.

OPPORTUNITIES

1. PRIMACY: We have the opportunity to be the first on the block, setting the course for this new market segment, and the potential to establish a pre-eminent name and loyal consumer base with two very brand loyal segments. We believe that this innovation will expand the total suncare category.

2. LINE BREADTH: Opportunities exist for a full line of products with multiple applications beyond traditional sunscreens (e.g., body quencher, insect repellent, etc.). We have the opportunity to write the rules for new suncare categories and segments.

3. DISTRIBUTION: We can open up and potentially "own" portable distribution channels (e.g., vending machines) in key recreational areas. We can do the same in sporting goods and specialty shop channels.

THREATS

1. EASE OF ENTRY: Co-packing capacity is available should competitors wish to enter the market. However, because we will likely be low-cost producer, we can expect to have more lenient and viable pricing structure in competitive situations if needed.

2. NEW TERRITORY: Line extensions of body quencher and others are entirely new territory for us or any suncare company. We have very limited experience in the proposed new "Body Quencher" category, although related to the SunSplash base line in form. Extensions into new areas such as these should be explored and tested for years two or three after the portable concept has been established and we have gained a loyal consumer base, rather than launched concurrently with the line in the first year.

We believe that the opportunities and payout potential outweigh the risks significantly, but we should pay very close attention to the marketplace as we follow through with our plans.

COMPETITIVE ANALYSIS

Based on the key attributes that we have screened in the suncare category for recreational and protection users, there are unmet consumer needs for "portability" and "disposable" sunscreen products. Currently, no products exist in the market that fulfill this need, except for one-ounce tubes of Amphobe Gel. Amphobe is premium positioned and would not likely venture into more mainstream pricing territory or even the lower echelons of prestige positioning and pricing, which we will be pursuing.

There is also considerable consumer demand for products that are considered "light" or "clean" in application and feel when applied to the body. Several companies have responded to these needs by producing products positioned as "greaseless," such as Caribbean Savvy Light Cream and Honduras Hank Invisible Tan. These products have a strong following, primarily because of these attributes, but are not likely to pose a threat to our venture because they are primarily applied in tanning or beach applications.

With consideration of production capabilities, an overall rack-up of competitors shows that Bronzebaby is the only other manufacturer with wet-fill equipment, and may therefore pose an immediate threat. They use this equipment primarily for promotional sampling and hotel supply. However, BB has been reported to be going up for sale this year, which will probably prevent them from beginning any new product development that drains capital from the bottom line. We can expect them to go up against us in year two after the buyout or merger takes place.

Surf n' Slope has been experimenting with spray bottles extensively and may be pursuing the portability concept in other forms. We do not expect them to be a leader in the new technology, but they are known for following up in second and third years with low cost "me-too's." However, they do have excellent distribution in the ski resort channels. They will have to be watched carefully, as we have in the past with all of our new product introductions.

Detailed competitive analyses are provided for each marketing function in the individual functional portions of this plan.

STRATEGIC DIRECTION

OVERALL DIRECTION: Develop a line of portable, disposable suncare products, using wet-fill technology and towelette delivery vehicle. Skew sunscreen SKUs toward higher SPFs. Investigate product form and packaging extensively and build other functional plans around final product innovation, benefits, and expected purchase behavior. Investigate possibilities for line extensions, within and beyond the suncare category, using the same or similar technologies as the base product—those that fulfill unmet needs for recreational users (e.g., carbonated water "refresher" towelettes). Develop as full a line as budget and capabilities will allow, taking advantage of economies of scope in technology.

TARGET AUDIENCE: *Recreational* users are the primary target (across all age groups, but with a contemporary and youthful image slant), and *protection-only* users (with a focus on mature, active adults) are the secondary target. Audience participates in a broad range of outdoor activities, from watching a baseball game to participating in a marathon. We will avoid the beach or tanning segment, where utility of the benefit diminishes. This split target yields average target demographics as follows:

Recreational Users:
18+; male & female split; 40,000+ HH income, 3.2 HH size, college educated, health conscious, active, sports-minded individuals.

Protection-Only Users:
50+; male skew 65%; 35,000+ HH income, 2.4 HH size, at least high school educated, health conscious, physically fit and active individuals.

POSITIONING STATEMENT: For *recreational* and *protection*-oriented suncare products users of any age, who enjoy outdoor activities, the *SunSplash* sunscreen towelette is the first sunscreen product that offers "on demand" portable and disposable protection and easy, clean, and uniform application, anytime and anywhere they need it.

PERFORMANCE CRITERIA: Generate gross sales of at least $14.5 MM (2.7 percent market dollar share) and net margins of at least 12 percent in the first year, with subsequent annualized sales growth of 25 percent through year three, and profitability growth to 18 percent by year three of operation.

MARKETING OBJECTIVE

To develop and launch a new breakthrough line of suncare products, to recreational (primary) and protection-only (secondary) suncare products users, that

1. Delivers key benefits of portability, disposability, and easy, clean application;
2. Expands the suncare category by at least 2 percent; and

3. Achieves a 2.7 percent market dollar share and generates gross sales of at least $14.5 MM and net margins of at least 12 percent, in year one.

KEY MARKETING STRATEGIES
(Functional Roles and Guidelines)

PRODUCT: Product plays the pivotal role, from which all else is derived. We need to structure the line and deliver key benefits. R&D will play a vital role in development of the technology for the towelettes. The launch product line will be the basic suncare products, based on their popularity in bottled and tube form with the target usage groups, and line extensions will be explored and tested in year one, for potential launch in year two or three (e.g., spring water body quencher, baby lotion, and insect repellent SKUs).

PACKAGING: Since a large percentage of category purchase decisions are made at the point of purchase, and this is likely to be even higher with an "on demand" disposable product, packaging and point of sale materials will play a major role in the marketing mix. Packet packaging itself must be portable, self-contained, easy to open, and environmentally safe (because of its disposability). Package must carry appealing graphics, with which the target groups will identify and associate benefits. Graphic design should be futuristic, clean, and energetic. Package alternatives will be in "single serve" and "multipack" configurations (optimal multipack count found to be six).

DISTRIBUTION: Distribution will play a significant role in both the movement of the product through the channels and solving the "take back" problem that all suncare products face at the end of the season. Winter resort channels should be pursued using broker network that we already deploy for our tube lines, and promotional activities should be designed to support their sales effort (e.g., sponsorship of ski events). Flowthrough of product can deliver a 30 percent increase in margins. Utilize alternative distribution channels such as hotels, resorts, sporting goods stores, sports stadiums, amusement parks, sports specialty shops, vending machines, etc., where spontaneous purchase or provided sampling will initiate trial.

PRICING: The category is still price inelastic, and consumers have indicated that they will be willing to pay a premium for the convenience of the disposable towelettes. We should assume that we will have competition in towelettes by year two and adopt the right strategy that will position the new form for others to follow, yet will not subject us to undercutting. Perhaps we can take higher margins on single serve SKUs because they are likely to be more impulse oriented and less price sensitive, and take lower margins on multipacks to encourage bulk purchase (perhaps through bonus packing of a free packet), because they are more likely to be compared to the cost of bottled products.

ADVERTISING: Advertising will play a larger role during the introductory period, to create awareness with a focus on usage and usage occasions, and a lesser role later on in the season due to the impulse nature of the purchase. We should utilize media that are most suited to communicate the product benefits to the target groups efficiently.

PROMOTION: Because packaging and point-of-sale communication of the benefits are critical to generating trial, in-store promotions will play a major role in helping to deliver the message. Price-oriented promotions are to be avoided. An incentive should be offered to purchase the multipacks, and we believe that strong point of sale and promotion will provide greater impact for the dollar spent.

PUBLIC RELATIONS: Public relations will play a major role in the marketing mix, as tangible benefits of protection and "on demand" sunscreen are newsworthy for the trade press, sports-related media, and medical trade. We can also leverage this PR for the entire company, which will help to further the corporate objectives of reestablishing the image of the company as the industry technology leader.

III. PRODUCT DEVELOPMENT PLAN
PRODUCT RESEARCH

COMPETITIVE RACK-UP: The following lists major competitors, their overall product line positioning, and the segments that they dominate or compete in as leading players (double check mark denotes segment leader).

	Posi-tioning	Tan-ning	Recre-ation	Protec-tion	Cos-metic	SPF Focus
Carib-bean Savvy	Main-stream	✓	✓			Low
Bronze-baby	Mid-Up scale	✓✓	✓	✓✓	✓	Full Range
Fait de Chaud	Up scale	✓			✓✓	Low
Surf n' Slope	Mid-down scale	✓	✓	✓		Low to Med.
Hon-duras Hank	Main-stream	✓				Low
Solar-Tech	Mid-Up scale	✓	✓✓	✓		Full Range

The following list the forms and application methods used by each competitor:

	Lotion	Oil	Gel	Cream	Hand Apply	Spray
Carib-bean Savvy	✓	✓			✓	
Bronze-baby	✓	✓	✓		✓	✓
Fait de Chaud	✓		✓	✓	✓	
Surf n' Slope	✓	✓			✓	✓
Hon-duras Hank	✓	✓	✓		✓	✓
Solar-Tech	✓	✓		✓	✓	

The target audience for portable sunscreen products are mid-upscale recreational adult consumers and mainstream older adult protection users. SolarTech dominates the recreation segment. We can expect no significant competition from Surf n' Slope at the outset because they are normally low-priced me-too producers. However, we should watch them for a low-cost entry in several years. Caribbean Savvy does not seem to be a threat because they are heavily committed to the low SPF products, which do not fit with the portability concept. Bronzebaby is in the best position to compete directly against us.

CONSUMER RESEARCH: Consumer focus group tests with target groups yielded the following key information:

- The concept of "sunscreen towelettes" had unanimous appeal to all groups.
- The *SunSplash* name won out over PortaScreen (and other names generated by our advertising agency) for appeal by a margin of 3:1. *SunSplash* name was indicative of "fun."
- Teens and young adults stressed the need for convenience during activities—most significant benefit.
- Yuppies with children suggested that a series with high SPF factors and extra moisturizers for sensitive skin be developed for small children.
- "Dark Tanning" series with low SPFs (under 6) was not seen as valuable to the target groups, especially the "protection" users.
- "High Protection" series with high SPFs (15 plus) was most valuable to *protection* users and had high utility with *recreational* users, confirming earlier exploratory research findings.
- Aloe-Vera "After Tanning Moisturizing" SKU had moderate to good appeal to all groups, more so to women.
- "Exhilarating Body Quencher" SKU with spring water was seen as innovative and new to the category. Considerable interest was voiced for Body Quencher.
- "Insect Repellent" SKU was received with some trepidation. The benefit was very much desired, but all feared bad smell and texture associated with traditional insect repellents. Participants felt that if not explicit (i.e., listed as a secondary benefit in the usage copy without alluding to specific properties), would be acceptable. After smelling and touching the prototypes, fears were allayed and interest grew.

- Consumers expressed concern over the "disposability" aspect of the packaging; they feared that it would be harmful to the environment. It would be an excellent idea to utilize the new biodegradable packaging we developed last year for our sampling programs.

PRODUCT PLANNER

OBJECTIVE	STRATEGIES	TACTICS
• To develop a new line of "portable" sunscreen products that appeals to recreational and protection only suncare product users, and delivers on primary benefits of "on-demand" sun protection, portability, disposability, and secondary benefits of ease of application and "clean," greaseless feel.	• Utilize wet-fill technologies to produce the line. • Develop a product line that reflects the most popular SPFs in the target usage segments. • Develop a product line that will allow the product to be easily and evenly applied and disposed of, in an environmentally safe manner. • Utilize sunscreen agents that work best with the delivery vehicle and leave a "light," greaseless protective film on the skin.	• Utilize wet Bilco wet-fillers to produce following SKUs, skewed to the higher SPFs: • SPF 6 • SPF 8 • SPF 15 • SPF 30 • Tanning Accelerator • Aloe After Tan Moisturizer • Utilize sunscreen impregnated biodegradable cotton fiber 4-fold 4″ × 6″ towelettes as delivery vehicle. • Include "greaseless" emollients and softeners in the formulation. • Add water-resistant and antisweat properties through use of new nonparaffin bases. • Make formulation clear to further "clean" claim. • Include insect repellent agent as a minor ingredient, without direct reference.

IV. PACKAGING PLAN

PACKAGING RESEARCH

COMPETITIVE RACK-UP: The following lists major competitors, their overall age/image targets, forms, and delivery vehicles.

	Age Target	Bottles	Tubes	Alternative Packaging	Graphics / Colors	Bulk Packaging
Caribbean Savvy	Teen	✓	✓		Warm	✓
Bronzebaby	All Family	✓	✓	✓	Warm	
Fait de Chaud	Adult	✓		✓	Avant Garde	
Surf n' Slope	Kids/ scale	✓	✓		Hot / Neon Youthful	✓
Honduras Hank	Teen	✓			Hot Funky	✓
Solar-Tech	All Family	✓	✓		Hot phisticated	

CONSUMER RESEARCH: Consumer focus group tests with target groups yielded the following key information:

- Packaging was seen as important to help position the product as contemporary to futuristic, because it is technology driven.
- Proposed package design with easy-tear top panel was most favored. Graphics that touted movement, activity, and moderated between fun and function had most universal appeal. Not too serious. Graphics that illustrate activity applications registered highest.
- "SolarTech Laboratories" tag lent considerable authenticity and trust to the product. When tested with competitive logos, SolarTech was seen as

giving all consumer groups the highest comfort level.

- The multiserve pack concept (e.g., six packets of SPF 8) was highly desired, especially if cost savings were involved.
- Multiserve variety packs (e.g., two packets of SPF 4 to 6, two of SPF 8, two of SPF 15) were not as valued as expected, and only highly valued for specific applications, such as "business" or spontaneous trips, where consumers would not have to worry about leakage and room in their suitcases.
- All saw single-serve packets for use either as a stand-alone in recreational or protection applications, rather than as a supplement to other lotions at the beach. In beach applications, portability was not a highly desired benefit, although it had appeal to a few of the group participants. Many group members concurred that single serve packets were convenient for any and all activities that required "light" baggage (e.g., bicycling, running, rollerblading), and said that they would use them frequently (i.e., more than once per week). Single serves were viewed as impulse purchases. Spectator sports applications (e.g., baseball games) were also brought up in all but one group and received well.
- Multiserve packets of the same SPF were viewed as premeditated purchases, rather than impulse like the single serve.
- Consumers also liked the idea of long shelf life, as compared with bottles, that once open, would separate or spoil after a year. Asceptically sealed towelettes have a minimum shelf life of three years.
- The concept of *SunSplash,* when applied to various competitors, was considered as a best fit with the SolarTech and Bronzebaby trademarks, as expected.
- Biodegradability of the packaging was important to several group members, and some suggested flagging the package with an environmentally safe symbol.

TRADE RESEARCH: Research conducted through the sales force with the trade, and during the course of exploratory alternative distribution channel discussions, yielded the following:

- Single-serve packages should be rackable, so that they could easily fit on J-hooks and other in-store merchandising fixtures.
- Graphics should be universal enough to appeal to target groups in any sports or protection situation (e.g., on the golf course, at the ball game, etc.). Graphics should also be able to traverse summer and winter applications, or at least preference summer but not alienate winter users.
- Multipacks graphics should be adjustable vertical/horizontal, so that the package can either stand upright, or be turned around and laid on its side.

PACKAGING PLANNER

Pouch: OBJECTIVES	STRATEGIES	TACTICS
To develop a primary package that: 1. Protects the product; 2. Aesthetically and functionally appeals to both recreational and protection target users, and communicates key benefits; 3. Adheres to FDA regulations for toxicity, child safety, and other federal/ state guidelines; 4. Can stand alone as a sin-gle- serve as well as in the multi-pack con-figuration; 5. Is universal enough to span product and dis-tribution chan-nel's merchandising needs.	• Configure the package size and shape to fit in typical pocket and on a typical peg hook. • Utilize a high resiliency biode-gradable pack-aging material that will not break down from the product ingredients and resists at least five lbs. of ten-sile pressure. • Utilize an easy open feature. • Utilize graph-ics that convey multiple appli-cation usage.	• Make package 2″ × 3″ × 1/8″ and include a J-hook slot. • Utilize biode-gradable plasto-seal materials technology. • Perforate the upper left-hand corner for easy opening. • Utilize the slo-gan "the any-time, anywhere sunscreen" on package. • Utilize a repre-sentative sample of sports icons.

Six-Pack Outer Package: OBJECTIVES	STRATEGIES	TACTICS
• To develop an outer box to house six individual packets that fits retailer requirements and graphic guidelines.	• Mirror single-serve packaging graphics and copy and further the portability perception and appeals best in variety to the target audiences. • Utilize a box configuration that implies mobility or portability. • Pack out six of same SPF in each multipack in expected demand splits, based on SPF levels desired with target groups on core SolarTech brands.	• Develop a CC1S card-stock box with top-cut handle to further perception of portability. • Pack out multipacks in following splits: • SPF 6 - 35% • SPF 8 - 20% • SPF 15 - 20% • SPF 30 - 15% • Tanning Accelerator - 5% • Aloe After Tan - 5% • Include promotional flag. • Mimic graphics on inner packets.
Case Package: OBJECTIVES	STRATEGIES	TACTICS
• To develop an outer carton with optimal quantity configuration, that can be used as a promotional vehicle.	• Develop a self-shipper. • Maximize quantity based on distribution channel.	• Create self-shippers that can be used as a counter display for single serve with interchangeable header cards. • Configure as 36 and 72 packs.

V. DISTRIBUTION PLAN

DISTRIBUTION RESEARCH

COMPETITIVE RACK-UP: The following lists major competitors and the key channels in which they compete.

	Drug Chains	Mass Merchandiser	Variety Stores	Supermarket	Summer / Beach Resort	Ski / Winter Resort
Caribbean Savvy	✓	✓	✓		✓	
Bronzebaby	✓	✓	✓	✓	✓	
Fait de Chaud	✓		✓		✓	
Surf n' Slope	✓	✓	✓		✓	✓
Honduras Hank	✓	✓	✓		✓	
SolarTech	✓	✓	✓	✓	✓	✓

CONSUMER RESEARCH: Consumer focus group tests with target groups yielded the following key information:

- Convenience was critical for a portable product—especially at "point-of-activity" for most users, especially for single serve. This translates to bicycle shops, golf shops, ski resorts, baseball stadiums, etc. Alternative markets such as these will increase the category. No one presently competes in retail sports channels.
- Six-packs were thought of more as planned purchases and sought in traditional channels, such as supermarkets, drug chains, and mass merchandisers, where we currently have strong distribution.
- Consumers also favored the idea that vending machines carry product in high traffic areas, for need-based spontaneous purchase.

TRADE RESEARCH: Research conducted through the sales force with the trade, and exploratory meetings and discussions with alternative distribution channel factions, yielded the following:

- Our sales planners were extremely interested in selling the product, especially if we crossed over into nonsunscreen applications (e.g., Body Quencher). They have been *waiting* for real innovation and will get behind the *SunSplash* launch.

- Our broker networks in drug, mass merchandise, variety, and supermarket channels were thrilled with the possibility of having a low-cost impulse item such as *SunSplash* at the registers during peak season. They view this as incremental volume. Early discussions with some of our key accounts indicate a willingness to provide duplicate facings—one on shelf in the usual section, and a second at counter.

- Alternative channels investigated were sporting goods stores, golf stores, resort hotel and casino chains, bicycle shops, running shops, and other specialty stores. Sporting goods "soft-goods and accessories" brokers cover all of these channels except the hotel chains, handled by a separate group of brokers and manufacturers' reps. Commissions range up to 8 percent as opposed to the 3.8 percent we are used to paying in traditional channels.

- The ski resort channels (in which we already sell our "Peak Protection" line), are extremely receptive to this type of product. However, we must offer some type of "resealable package" or receptacle, so that packages don't end up all over the slopes. This channel affords us tremendous profit leverage, as we can flow through our takebacks at the end of each summer season (averaging 36 percent, 7 percent below industry average) directly into the ski/winter resorts channels. All we need to do is make the packaging universal and change the header card on the shipper/display.

- Convenience stores were also explored and were found to be an excellent volume distribution channel, especially for the protection-oriented user. The three largest chains were all very receptive to the products, primarily because of its high-margin price point.

- The Body Quencher line extension was viewed as an excellent enhancement to the line. We expect to get an average of 4.2 SKUs in each traditional channel site and 2.8 in alternative channels.

CHANNEL DISTRIBUTION PLANNER

OBJECTIVES	STRATEGIES	TACTICS
• To gain distribution in all major traditional suncare channels (e.g., drugstores, supermarkets, and mass merchandisers) and achieve a minimum of 70% ACV nationally. • Get at least 50% of SolarTech trade accounts to stock 1+ case and carry at least three SKUs.	• Utilize and motivate current SolarTech brokered sales forces, and leverage relationships with key SolarTech accounts.	• Offer sell-in bonus commissions of +1% to brokers. • Offer dealer loaders of shipper displays and other POS. • Offer introductory 5% distribution allowance. • Offer 5% additional display allowance for counter setup in key accounts.
• To generate additional 20% of volume movement through the following alternative channels: • Summer hotel/resort • C-store • Military commissary • Winter hotel/resort • Amusement parks • Specialty sports shops • Sporting goods stores • Sports stadiums • Vending	• Utilize brokers and distributors in alternative retail channels. • Utilize food service distributors for park & stadium concessions. • Utilize same ski soft-goods brokers currently used for *Peak Protection* line in ski resort channels. • Utilize vending distributors in two test sunbelt markets.	• Utilize Swanson & Carly national manufacturers rep firms for alternative retail channels at 4.3% commission rate plus standard SolarTech performance bonus structures. • Tray pack product for vending channel to conform to machine insertion guidelines. • Test vending channel in Miami and Atlanta markets.

PHYSICAL DISTRIBUTION PLANNER

OBJECTIVES	STRATEGIES	TACTICS
• To maximize shipping efficiency across channels and minimize shipping costs.	• Use optimal cost-saving ground transport mediums. • Pack in skid configurations and utilize break-bulk warehouse in central states. • Set up tracking system.	• Utilize McCann warehouse and fulfillment center in Michigan. • For key accounts, ship direct product overland bulk. • For small accounts and alternative channels, utilize LTL shippers where applicable. • Utilize bar codes for outer containers for tracking.

VI. PRICING PLAN

PRICING RESEARCH

COMPETITIVE RACK-UP: The following lists major competitors and pricing index (performance/price ratio) in each usage segment (based on industry averages):

	Avg. Retail cost / ounce	Tan- ning value index	Recre- ational value index	Protec- tion value index	Cos- metic value index	Porta- bility value index
Carib- bean Savvy	$1.45	111	102	78	63	89
Bronze- baby	$2.05	109	96	102	104	104
Fait de Chaud	$3.05	103	83	93	116	72
Surf n' Slope	$1.02	92	89	95	42	101
Hon- duras Hank	$1.55	101	87	74	59	88
Solar- Tech	$2.05	102	106	102	67	103

SolarTech was viewed with a high performance/price ratio, as compared with competitors, for target users of *SunSplash*. In addition, the value of a portable sun-screen towelette when tested across all major brands yielded the second highest value for SolarTech, far above other major competitors who don't compete in segments where portability is an unmet need.

CONSUMER RESEARCH: Consumer focus group tests with target groups yielded the following key information:

- Single-serve units SRP under $1.00 were acceptable to the majority of participants, with a mean level of $0.79.
- Six-pack units SRP under $5.00 were similarly acceptable, tracking lower than the unit price, with mean level of $4.14, approximately $0.69 each.
- "One free packet with purchase of five" tested more favorably with consumers (buy five at regular price and get one free—$3.95), than "buy six at $0.10 off each" ($3.95 also). Consumers perceived free packet as more valuable than discount. Odd pricing also fares well at the $3.95 price point.

PRICING PLANNER

OBJECTIVES	STRATEGIES	TACTICS
• Generate overall gross margins of at least 65 percent over cost of goods, while achieving distribution and sales targets.	• Take an initial skimming prestige-oriented pricing strategy, justified by a strong A&P image-building program, and adjust as competitors come into play. • Build volumes to achieve economies of scale through moderation of above strategy. • Support trade with introductory trade allowances to boost initial distribution and shelf space for the season, but avoid price-oriented consumer promotion programs.	• Price single-serve at $0.79 each and six-pack at $3.95, positioned to the consumer as "buy five, get one free" bonus pack. • Offer 5% introductory trade allowance (see distribution) to penetrate trade accounts and secure shelf space.

VI. ADVERTISING PLAN

RESEARCH

COMPETITIVE RACK-UP: The following lists major competitors, the types of media that they used, the estimated number of GRPs put against consumers, estimated budget, and the overall affect on sales volumes during advertising periods:

	TV	Print	Out-of-Home	In-Store	Budget	Sales Change
Caribbean Savvy	0	110	140	30	$8.3 MM	+4%
Bronze-baby	140	160	160	15	$10.6 MM	+7%
Fait de Chaud	120	110	0	40	$4.4 MM	+9%
Surf n' Slope	0	40	120	10	$3.9 MM	–3%
Honduras Hank	0	80	160	20	$6.7 MM	+1%
Solar-Tech	120	120	140	30	$9.5 MM	+6%

Overall category spending levels were up by 11.6 percent over last year. Fait de Chaud's volume gains probably were derived from the fact that they have never spent behind their brands in any medium except print, until last year. A more detailed analysis showed that in general, TV was very effective in delivering incremental volumes for brands that are more image driven, and did not do much for brands that are not. Print and outdoor advertising continue to be the most efficient media across audiences.

A further analysis was conducted on each target usage segment. It was found that outdoor advertising was the most efficient medium to reach the beach user segment; targeted print media was most efficient with recreational users; and a combination of print and out-of-home efforts was most efficient with protection-only users.

CONSUMER RESEARCH: Consumer focus group tests with target groups yielded the following key information:

- The idea of the "sunscreen on demand" requires a very visual medium that can show action to convey the key benefits of the product. Television spots depicting usage occasions were explored in animatic form and tested with excellent unaided recall and purchase intent scores—26 percent above any other line we've tested or run. Television should definitely be included to create awareness of the "process," and to indicate life-style image.

- Slogans were developed and tested, with one winner emerging by a wide margin—"The any-time, anywhere sunscreen." Storyboards were also tested for several sports-oriented print ads for the multipack. The clear winner in theme and headline was "Take this six-pack to your next _____."
- Print ads in targeted sports magazines that would reach recreational users tested as very efficient. Other ads in targeted mature market books, focusing on on-demand protection benefits, is also a good idea.
- Outdoor advertising in key BDI cities, especially near city parks, should be utilized.

ADVERTISING PLANNER

OBJECTIVES	STRATEGIES	TACTICS
• Generate awareness of SunSplash in at least 60% of suncare product recreational and protection-oriented users (33.1% of total user market) — 10.9 million consumers. • Of those suncare product users who become aware of the product's benefits, establish positive brand perceptions in at least 75% of the audience—8.2 MM consumers. • Of those users who register positive brand perceptions, generate a 50% trial purchase intent level—4.1 MM consumers.	• Utilize broad-reach medium during introductory period. • Utilize targeted media related to life-style of target throughout key seasons, i.e., summer outdoor activities and winter ski season. • Develop life-style-focused creative that communicates the portability, disposability, convenience, and "no mess" benefits.	• Television during introductory period—6-week flight, mid-April through end of May, generating at least 450 GRPs, with a higher concentration on reach than on frequency. • Full-page magazine ads in June and July outdoor sporting activity books, and in *Modern Maturity*. • Full-page magazine ads in November and December skiing books.

CREATIVE STRATEGY

OBJECTIVE: To persuade active adults that Sun-Splash sunscreen towelettes are the easiest, most convenient way to protect themselves from the sun while engaging in all of their favorite outdoor activities.

TARGET AUDIENCE: The SunSplash user loves outdoor activities. He or she participates in sports or activities such as tennis, golf, walking, bicycling, rollerblading, skiing, etc. It doesn't really matter how old he or she is. He likes to watch sporting events in person, not on TV. He likes to barbecue for his family. She likes to work in the garden. They've been to the U.S. Open tennis tournament. They don't like to fuss about their appearance—they are "wash and wear" people. They like fresh foods that are low in fat. They drink bottled or sparkling water. They don't spend free time baking in the sun on a beach—they prefer to sightsee or play golf or tennis on vacations.

KEY CONSUMER BENEFIT: SunSplash sunscreen towelettes will allow the user to enjoy the benefits of complete sun protection anytime, anywhere. There is no need to carry bulky bottles or to deal with messy oils. When you carry a packet with you, there is never a reason to worry that you will be caught "off-guard" and unprotected from the sun's harmful rays.

REASON TO BELIEVE: SunSplash sunscreen towelettes come in convenient, easy-to-carry, easy-to-open disposable packets. Because the greaseless sunscreen lotion is on a towelette, it is a clean, even application.

TONE AND MANNER: Today, more than ever, people are concerned with staying active and healthy. This begins at a young age and continues into mature adulthood. Life is good for these people—they feel good about themselves, and this reflects in the way that they enjoy life to its fullest. They are smart about the sun's harmful effects, but they don't have to let that stop them from enjoying all of their favorite outdoor activities. The tone of the advertising should therefore reflect a "winning attitude."

VIII. PROMOTION PLAN

PROMOTION RESEARCH

COMPETITIVE RACK-UP: The following lists major competitors, the major types of offers used in the industry, and estimated budgets spent during drop periods.

	Sampling	Price-Off	Bonus Packs	Displays	Trade Allowances	Total Budget
Caribbean Savvy	$0.5 MM	$1.8 MM	$1.4 MM	$2.4 MM	$3.3 MM	$9.4 MM
Bronzebaby	$0.5 MM	$0.6 MM	$0.6 MM	$2.2 MM	$4.6 MM	$8.5 MM
Fait de Chaud	$0.0 MM	$0.3 MM	$0.8 MM	$1.6 MM	$3.0 MM	$5.7 MM
Surf n' Slope	$0.1 MM	$2.1 MM	$0.0 MM	$0.5 MM	$3.4 MM	$6.1 MM
Honduras Hank	$8.1 MM	$0.9 MM	$0.3 MM	$2.0 MM	$3.7 MM	$8.7 MM
Solar-Tech	$0.7 MM	$0.4 MM	$0.8 MM	$2.1 MM	$4.2 MM	$8.2 MM

Overall category spending levels were up by 26.2 percent over last year, reflecting a more aggressive posture in the industry for promotions and the allowances that had to be paid to execute programs. Further analyses showed that sampling was efficient only for Honduras Hank's Lite introduction. Point of sale displays seemed to have had a significant impact, as many of the key players scrambled to get long-term premium store space by providing "permanent display." An opportunity that can be capitalized upon with *SunSplash* is its ability to hang on J-hooks in several places in the store.

Price-offs gave Surf n' Slope and Honduras Hank significant bumps, probably because they pulled share away from the private labels. For SolarTech, price-offs, once again, only helped move product that we were going to pull from the line.

CONSUMER RESEARCH: Consumer focus group tests with target groups yielded the following key information:

- As mentioned in the packaging module, bonus packs (e.g., "buy five get one free") held good value for consumers.
- As trial purchase is key for this product, we explored many different avenues to reach the consumers through sampling. Foremost, loyal consumers that use our bottled products could be sampled to through an on-pack of the towelette. Sampling can also be done through outdoor events, in concert with sponsorships developed by the PR department. For example, sampling at marathons, triathlons, baseball stadiums, Special Olympics, etc., could prove very beneficial. It was found that recreational and protection users are far more brand loyal than tanning-usage segment consumers. Once they believe in a product, it becomes part of their "equipment." In this vein, consumers were very excited about receiving samples through tie-in purchases of sports apparel and equipment. Consumers felt that being associated with well-known sports brands would lend significant credibility to *SunSplash*.
- Various point-of-sale displays, shelf-talkers, and other merchandising products were tested. Merchandising in traditional channels that depicted action and focused on the three key benefits, built around the slogan "The anytime, anywhere sunscreen," were most effective. Mature adults, more apt to buy the six-packs than single-serve, responded more to creative advertising geared toward protection than activity. In alternative channels, single-serve was more favored to all target audiences, and counter displays were perceived as extremely influential.

TRADE RESEARCH: Research conducted with the trade through the sales force and exploratory meetings and discussions with alternative distribution channel factions, yielded the following:

- Counter displays during peak season were universally accepted by retailers, because of anticipated high stock turns and margins.
- Tie-in on in-pack promotions with sports apparel and equipment companies were desired in concert with other *SunSplash* merchandising activities,

and viewed as added value to sports products, as well as a traffic pull for loyal consumers. Several chains also expressed interest in using *SunSplash* packets as promotional giveaways with retailers' own in-store merchandising programs (e.g., buy a bicycle water bottle, get a *SunSplash* packet free). These opportunities should be explored as well.

CONSUMER PROMOTION PLANNER

OBJECTIVES	STRATEGIES	TACTICS
• Generate trial of SunSplash with at least 10% of suncare users during peak season across key SolarTech markets. • Generate repeat purchase among at least 50% of tryers. • Generate multiple purchase among heavy recreational users.	• Create awareness and excitement at the point of purchase. • Provide free samples and continuity-based purchase incentive at high visibility events that attract large concentrations of recreational users. • Utilize package-delivered incentive to encourage trade-up purchase of multipacks. • Utilize tie-ins with well-known sports products in sporting goods channels.	• Develop impactful point of sale displays on selfcontained shippers, with changeable header card tailored to different distribution channels (i.e. ski graphics for ski shops, golf graphics for golf shops, generic activity graphics for general channels). • Sample at baseball and tennis games attracting large crowds, and provide an informational brochure and coupon for next purchase. • Utilize ongoing package promotion on six-packs, indicating that there is a FREE towelette with purchase of five. • Explore tie-in opportunities during sell-in.

IX. PUBLIC RELATIONS PLAN

PUBLIC RELATIONS RESEARCH

CONSUMER RESEARCH: Consumer focus group tests with target groups yielded the following key information:

- Psychographic studies of our target audiences showed that consumers who engaged in outdoor recreational activities aspire to be like admired sports figures. Because of the high level of transference and aspirational brand loyalty, we believe that there is an opportunity to appoint a sports spokesperson with universal appeal and/or pursue endorsements from various athletes in various sports.
- Also, based on the above, we should pursue sponsorships for channels that need a strong push in the contraseason, such as winter resorts. Being one of the official sponsors of the U.S. Ski Team could propel *SunSplash* to very large numbers in the off-season and gain continuity of purchase by those loyal users that can be extended into the warmer seasons. High winter volumes would also allow us to increase our costs of scale, lower our production costs, and ultimately our financial exposure during peak season.
- Advertorials might work well for our type of product, perhaps with endorsements from the medical as well as sports community. This tactic seems to be extremely acceptable to the mature adult target.
- Consumers in our target groups are somewhat to very concerned about the dangers of the sun on skin, especially the *protection-only* faction. This represents an opportunity to take advantage of the hot topic in the press and show how SolarTech is helping to minimize this problem by making available "instant" sunscreen. A lot of mileage can be gained from this tack, and it should be pursued with diligence.

PUBLIC RELATIONS PLANNER

OBJECTIVES	STRATEGIES	TACTICS
• During the key introductory period of April through June, generate awareness and positive perceptions among 25% of recreational and protection suncare products users.	• Utilize athlete endorsements. • Sponsor targeted events with both local and broad coverage.	• Sign John Brody, former Olympic champion and triathloner. • Become one of the sponsors of the New York and SF marathons, both with high TV exposure. • Press releases to all major media and targeted magazines.
• Generate goodwill and support in the medical communities.	• Utilize endorsements and the trade and popular media to tell story of "on-demand" protection.	• Get American Dermatology Institute endorsement. • Utilize press releases with ADI sanctions.
• Leverage technology innovation in overall corporate relations.	• Include in corporate trade marketing program.	• Develop themed trade show booth simulating use of towelettes in action settings.

X. BUDGETS

Following is the budget rack-up summary for each of the functional areas:

PRODUCT DEVELOPMENT	$0.3 MM
PACKAGING DEVELOPMENT	$0.3 MM
DISTRIBUTION (TRADE)	$1.6 MM
ADVERTISING	$2.2 MM
PROMOTION	$1.6 MM
PUBLIC RELATIONS	<u>$0.2 MM</u>
Total:	$6.2 MM

BIBLIOGRAPHY

Aaker, David. *Managing Brand Equity: Capitalizing on the Value of Brand Name*. New York: The Free Press, 1991.

Aaker, David, and George Day. *Marketing Research*. New York: John Wiley & Sons, 1990.

Awad, Joseph F. *The Power of Public Relations*. New York: Praeger Publishing, 1985.

Baker, Steven. *The Advertiser's Manual*. Steven Baker, 1988.

Barban, Cristol. *Essentials of Media Planning*. Lincolnwood: NTC Business Books, 1987.

Boon, Louis E., and David L Kurtz. *Contemporary Marketing*. Chicago: Dryden Press, 1989.

Boyd, Harper, Jr., and Orville Walker, Jr. *Marketing Management: A Strategic Approach*. Homewood: Richard D. Irwin, Inc., 1990.

Brody, E. W. *The Business of Public Relations*. New York: Praeger Publishing, 1987.

Bruneau, Edmond A. *Rx for Advertising*. Spokane: Boston Books, 1986.

Churchill, Gilbert, Jr. *Marketing Research: Methodological Foundations*. Orlando: Dryden Press, 1991.

Crawford, C. Merle. *New Products Management*. Homewood: Richard D. Irwin, Inc., 1987.

Cundiff, Edward, Richard Still, and Norman Govoni. *Fundamentals of Modern Marketing*. Englewood Cliffs: Prentice Hall, 1980.

Dunn, S. Watson, Arnold Barban, Dean Krugman, and Leonard Reid. *Advertising: Its Role in Modern Marketing*. Orlando: Dryden Press, 1991.

Farlow, Helen. *Publicizing and Promoting Programs*. New York: McGraw Hill, 1979.

Hamper, Robert J., and L. Sue Baugh. *Strategic Marketing*. Lincolnwood: NTC Publishing Group, 1990.

Harckham, Arthur. *Packaging Strategy: Meeting the Challenge of Changing Times*. Lancaster: Technomic, 1989.

Hisrich, Robert D., and Michael P. Peters. *Marketing Decisions for New and Mature Products*. Columbus: Charles E. Merrill Publishing, 1984.

Husch, Tony, and Linda Foust. *That's a Great Idea! The New Product Handbook*. Berkeley: Ten Speed Press, 1987.

Lesly, Phillip, ed. *Lesly's Handbook of Public*

Relations and Communications. Chicago: Probus Publishing, 1991.

Priemer, August. *Effective Media Planning*. Lexington: Lexington Books, 1989.

Robertson, Thomas S., Joan Zielinski, and Scott Ward. *Consumer Behavior*. Glenview: Scott, Foresman and Company, 1984.

Sacharow, Stanley. *The Package as a Marketing Tool*. Randor: Chilton, 1982.

Schultz, Don. *Essentials of Advertising Strategy*. Lincolnwood: NTC Business Books, 1989.

Stanley, Richard. *Promotion*. Englewood Cliffs: Prentice Hall, 1982.

Stanton, William J. and Charles Futrell. *Fundamentals of Marketing*. New York: McGraw-Hill, 1987.

Steinbrink, John. *The Dartnell Sales Manager's Handbook*. Chicago: Dartnell, 1990.

Surmanek, Jim. *Media Planning: A Practical Guide*. Lincolnwood,: NTC Publishing Group, 1989.

Tull, Donald S. and Del I. Hawkins. Marketing *Research: Measurement and Method*, New York: Macmillan, 1990.

Ulanoff, Stanley. *Handbook of Sales Promotion*. New York: McGraw-Hill, 1985.

Weitz, Barton A., and Robin Wensley. *Strategic Marketing: Planning, Implementation and Control*. Boston: Kent Publishing, 1984.

White, Roderick. *Advertising: What It Is and How to Do It*. New York: McGraw-Hill, 1988.

Wilcox, Dennis, Phillip Ault, and Warren Agee. *Public Relations Strategies & Tactics*. New York: Harper & Row, 1989.

INDEX